MW01129662

When Death Falls Apart

∴

When Death
Falls Apart

∴

MAKING AND UNMAKING
THE NECROMATERIAL TRADITIONS OF
CONTEMPORARY JAPAN

Hannah Gould

THE UNIVERSITY OF CHICAGO PRESS
CHICAGO AND LONDON

The University of Chicago Press, Ltd., London
© 2023 by The University of Chicago
All rights reserved. No part of this book may be used or reproduced
in any manner whatsoever without written permission, except in
the case of brief quotations in critical articles and reviews.
For more information, contact the University of Chicago Press,
1427 E. 60th St., Chicago, IL 60637.
Published 2023
Printed in the United States of America

32 31 30 29 28 27 26 25 24 23   1 2 3 4 5

ISBN-13: 978-0-226-82899-2 (cloth)
ISBN-23: 978-0-226-82901-2 (paper)
ISBN-13: 978-0-226-82900-5 (e-book)
DOI: https://doi.org/10.7208/chicago/9780226829005.001.0001

Library of Congress Cataloging-in-Publication Data

Names: Gould, Hannah, 1971– author.
Title: When death falls apart : making and unmaking the necromaterial
    traditions of contemporary Japan / Hannah Gould.
Other titles: Making and unmaking the necromaterial traditions of
    contemporary Japan
Description: Chicago : The University of Chicago Press, 2023. | Includes
    bibliographical references and index.
Identifiers: LCCN 2023015012 | ISBN 9780226828992 (cloth) |
    ISBN 9780226829012 (paperback) | ISBN 9780226829005 (ebook)
Subjects: LCSH: Funeral rites and ceremonies—Japan. | Dead—
    Religious aspects—Buddhism.
Classification: LCC GT3284.A2 G68 2023 | DDC 393.0952—dc23/
    eng/20230406
LC record available at https://lccn.loc.gov/2023015012

♾ This paper meets the requirements of ANSI/NISO Z39.48-1992
(Permanence of Paper).

Dedicated to those who care for the dead.

Contents

Textual Conventions

Japanese names are presented family name first except for authors publishing in English. Private individuals are referred to by pseudonym. Companies and their official representatives are named, with permission. Individual workers were given the choice of whether to be named or to be referred to by pseudonym.

All translations are by the author unless otherwise stated. The modified Hepburn system for the romanization of Japanese is used throughout.

Japanese loan words are the same in singular and plural form, thus "one *butsudan*" or "many *butsudan*."

The Stuff of Death and the Death of Stuff

At the height of summer in Japan, when humidity levels rise past 80 percent and the air feels like a tight hug, death seems closer. This is the period of O-bon (お盆), an annual festival dedicated to the ancestors, when the barriers between this world and the next are said to be at their thinnest and people try to wrangle holiday leave and finances sufficient to visit their hometowns and ancestral graves. Midsummer is a busy season for Japan's deathcare sector, as elderly victims of heatstroke join the ranks of the recent ancestors. The Buddhist grave and altar company in Osaka where I undertook fieldwork sold decorative lanterns, sets of offerings, and ancestral tablets. Local temples ordered extra boxes of incense to give to parishioners and held festivals to welcome home ancestors and pacify the neglected dead, all accompanied by folk dancing, food stalls, and fireworks.

In the summer when I began this work, yet sharper reminders of mortality hovered in the air. Between May and August 2017, North Korea tested five nuclear-capable missiles, including an intercontinental ballistic missile, that soared over remote islands before crashing into the Sea of Japan. People in Hokkaido awoke to emergency text messages, breaking news alerts, and on some occasions, evacuation orders. The creeping sense of "precarity" that is said to tinge contemporary Japanese society, an affect of unease that "crimps the familiar and routine" (Allison 2013, 4), crystallized into more immediate dystopias. Over the course of the year, the missiles were joined by record numbers of "ghost ships" arriving at night on the northern coastline, their battered wooden hulls transporting the corpses of lost North Korean fishermen (or perhaps would-be escapees).[1] Several Buddhist temples in the area agreed to hold rites for these dead — despite some local protest — lest their souls become *muenbotoke* (無縁仏), Buddhist specters trapped wandering the in-between. This indeterminate state is described as a pitiful fate for the dead and a potential threat to the living (Ikegami 2014).

Since then, death's spectral presence in everyday life seems only to have intensified. October 2022 saw the return of North Korean missile tests. And

UNCLAIMED DEAD

although Japan has been relatively lucky in its experience of COVID-19, re-porting some of the world's lowest death rates, the impacts of the pandemic have been unevenly felt by the most vulnerable populations (Slater 2020). Globally, COVID-19 has disrupted funerary traditions and stretched the in-frastructure of our deathcare systems to a breaking point. In Japan, these tra-ditions and structures were already crumbling under the weight of slower, transformations, such as an aging population, urbanization, and economic decline. By the time I entered the field, many of the socioreligious systems people had long relied upon to secure a "good death" were already fragile, if not failing.

In that first summer of fieldwork, the sweating, ripening, decaying pos-sibilities of bodies—my own and others—seemed closer to the surface and more difficult to manage. Workers at the Buddhist grave and altar store wrapped white towels around their necks to avoid dripping sweat onto the altars they were installing. The fashion retail giant Uniqlo advertised sweat-absorbing undershirts with antimicrobial properties, jackets with built-in battery-powered fans became a trend among construction workers, and train carriages on morning and evening commutes were filled with the heady scent of "8×4," a popular aerosolized talcum (in "floral," "soap," and "citrus") that was applied at regular intervals throughout the day.

I sat on the platform of a local train station in Osaka, brushing at the gray smudge of sweat, sandalwood incense, 8×4, and human ash that clung to my skin. The effect reminded me of the ladies of Maycomb in Harper Lee's *To Kill A Mockingbird*, who "bathed before noon, after their three o'clock naps, and by nightfall were like soft teacakes with frostings of sweat and sweet talcum" (1960, 5). I had just returned from my first interment ceremony (納骨式 *nōkotsushiki*), where an unexpected gust of wind had redistributed ashes among the crowd.

The ceremony was performed at a large memorial park in southwest Osaka. Lines of black and gray marble graves, each containing the remains of an entire household's dead, magnified the summer sun to a ferocious in-tensity. Enomoto, a soft-spoken Buddhist goods retailer, prepared for the ceremony. He washed down the Yamazaki family grave, replaced the candle stub, and arranged a low wooden altar laden with incense chips, a brazier, and a brass bell. In truth, there was not much to clean. The grave had been erected only five years earlier, upon the death of the father. Today, three school-age children, accompanied by their aunt and uncle, were coming to inter their mother.

We were expecting a Buddhist priest to accompany the family, to perform the final rites. But the family arrived alone; they'd had enough of priests, we were told. They appeared unsure how to proceed, so Enomoto gently directed them through the process of offering incense and flowers and striking the bell. He then propped open the stone cap that covered the grave. The eldest daughter stepped forward with a sizable white box and a determined look. She untied the silk wrappings and lifted the lid off a ceramic urn to reveal a mixture of fine ash and large bone fragments. Enomoto held out a fine muslin bag and she tilted the urn.[2]

Then, some of her mother escaped with the wind.

Enomoto, entirely unfazed, scooped up the ashes from the table and placed the bag inside the grave. The eldest daughter held up her hands before her face, turning them this way and that, as if intrigued to see how the residue of her mother clung to her skin. Enomoto struck the bell and we folded our hands in prayer. I assumed the position taught to me: hands folded around a string of Buddhist prayer beads, head down, back bowed at a forty-five-degree angle.

The family's youngest daughter, about six years old, chose this moment to run around the cemetery with a half-closed umbrella over her head. She laughed and screamed that she was a *kasa o-bake* (傘お化け), a kind of "household good turned god"—an everyday item that has acquired a spirit of its own. Her aunt smiled and gathered the girl into her arms. She brushed ash off the eldest daughter's school uniform and, after a few moments, turned toward the car. After the family left, Enomoto and I cleared the offerings and extinguished the candle. I cradled the bulky altar awkwardly against my arms and face, where it left a thin coat of ash on my skin. "It's just carbon," Enomoto instructed.

In Caitlin Doughty's popular memoir of her time working at a crematorium, *Smoke Gets in Your Eyes* (2015), she describes greeting clients at her second job—child minding—with human ash still lodged in her clothes and hair, and speculates about how her wards' parents would react if they knew. On the train that afternoon, I felt the same sense of harboring a secret from those around me. When I returned home to wash and change, it struck me that the shower drain was an ignoble fate for even a small portion of that mother's mortal remains. In tiny particles, ash persists and travels. It sticks to people, mixes into water, and floats away, despite the best attempts of Buddhist ritual to dispose of it properly, to fix it in time and place. In this sense, ash is like the dead; it is hard to wholly preserve and hard to wholly dispense with.

Employees of the company were in contact with the family several times after the ceremony to answer questions about memorial services and maintenance of the grave. They hoped as well to sell the family a *butsudan*, a Buddhist altar for use in ongoing rites for the dead in the home. Family members expressed a need to do something, to *buy* something, for the dead, but were

LOCKED INTO A CONTRACT

uncertain what to purchase. Their indecision was understandable. In the following weeks, I visited many cemeteries and homes, not to perform new interments but to desacralize and remove old graves and altars that were no longer wanted or needed, either because there was nobody now living to care for them or because their upkeep had become a burden. What, I wondered, would the Japanese tradition of graves and altars do for this family?

This is a book about graves and altars, incense and flowers, bones and ash: the materiality of encounters between the living and the dead in formal rituals and everyday observances in contemporary Japan. It is about what it means for those material traditions to persist through time and across generations. But mostly, it is about what happens when they die. In contemporary Japan, the necromaterial tradition of ancestral graves and altars, and the ritual practices and social relations they animate, has reached existential crisis point. What happens when material traditions of death, sometimes quite literally, fall apart? How do people handle their material, social, spiritual, and economic remains? Who is left holding the pieces? And whence does new life—which is to say, new death—emerge?

When Death Falls Apart shows how encounters between the living and the dead happen materially, by giving attention to where transformations in death ritual intersect with the lifecourse of the objects that animate them. I use "lifecourse" here because, as an anthropologist informed by studies of material culture and religion, I approach both humans and nonhumans, bodies and *butsudan*, as entities that live, die, and change. Specifically, this work is interested in shifting engagements with one major artifact of Japanese death culture, the domestic Buddhist altar, or *butsudan* (仏壇). In noisy carpentry studios, flashy funeral showrooms, and cramped kitchens where women prepare memorial feasts, this ethnography narrates how *butsudan* are made, circulate within economies, come to mediate intimate exchanges between the living and the dead, and then fall into disuse or, perhaps, can be remade. Attention to the now fragile lifecourse of *butsudan* is not simply academic. For workers like Enomoto, the precariousness of Japanese necromaterial traditions is an increasingly pressing concern. As I will describe, this pathos for the passing of things (もののあはれ *mono no aware*) generates creative new redesigns for death, alongside personal and professional acts of mourning.

BUTSUDAN AS NECROMATERIALS

Death creates an absence, but it also breeds abundances, in the rich array of objects used to handle the corpse; to commemorate, care for, or pacify the dead; and to console and comfort the living. Any study of death and material culture thus potentially encompasses a broad swath of stuff: the corpses, coffins, catering, the deceased's possessions, headstones, floral arrangements, and more. I coin the term "necromaterials" here to invoke this collection without recourse to the language of "memorials" and to reach beyond the categories of "funerary goods" or "grave goods."

The language of memorials dominates English's rather paltry resources for describing the stuff of death. It also tends to frame objects as "materialised memories" (Hallam and Hockey 2001, 203) that bring the living and the dead into relation through the dialectic of remembering and forgetting. Gygi describes how the dead are preserved in the minds of the living, and in the personal and collective forms—songs, histories, statues, tattoos— used to bolster human memory. Concomitantly, the erasure of one's name from history, a funeral devoid of mourners, and other instances of forgetting resonate as "bad deaths." While memory has proved one of the most productive frames for theorizing the interplay between death and material culture (see in particular Connerton 1989; Hallam and Hockey 2001; Kidron 2009; Miller and Parrott 2009; Nelson and Olin 2003; Verdery 1999; and, on forgetting, Weiss 1997), several scholars publishing in Japanese now challenge the universality of "memorialism" (メモリアリズム) or an "ideology of commemoration" (記念主義 kinen shugi) and its applicability to Japanese death culture (e.g., Shintani 2007; Naitō 2013; Yamada 2018).

Memorialization should not be viewed as the only or ascendant configuration of the "necrosocial" (Kim 2016). Instead, what I set out to describe in this ethnography is a relation of kuyō (供養), a material practice of care or "concern" (Traphagan 2004) that is premised on exchange. In Japan, the living offer, as well as memory, gifts of incense, food, Buddhist sutra readings, and recent gossip. In return, the dead can provide guidance and protection. While kuyō is centrally concerned with such acts of caring for and nurturing the dead, it also includes the dynamic of separation, in the form of the timely dissolution of the bonds between the living and the dead. The posthumous practice of a "good death" is thus one in which necrosocial bonds are acknowledged, nurtured, and ultimately resolved. The dead become a problem both when they are abandoned and when they linger too long in the world of the living. This framing shifts our thinking on necrosociality from a dialectic of remembering and forgetting to one of presencing and absencing, giving and receiving, with implications for what efficacious death rites look like, who can perform them, and under what conditions.

Butsudan (plates 1 and 2) are among the most important necromaterials in the Japanese Buddhist tradition of death, and the most important site for the domestic practice of kuyō.[3] Typically located in the head household of the patrilineal family line, they comprise a decorative double-door cabinet that enshrines a central Buddhist icon (ご本尊 *go-honzon*), ancestral tablets (位牌 *ihai*), and an array of ritual goods (仏具 *butsugu*).[4] In and around *butsudan*, people might place freshly cooked rice as an offering each morning, host formal celebrations for New Years and O-bon, burn incense and chant sutras, or introduce the ancestors to new children born into the family.

Conventional or "traditional" Japanese deathways arise from late nineteenth- and early twentieth-century invention and debate, and thus are largely a product of modernity (Kawano 2010, 54).[5] A shift in control of funeral and interment services from community-based funeral associations and families to Buddhist temples and then private corporations has further led to their regularization across Japan (Suzuki 2000, 49–59). While Japanese folkloristics and anthropology scholars have cataloged deeply significant regional variations that persist, the model I sketch out here is, inevitably, a general one. What follows is also an account of a "good death," a normative ideal unattainable for many. It begins with good dying. Susan Long's research (2004, 2005, 2008) shows how end-of-life decisions are made and experienced, and how they interact with culturally specific models of ideal dying experiences in Japan, particularly *pokkuri* (ぽっくり), a sudden death, or *rōsui* (老衰), a gradual decline. In complement to this excellent body of work, my ethnography focuses on posthumous rites.

After a death, relatives and deathcare professionals engage in a multidecade ritual process. A wake (通夜 *tsuya*) may be held immediately, with family and close friends in attendance. Funerals (葬式 *sōshiki*) are generally held the next day or soon after, usually at a commercial ceremony hall or temple. The body is typically cremated following the funeral, and the cremains are placed into an urn, which is kept at a temporary altar (祭壇 *saidan*) in the home or, sometimes, sent directly to the cemetery.[6] During this time, the deceased's soul is said to wander in between worlds, until the forty-nineday ceremony (四十九日 *shijūkunichi*), at which the cremains are transferred to a grave (figure 0.1) and the spirit of the deceased is enshrined in an ancestral tablet, placed on the *butsudan*. The grave is often located in the ancestral hometown at a Buddhist temple where the household is registered, or in a municipally run cemetery. In this way, the Japanese dead are multiply located, present simultaneously in the grave and the altar, and said as well to reside in the mountains, returning home during O-bon (Maeda 1976, 140).[7]

Multiple scholars describe graves and altars as connecting people across worldly and transcendental realms, in a relationship that supports the perpetuation and well-being of the household, both its living and dead members (e.g., Jeremy and Robinson 1989, 13; Nakamaki 2003, 14–16). In formal

Figure 0.1. A typical suburban gravesite, showing different styles of grave. Osaka, 2018.

Buddhist rites and informal offerings, the living care for the dead, perhaps maturing them into Buddhas (仏 *hotoke*) and subsequently (or alternatively) ancestors (先祖 *senzo*). In return, the dead offer guidance and protection to the living, including good fortune and blessings of future generations. This reciprocal relation is known as the "Posthumous Security Assurance System" (死後の安心保証制 *shigo no anshin hoshōsei*) (Himonya 1994, 64– 65; Suzuki 2013a, 17–18) or the "total life care system" (Traphagan 2004, 79). Paying into the system by performing rites when you are alive raises the chances that your descendants will prosper and provide you such care when you die.

The temporality of necrosocial relations that this system sets up is vital to understanding *kuyō* as a practice concerned equally with nurturing and disentangling the bonds between the living and the dead. Posthumous rites at the grave and *butsudan* are scheduled at successively larger intervals: seven days, then fourteen days, forty-nine days, one year, three years, and so on, up to thirty-three, fifty, or one hundred years (depending on the Buddhist school, region, and religiosity of participants). In this manner, the bonds between the dead and the living slowly dissipate. Effected too soon, the separation might be encountered as violent or disruptive. On the other hand, the specter of the pitiful dead in Japan remains the lingering *muen-botoke*, who has not received proper *kuyō* and so overstays one's welcome among the living.

The performance of *kuyō* is thus premised on, and contributes to, an intergenerational cycle of death and birth that projects the household into the future. Ideally, the cycle has no end, continuing well beyond the lifespan of its individual members. When this model prevails, rituals practices and material goods (*butsudan* and graves) are passed down between generations in an unending chain. But when the continuity of the household becomes uncertain, the future of Japanese deathways is threatened.

THE END OF *BUTSUDAN*?

Although *butsudan* were once present in the vast majority of Japanese homes, remain the most visible marker of household religious affiliation, and contribute to a multibillion-yen religious goods industry, they have received remarkably little dedicated study, in English or Japanese.[8] Upon hearing of my research project, scholars, Buddhist priests, and industry workers alike often expressed shock—sometimes accompanied by laughter—that anyone would specialize in the study of *butsudan* (let alone a young, foreign woman). This reaction speaks to the unfortunate place of *butsudan* at a convergence of biases that structure how anthropology has addressed the study of death, materiality, and religion.

Only in recent decades has materiality become a substantive focus in studies of death and religion. We have abundant mappings of Japanese religious cosmology (e.g., Ooms 1967) and shifting kinship relations enacted through ancestor veneration (e.g., Morioka 1984), but few if any descriptions of the crafting, material agency, or sensory experience of *butsudan*. The study of Buddhism in particular has suffered from popular and scholarly assumptions about its "amaterialist" or even "antimaterialist" nature, only more recently giving way to interest in Buddhist economies, technologies, and waste (e.g., Brox and Williams-Oerberg 2022). In the last two decades, foundational publications on the material cultures of death (e.g., Hallam and Hockey 2001) have come to anchor a "growing field of inquiry for anthropologists" (Graham 2016, xi; also Toulson and Newby 2019, 11).[9] As Barbara Graham argues in her ethnography of Irish death culture, materiality is "the crucial element in the transformations, negotiations and reintegrations that inform ongoing relationships between the living and the dead" (2016, ix). The frequent omission of materiality in studies of Japanese death is regrettable, not simply as a gap in the literature but because it skirts more fundamental questions about the nature of religious practice, about how exchanges between distant groups, such as the living and the dead or humans and buddhas, are carried out.

Moreover, *butsudan* are objects of "domestic religion," almost always located in private homes.[10] During fieldwork, I was repeatedly warned that *butsudan* are "home things" (家のもの *ie no mono*), a deprecatory phrase suggesting they are not worthy of scholarly attention. As Colleen McDannell argues in her study of American Protestant material culture, domestic, layperson artifacts are sometimes derided as kitsch and are often treated less seriously than institutional and elite forms of religious goods (1995, 223). And despite the aforementioned burgeoning interest in Buddhist materiality (e.g., Gerhart 2009; Winfield and Heine 2018), in general, popular religious paraphernalia that exists outside temple art is still underserved (but see Daniels 2003, 2010a; Starling 2019). Because they are located in people's homes, the study of *butsudan* also presents methodological challenges. Gaining access to the domestic sphere is notoriously difficult, often requiring a long-term commitment to a community. Even then, in Japan, entertaining guests in one's home is less common, with public access restricted to certain areas. In contrast, investigations of the changing form of public graves has flourished in Japanese and English (e.g., Suzuki and Mori 2018; Uriu et al. 2018; Yamada and Doi 2022).

Finally, there exists an uneasy relationship between *butsudan* and normative ideals of Buddhism. *Butsudan* are highly syncretized and flexible assemblages that blend the icons, rites, and symbols of Buddhism, Confucianism, and folk traditions of ancestor veneration. Such ambiguity is made plain when *butsudan* are described as "where *hotoke* resides," as the term *hotoke* (仏 or ほとけ) can simultaneously mean "Buddha," "ancestor," and "spirit of the dead" (Gorai 1994, 192–200; Rambelli 2010, 66; Nakamaki 2003, 15). Further, as Smith (1974) uncovered, *butsudan* use is overwhelmingly ruled by unorthodox conventions of regional or household practice. There is thus a sense in which *butsudan* are "not really Buddhism," or are an example of what I have described elsewhere as "bad Buddhism" (Gould and McKay 2020). Indeed, *butsudan* are totemic of a broader critique of Japanese Buddhism as "funerary Buddhism" (葬式仏教 *sōshiki bukkyō*), said to be only concerned with death and generating income from the provision of funeral services (Tamamuro 1963). But the material, domestic, syncretic, improvised nature of *butsudan* is exactly why they spark my interest. The *butsudan* is where quotidian life of the domestic sphere meets death, making these objects outstanding departure points for an ethnographically grounded understanding of contemporary Japanese cosmology.

Over and beyond these objections, the most thought-provoking reaction I receive to my research is a concern for its continued relevance, because *butsudan* appear to be dying. Although *butsudan* retail still generates significant profit, sales figures have plateaued. The frequency of ritual practice at the *butsudan* has also declined (Ishii 2007, 76; Reader 2011, 241–42; 2012). Finally, the domestic artisan sector for *butsudan* production is struggling to survive (Araki 2005). This narrative of decline extends to other aspects of Japanese death culture. Japanese funerals have been significantly condensed in recent years, under the cumulative impact of financial pressures, demographic shifts, and COVID-19 lockdowns. A 2022 nationwide survey conducted by Kamakura Shinsho found that more than half (55.7%) of respondents conducted the funeral as *kazokusō* (家族葬), with only close family in attendance.[11] The same period saw a rise in "one-day" combined wake, funeral, and cremation rites (5.2% in 2020; 6.9% in 2022) and "no service" or direct cremation (4.9% in 2020; 11.4% in 2022) (Kamakura Shinsho 2022).

Such changes may be read cumulatively as reflecting a broader collapse within Japanese society and religious life. As with the contemporary pension system, serious cracks now appear in Himonya's Posthumous Security Assurance System. The delivery of this model relies heavily upon the perpetuation of the household (家 *ie*), which in recent decades has moved toward a nuclear-family structure (Suzuki and Mori 2018, 3). In Japanese, the household is the "elementary social unit" encompassing both consanguineal kin and nonconsanguineal connections, living and dead, across multiple generations (Nakamaki 2003, 15). With the rise of the nuclear family, the fate of the household is subject to extensive debate (see Ronald and Alexy 2017), although it retains power in relation to death, at the very least as a rhetorical device (Boret 2014, 62–65). The household is also "the bedrock of temple Buddhism" (Rowe 2011, 4), a relationship formalized during the Edo period (1603–1868) when the temple-parishioner patronage system (檀家制度 *danka seido*) legislated that each household register its affiliation with a temple and enshrine a Buddhist image (Rambelli 2010, 73; chapter 1).

Within a rapidly aging society, Japan's yearly death rate is set to climb, leading to what Daisuke Uriu and colleagues (2019) have called a "death-ridden society" (多死社会 *tashi shakai*). Combined with the low birth rate, there are now more and more terminal households with no living descendants to inherit the grave, altar, or responsibility to care for the dead. Even when descendants exist, the model no longer proves attractive or feasible for many, who have "limited availability of memorial care resources" (Kawano 2014, 55; see also Kotani 2018, 115–19). Transforming gender roles and a drop in the marriage rate has led people to seek graves outside of the household structure, either as single persons or in new forms of social collective. Those who do wish to purchase an ancestral grave in an urban center face severe shortages and exorbitant costs (Boret 2014, 90–92). As such, columbaria and tree burial have come to rival conventional graves as a percentage of new grave purchases (Ceremonial Occasions Research Institute 2021, 134).

Finally, secularization and negative attitudes toward organized religion have soured relations between temples and laity. Not only is there increased competition from secular funeral providers, but accusations of profiteering in interactions with bereaved families have been particularly harmful to Buddhism's public image (e.g., Covell 2009). Although Buddhist clergy still attend a majority of funeral services and appear to have a monopoly over rites of consecration and desacralization (Tanabe 2012, 178), Hikaru Suzuki argues that ideal funerals today are less formal or religious and more "tailor-made, authentic, aesthetic, and intimately shared with family and friends" (2013a, 13).

Transformed Japanese deathways have become a marked social problem with public debates raging about their perceived practical and moral consequences (e.g., Ukai 2016). For some, this shift represents a growing freedom of choice that releases people from antiquated, expensive, and patriarchal modes of death. The emergence of new forms of graves, including individual interments (Rowe 2011), ash scattering (Kawano 2010), tree burial (Boret 2014), and high-tech columbaria (Uriu et al. 2018), has been the focus of analysis of this kind. For others, however, news stories of lonely deaths, abandoned cremains, and grave closures are evidence of a collapse of not only religious tradition but moral character (see Allison 2018). I do not think it an exaggeration to state that the increasingly marginal position occupied by *butsudan* in Japanese family life contributes to a growing sense of unease, if not "crisis" for religious institutions and industries. It also provokes broader questions about contemporary Japan: how could something once so fundamental to how the living relate to the dead, die?

When Death Falls Apart is not intended as a eulogy for *butsudan*. But I think there is something compelling about thinking with an unstable artifact of death culture, because it brings to the surface the processes via which necromaterials and the relations they animate are made and unmade. As Rebecca Solnit reminds us: "The process of transformation consists almost entirely of decay" (2006, 81–83). In paying attention to the lifecourse of *butsudan* in contemporary Japan, I hope that I might thus challenge the assumptions about memorial permanence that shape our understandings of necromateriality.

It is this transformation of death culture that anthropologists have recently been accused of failing to comprehend (Simpson 2018, 1), with a few notable exceptions (e.g., Ariès 1974; Barraud et al. 1994; Jindra and Noret 2011; Vitebsky 2017). Anthropological approaches to the material culture of death, for example, have overwhelmingly focused on the production of permanent—or at least durable—monuments, elite rather than non-elite goods, and artisanal rather than mass-produced goods (Toulson and Newby 2019, 7). Death as transformation (not "transforming death") we appear to be far more comfortable with. Following Hertz (1907), anthropologists are accustomed to examining mortuary rituals as rites of passage that transmute the status of the deceased, symbolically conquering death via the production of new life. This approach has proved influential in work in Japan, focused on the passage of the dying from spirit to buddha, ancestor, and household god (e.g., Ooms 1967, 1976; Plath 1964).

Drawing on the anthropology of death and disposal, Buddhist studies, death studies, and material religion, this book sets forth a path for looking at transformations to death cultures as entangled in the lifecourse of necro-materials. I propose to start with *butsudan*, taking as axiomatic that necro-sociality does not exist in advance of the stuff that is suspended between the living and the dead. As founders of material religion studies articulate, the question of how religion "happens materially" should not be confused with "the much less helpful question" of how religion is expressed in material forms (Meyer et al. 2011, 210). So while I approach *butsudan* as religious media that render the sacred "visible and tangible" (Orsi 2013, 74) or "tangible and proximate" (Kieschnick 2003, 23), I do not presume to know what that "sacred" constitutes before engagement with these objects in the field.

The lifecourse of *butsudan* both drives this book and structures its chapters. The cultural biography approach, articulated by Igor Kopytoff, Arjun Appadurai, and others in the 1986 work *The Social Life of Things*, has been a compelling model for conducting object-based ethnography. It decenters the human and uncovers how value is created through the circulation of goods (as per Weiner 1992), not just the labor of production. But it can codify some problematic assumptions about material culture. For instance, the cultural biography approach tends to assume the material and conceptual endurance of objects across time and space. However, it is far from clear that there always exists a single, continuous "*butsudan* thing" to be followed. In studies of material religion, David Morgan describes the importance of shifting "from object-centred to practice-centred" approaches, which study "the way things get put together" (2016, 642) and, I would add, fall apart. In my pursuit of the *butsudan* lifecourse, then, I focus on the different practices via which *butsudan* come together, fall apart, and might be remade into entirely new entities, without assuming a single or unifying thread.

Biographical approaches can also shift focus from material agency. As Inge Daniels argues, a passive view of mobile objects that does not adequately account for the consequences of their materiality (2009, 386; also Mansfield 2003; Weiner 1992, 58–59). *Butsudan* are deeply symbolic, but they are not just signs, and their material form and sensory qualities shape their lifecourse. Consideration for the agency of materials is particularly pertinent for anthropologists working in Japan. A long history of scholarship describes the material world of Japan as significantly enlivened (if not animated) in ways that challenge or blur the dominant subject-object dualism of Western cosmologies. As I discuss later (chapter 4), manifold theories of Japanese materialism exist, from animism to dramaturgical approaches. For example, Japanese scholars working on the collective project of *mo-nogaku* (モノ学) argue that the basic Japanese category of "stuff," or *mono*, in fact encompasses the phenomena of "people," "spirits," and "things/ matter" (see Kamata 2009; Shimazono 2009). From the *kasa o-bake*, or "umbrella turned god," to robotic pets that receive funeral ceremonies, it is not necessary to commit to any particular theory to appreciate that Japan is a context in which the liveliness of nonhumans can inflect everyday life and the bonds between (non/human) *mono* might carry moral weight. Moreover, certain *mono*, including altars, gravestones, and human ash, appear particularly enlivened, such that the intersection of their lifecourse with that of humans becomes marked, even in a state of abandonment or decline.

FIELDWORK WITH *BUTSUDAN*

Following the *butsudan* lifecourse has meant investigating Japanese death and religion in spaces and with actors that have not previously been described in the literature and, indeed, that are often hidden from public view. Manufacturers, marketers, retail workers, crematoria operators, waste workers, and entrepreneurs form a group of what I call "religious third actors," who sit outside, but directly support, official religious institutions and their relationships with laypeople. This sector has increasingly come to replace households and community groups in performing many of the labors around death. Those in retail positions are also some of the most publicly accessible agents of Buddhism in Japan, and a preferred point of contact for those wishing to avoid expensive or binding relationships with temples. The sector thus wields significant power (if not always authority) in the transmission of religious knowledge and, as I contend, the future of death in Japan. By locating my ethnography here, I want to show how, in a secularizing, capitalist society like Japan, ritual is sustained and potentially remade by these professionals, as much as through top-down construction by Buddhist priests or a ground-up community movement.

When Death Falls Apart is based on ethnographic research conducted in the deathcare sector across Japan between 2016 and 2019, and then in 2022 after COVID-19 travel bans were lifted. *Butsudan* are mobile objects that draw together raw materials, artisan traditions, and religious symbols from disparate locations across Asia and circulate within nationwide companies and online shopping networks. I engaged *butsudan* at different stages of this mobile lifecourse, learning to apply gold leaf with artisans, making tea for potential buyers, helping to install *butsudan* in homes, staying in people's homes to observe daily altar rituals, and attending memorial services at temples. My fieldwork was punctuated by three intense periods of full-time work with Buddhist grave and altar companies: six weeks at Takimoto Bukkōdō in downtown Osaka, then three weeks at Ōgoshi Butsudan in Takaoka in Toyama Prefecture, and three weeks at Hasegawa Butsudan in Tokyo. The companies vary widely in location (Ōgoshi is in a rural area, Takimoto and Hasegawa in large cities), the religious affiliation of their customers (Ōgoshi and Takimoto serve largely Jōdo Shinshū populations), the socioeconomic background of their immediate surrounds (Hasegawa is located in Ginza, Japan's most exclusive shopping district), and their artisan traditions (Ōgoshi Butsudan is associated with bronze, lacquerware, and gold leaf). Workers at all three *butsudan* stores possess immense religious knowledge and embodied skill. They are expected to study and memorize the iconography of each component of altars across all Buddhist schools, regional styles, and aesthetics.

For those interested in religious capitalism, then, *butsudan* stores demonstrate a blending of religion and corporate culture par excellence. Morning meetings at Takimoto, for example, began with a recitation of sutras, followed by a reading from the official corporate history. Fieldwork in this corporate religious world is rewarding but comes with precarious politics. Within a tight-knit industry, I became a well-known figure, and my alliance with particular firms limited my ability to engage with their rivals. It also distanced me from Buddhist priests, many of whom regard the profit-driven industry as parasitic and expressed open disdain for *butsudan* companies. Further, when working with industry, one cannot ignore the commercial pressures that structure interactions in the field. On several occasions, R & D teams requested my expert opinion on the future direction of the industry. At other times, I was asked to sign confidentiality agreements to protect new product designs. Almost all companies were eager to leverage our relationship to promote their brand, whether through social media posts, human interest stories placed in newspapers, or more formalized consultancies. For this reason, and with permission, many of the companies and individuals I describe in this text are referred to by name.

THE BOOK

When Death Falls Apart unfolds across the *butsudan* lifecourse, a structure that privileges the altar itself, responding to my informants' desire for greater attention to this artisan tradition and enabling a consideration of how nonhuman and human lives intersect. In the process of writing, I have inevitably found this lifecourse to be far less linear than the structure of a book, which is to say, there are not nearly as many alternative routes, shortcuts, and U-turns included here as I would like.

The first chapter, "Crafting," analyzes how necromaterial religious traditions are made and then modernized. In the first part, dissecting the material assemblage of an altar allows me to interrogate how *butsudan* were standardized into the "sensational form" (Meyer 2009) that is popular today. The second part describes how the specter of this (invented) material tradition shapes the prospects of embattled *butsudan* artisans, facing their own intergenerational crisis.

Chapter 2, "Retail," takes place on the showroom floor and in the delivery truck, as I describe selling *butsudan* and installing them in people's homes. This chapter probes the embodied affect of concern, or "pull of the dead," that motivates many to continue to invest in altars. *Butsudan* retail is described as a process of maintaining, severing, and resolving necrosocial bonds (縁 *en*), tied up in considerations of practicality, cost, and aesthetics.

Chapter 3, "Practice," takes us into the home via two extended narratives. Analyzing everyday observance at the altar, I use Japanese-language scholarship to challenge the dominance of "memorialism" as *the* mode of contemporary necrosociality. This chapter develops my theorization of *kuyō* as material practice aimed at both caring for the dead and, ultimately, dissipating their bonds with the living.

The practice of *kuyō* involves making materials that are themselves mortal, and chapter 4, "Disposal," explores what happens when graves and *butsudan* become waste. The disposal of altars is complicated for emotional, spiritual, and practical reasons, often requiring the same disposal rites as the human dead. However, not all *butsudan* receive this level of care, and innovative disposal practices reveal attempts to create death rites that are less taxing and enduring.

Chapter 5 looks beyond *butsudan* to experimental designs for necromaterials gaining popularity in Japan. Following two emerging products from the deathcare industry into the world, it explores the labor involved in creating new ritual practice, as well as how these designs can (intentionally or unintentionally) restructure the social and sensory dimensions of exchange with the dead. The consequences of the decline of graves and *butsudan* are impending and grand, for artisans, laypeople, religious leaders, and scholars. And so finally, in the conclusion, I turn to contemplate what a "good death" for necromaterials like *butsudan* might look like.

This research has deep roots but owes its immediate origins to two personal rites of passage that transformed my personal kinship networks: a death and a marriage. The death was my father's. He died of cancer in the space of a year, just after I completed my undergraduate thesis in anthropology. His death continues to be a lesson of understanding absence, of learning what is meant by that strange and sudden reality of somebody's material nonexistence. The process of organizing his funeral introduced me to a plethora of new goods. All at once, our family was to select from coffins, flowers, and headstones accompanied by naff brand names and hefty price tags. I found it difficult to hold these objects in my mind together with the memory of my father. How did these products from a funeral home catalog come to be the things we use to represent his person? Why does this matter, matter?

My specific interest in *butsudan* was brought about by my marriage, shortly before my father's death, to Daisuke, the eldest son of a family from Hiroshima. On my many previous trips to Japan, I had neither the occasion nor the intimacy to interact with *butsudan* in someone's home. Now, on visits to my in-laws, I occasionally sleep on *tatami* mats in a room occupied by an ornately decorated gold altar. Daisuke expresses little interest in this particular *butsudan*, except to move our futons away from its doors because he feels it is somewhat "gloomy." He is also reluctant to inherit an ancestral grave or the ritual responsibility to look after the dead, despite his ostensible obligation to do. His views are not atypical of younger people in Japan today.

Put simply, in the same broad moment in which I was choosing between an array of unsatisfactory goods designed to memorialize my father, I came to empathize with young people in Japan, struggling to connect with a necromaterial tradition of their own.

At the best of times, the tether between the dead and the material objects they animate can appear tenuous. In a world where the traditions, rituals, and public infrastructures of death, as well as life, appear increasingly unstable, this tether is often frayed. I hope that *When Death Falls Apart* provides a method to examine change in death ritual through examining the dynamic lifecourse of necromaterials. But more than that, I offer it as an empathetic account of people's attempts to make, and remake, the stuff of death in disarray.

CHAPTER 1

Crafting

One of the most extraordinary examples of *butsudan* artisanship I have ever encountered is a golden altar in the Jōdo Shinshū tradition, located in the Toyama countryside (plate 3). At over two meters tall and three meters wide with its folding doors outstretched, it dominates the formal sitting room it occupies. Every surface is embellished with lacquer finishes, gold leaf, and decorative metalwork. A soft light radiates from the altar, as candles and electric lights reflect off the golden surface. High-purity gold leaf was used to cover the interior, and the reflected glow is described to me not as "shiny" (キラキラ *kira-kira*) or "glittery" (ピカピカ *pika-pika*) but as a subtle, buttery yellow. I am told that Shinran, a thirteenth-century Buddhist reformist and founder of the True Pure Land school, taught that *butsudan* should be golden so as to convey the grandeur of the Gokuraku Pure Land, the realm of Amida Buddha, and thus impress the grace of Amida's teachings upon all those who view it. The effect of the gold is certainly stunning; I have seen many *butsudan*, but still, the majesty of this altar leaves me in awe.

The altar is located in the newly built, palatial home of the president of one of Toyama Prefecture's largest yellowfin fishing companies. On the day of my visit, President Yamashita arrives to greet me straight from the factory floor, still dressed in overalls. He shrugs off his long rubber boots at the entryway and folds his massive frame to sit with legs crossed beside the altar, looking every bit the "big man" of the village. The *butsudan* was only completed in the last year. He had, he says, originally planned to keep the altar he inherited but eventually decided that "if my family was getting a new home, then my ancestors should have one too." The old *butsudan* was given to his younger brother, and the president was persuaded by local artisans to commission a new design.[1] I visited the altar with Ōgoshi-san, president of Ōgoshi Butsudan in Toyama, who managed the altar's production. Ōgoshi Butsudan is one of the largest *butsudan* retailers in the region, specializing in the grand, golden altars still preferred by many Jōdo Shinshū followers, particularly those with spacious homes in rural areas. Beginning life as a joinery company, Ōgoshi now employs nine artisans who make and repair custom altars, alongside a team of retail assistants who also sell prefabricated models. New commissions like President Yamashita's are rare but valuable, and an opportunity to demonstrate the full skills of the artisans.

This *butsudan* is testament to Yamashita's standing in the community and ability to amass the economic and religious resources required for its construction. It is a Mikawa altar (美川仏壇 *mikawa butsudan*), a design style established during the Ashikaga/Muromachi period (1336–1573) in Hakusan City, Ishikawa Prefecture (BKSSK 2015, 333). Between 2016 and 2017, artisans from Ōgoshi Butsudan assisted specialists in joinery, lacquer (漆 *urushi*), gold leaf (金箔 *kinpaku*), raised lacquer (蒔絵 *makie*), metal embossing (金具 *kanagu*), and wood carving for the transom or crosspiece (欄間 *ranma*). Each required several months, if not years, to complete their work. The total cost was over fifteen million yen.

Yamashita received special permission from the head temple, which his family has supported for many generations, to reproduce famous religious artworks on the folding doors. The right-hand doors display the *Nigabyakudō* (二河白道), an allegory of adherents' faith that they will be reborn into the Pure Land.[2] The left-hand doors display the Amida triad (阿弥陀三尊 *amida sanzon*): Amida Buddha flanked by two attendant Bodhisattva, who are enlightened and compassionate beings. The images were crafted through the application of layers of gold and silver dust, charcoal, and paint to the lacquered surface, using a special brush made from mouse hair. Across the front of the drawers set into the altar, the Tateyama mountain range is reproduced in inlaid crushed nacre (mother-of-pearl). In Buddhist iconography, the Buddha often appears above an image of the sacred Mount Sumeru, the cosmic mountain and center of the Buddhist universe. On this *butsudan*, President Ōgoshi decided to reproduce Amida Buddha atop the same local mountain range that appears on the Yamashita company logo, visually merging the company's fortune and the prosperous realm of Amida.

President Yamashita sits back as we examine the altar, deferring to Ōgoshi's expertise for explanations and occasionally interjecting a question about certain artisans. As a final act of greeting to Amida, and by extension the household, Ōgoshi gives a full recitation of a sutra, in a clear, deep voice. I join him in the final strains, while President Yamashita silently surveys the scene. The *butsudan* struck me as pristine; there were no sweets or mounds of rice placed on offering trays, as is common. Writing on China, John Kieschnick suggests that Buddhist artworks are "seldom if ever only channels of communication between individual devotees and the deities they worshipped; they were at the same time attempts to win or assert social prestige" (2003, 11). Commissioning this *butsudan* was as much an act of patronage to the local religious and artisan industry as it was an act of piety. Or perhaps, patronage as piety.

Altars are materially and symbolically dense artifacts, the condensation of hundreds of hours of hand labor and hundreds of years of history. When I began my research, the complexity of this assemblage was intimidating, and it was only as I pored over industry textbooks and completed fieldwork that I gained some measure of competency. Colleagues at the Osaka *butsudan* store created a training course and tests for me, including packing the *butsudan* frame for transport, arranging the interior in the styles of different schools and regions, and, conversely, recognizing the Buddhist school of an altar from a quick glance at its decorative elements or icon. Time spent with *butsudan* artisans taught me other forms of embodied knowledge, such as how to take shallow breaths and sway one's body in motion with gold leaf, so that the micron-thin sheets of gold do not crumple or fly away. At the same time, it slowly became clear that my initial hesitancy is the norm for most Japanese; contemporary knowledge of *butsudan* is unequally shared. Much of what I describe in this chapter is acquired from expert sources and only sometimes filtered through to consumers, whose own ideas about *butsudan* will emerge more fully later.

The origins of *butsudan* are contested. Throughout their history, *butsudan* have proved flexible symbols, deployed to represent (and indeed enforce) a socioreligious kinship structure, an emperor-centered family-state model, and an apparently essential and timeless ethnic tradition of ancestor veneration. In Japan, *dentō* (伝統), or "tradition," is powerful currency in discussions of history, social policy, and national identity, and in defining, through opposition, the modern era. In *Mirror of Modernity*, Stephen Vlastos suggests that "especially since 1945 and the eclipse of the ideology of the emperor-centered family-state, Japanese have come to know themselves, and to be known by others, through their cultural traditions" (1998, 1). It is this highly self-conscious discourse about the value of traditions that distinguishes contemporary Japan (Cox and Brumann 2010, 2).

It is tempting to read *butsudan* as an "invented tradition," following Hobsbawm and Ranger (1992). This framing has been used to dissect many bastions of Japanese culture, including martial arts, the village, and tea ceremony, which all turn out to be rather modern (Vlastos 1998, 1). Despite frequent appeals to their primordial origins, *butsudan* are no different. However, when used to narrowly construe tradition as artifice or fiction, the concept of invented traditions can obscure the labors involved in invention, "leaving only manipulation and mystification" (1998, 11). It can overlook people's intimate engagement with distinct genealogies of knowledge and the labors of their intergenerational transmission. For *butsudan* artisans, this includes the embodied skill of craft, passed down via physical repetition. I thus deploy terms like "assembly" and "making," rather than "invention," to direct attention to the tactile relationships between artisans and materials that bring *butsudan* to life.

In her study of Japanese modernity, *Discourses of the Vanishing* (1995), Marilyn Ivy expresses similar discomfort, arguing that theories of the "invention of tradition" rely upon untenable distinctions "between invention and authenticity, between fiction and reality, between discourse and history" (1995, 21). Ivy proposes an alternative model of vanishings, in which cultural traditions are understood as "gone but not quite, suspended between presence and absence" (1995, 20). Such vanishings are phantasms, "recurrent yet elusive forms of absence that haunt the historical present of that place called Japan" (1995, 242). This phantasm also appears to haunt scholarly narratives about artisans, such as the work of Richard Sennett, which resonates with me as a salvage ethnography. For Sennett, craftsmanship names "an enduring, basic human impulse," that is, "the desire to do a job well for its own sake" (2008, 9), and should be protected from capitalist efficiency, automation, and planned obsolescence. The image of a vanishing *butsudan* tradition looms large over the entire altar lifecourse, such that one cannot discuss their beginnings without reference to their twilight. It functions both as an urgent plea, pointing to the real material and financial consequences for artisans, and as a rhetorical device, cultivated and commodified in order to raise revenue and drive change.

This chapter breaks *butsudan* into their component parts to introduce the complexities of altar assemblages and to probe the origins (and end) of this material religious form. The *butsudan* tradition has been made slowly, by calloused hands carving wood, the application of lacquer, and hand-beaten brass bells. It is equally made through debates about the origins of ancestor veneration, arguments about what *butsudan* rituals are "correct," and a codification of industry standards around what counts as a "traditional artisan good" (伝統工芸品 *dentō kōgeihin*). I thus describe *butsudan* as largely improvised, multisensory assemblages, which are only partially regulated by religious and industry standards.

ASSEMBLY

Disassembly and reassembly of *butsudan* usually occur when altars are tendered for repair or during cleaning in preparation for a special anniversary or formal service. Each component is removed, cleaned or remade, and then put back in place. It is a difficult process, as grandiose, golden altars may comprise over five hundred individual parts, and even a modest, modern altar might be furnished with ten separate ritual instruments. As a discursive device, taking apart *butsudan* allows one to appreciate the histories of labor that go into each component. The material accumulation at *butsudan* is both broad and deep. Broad because they draw together diverse cultural, religious, and artisan traditions into a single assemblage. Deep because each component possesses an iconography and history that is almost infinitesimally detailed, from rival interpretations of the open and closed beaks of the golden cranes that adorn the candlesticks on altars in Eastern Jōdo Shinshū, to the Heian era (794–1185) poetry referenced in the embroidered cushions used to support brass bells. As many of my seniors at *butsudan* stores proclaimed, even after fifty years working in the industry, one can never hope to learn all there is to know about *butsudan*.

Traditional *butsudan* fall into two styles. The first, *kin butsudan* (金仏壇), or "golden altars," are decorated with Japanese lacquer and gold leaf. They are almost exclusively used by members of the Jōdo Shinshū school of Buddhism, and there are two chief decorative variants corresponding to its East (東 *Higashi*) and West (西 *Nishi*) branches. The second, *karaki butsudan* (唐木仏壇), or "exotic wood altars," are made from woods like ebony, rosewood, or Yakushima cedar, which is carved to show off the wood grain.[3] *Karaki butsudan* are favored by almost all schools of Buddhism outside of Jōdo Shinshū. Each style has distinctive architectural and decorative features; the intricately carved roofs, patterned ceilings, columns and railings, latticework, lanterns, and central dais broadly mirror the design of the main altar at the head temple of the Buddhist school to which the altar belongs (figure 1.1). A third style of *butsudan* gained popularity in Japan from the 1990s. Known variously as "modern" (現代 *gendai*), "city" (都市 *toshi*), or "furniture" (家具調 *kaguchō*) *butsudan*, they are typically smaller and less ornate. Within the three general styles, *butsudan* further vary according to (1) the Buddhist school; (2) the regional artisan tradition; (3) the physical dimensions, often determined by their position in the home; (4) the design aesthetics of the maker or retailer; and (5) the personal preferences of the customer.

The interior of a *butsudan* has been described as a hierarchical structure with three tiers (Gorai 1994; Sasaki 1993; Rambelli 2010). The top tier contains the main Buddhist icon (ご本尊 *go-honzon*) and attendant guardian deities and symbolizes the enlightened realm of the Buddha. The middle tier houses the ancestral tablets (位牌 *ihai*) and is the realm of the ancestors.[4] The bottom tier, which contains food offerings and ritual instruments, symbolizes the mundane world of the living. Sasaki describes *butsudan* as thus producing a "religious cosmos" in miniature (1993, 27–34; 1996, 170),

Figure 1.1. An example of the intricate architecture of the interior of a golden *butsudan*, Takimoto Bukkōdō, Osaka, 2018.

with ancestors mediating between living humans and Buddhas. As I shall describe, however, *butsudan* in people's homes rarely maintain this strict hierarchy.

On the top tier, the *go-honzon* (item 3 in figure 1.2) is a painted scroll or carved wooden statue representing one manifestation of the Buddha. The Buddhas primarily enshrined in Japanese *butsudan* are *Amida Nyorai* (阿弥陀如来), the Buddha of Infinite Light; *Shaka Nyorai* (釈迦如来), the Historical Buddha; and *Dainichi Nyorai* (大日如来), the Cosmic Buddha. The central figure is accompanied by flanking figures (item 4), usually Bodhisattva or important teachers in the school, or by a calligraphic mantra.[5] Despite Rambelli's suggestion (2010, 66) that families are awarded a "high degree of freedom" over the selection of *go-honzon*, in my experience, most do not exercise it; *butsudan* almost always exhibit the triad of figures set out by Buddhist schools and sold at *butsudan* stores.[6] Exceptions may result from a religious conversion somewhere in the family history or a personal connection with one particular Buddha, especially the ever-popular *Amida Nyorai* (Sk. *Amitābha*, Buddha of Infinite Light) or *Kannon Bosatsu* (観音菩薩; Ch. *Guanyin*, Goddess of Mercy). In general, personalization is more common in the lower tiers.

The second tier of the *butsudan* houses the *ihai* (ancestral tablets). In the case of Jōdo Shinshū, which typically does not use *ihai*, the ritual implements otherwise located on the third tier are raised one level. *Ihai*, made from lacquered or polished wood, are generally around twelve centimeters high and three centimeters wide (depending on the size of the *butsudan* and status of the deceased). The front is engraved with an individual's Buddhist name (戒名 *kaimyō*), and the back lists their profane name, age, and date of death. In most schools of Buddhism, *kaimyō* are purchased posthumously from temples at great expense to the family (Covell 2009). *Ihai* appear to have been introduced from China during the Sung dynasty (960–1279) (Hirayama 1949, 65), just as Buddhist and Confucian memorial practices were being syncretized (Rambelli 2010, 76). Some propose, however, that *ihai* derive from the votive tablets placed on "spirit shelves" and used in funerals in Japanese folk religion as practiced before Buddhism's arrival (Yanagita 1946; see Hirayama 1949, 53). More than records of the deceased, *ihai* are considered "receptacles (依り代 *yorishiro*) or even duplicate bodies (分身 *bunshin*) of individual ancestors" (Rambelli 2010, 75; see also Irizarry 2014). Several copies of *ihai* may be made and distributed among family members or enshrined in temples to ensure the dead receive sufficient care (Irizarry 2014, 165). This "mechanical reproduction" (Benjamin 1936) of religious items does not appear to reduce their indexicality or sacredness. *Ihai* are not the only signs of the dead included in contemporary *butsudan*, which might also contain items like a wristwatch or ashes. Personal photographs of the deceased in particular have become common features of modern *butsudan*, sometimes replacing the presence of an *ihai* or Buddhist icon altogether. Further, *butsudan* are only one site for materializing the dead.

The bottom tier of the *butsudan* contains the *butsugu* (仏具), Buddhist ritual implements used for making offerings. They come in sets of five (五具足 *gogusoku*) or three (三具足 *mitsugusoku*): one or two candlesticks (figure 1.2, item 12), one or two vases of flowers (item 14), and an incense brazier (13). In addition, cups filled with tea (9), stands piled with sweets or fruit (15), and bowls of rice (10) are given as offerings. The typical gifts made at *butsudan* span the "five offerings" (五供 *gokū*): incense, flowers, candlelight, water, and rice (Taniguchi 2013, 38–39). Each possesses a string of doctrinal interpretations and folk meanings. According to the *Housewives' Guide to Graves and Butsudan*, for example, flowers represent the love and beauty of the Buddha, candlelight represents wisdom, and incense cleanses the profane body of the person making offerings (Shufunotomo 2011, 172). Jōdo Shinshū priest Taniguchi Kōji suggests that flowers placed at the *butsudan* face toward the living, so as to brighten their smile for the Buddha, while incense transmits the dharma: "listening to the incense means listening to

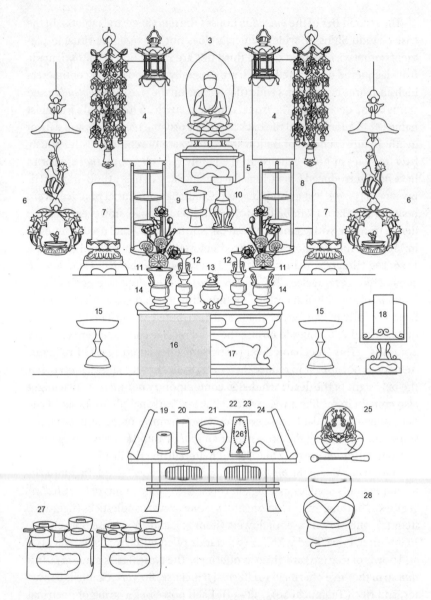

Figure 1.2. Diagram of the standard composition of a *butsudan* interior. Adapted with permission from *Butsudan Butsugu Gaidansu* (BKSSK 2015, 385)

CRAFTING   >   25

1	隅瓔珞 *sumiyōraku* hanging corner ornament		15	高杯 *takatsuki* offering dish
2	吊灯籠 *tsuritōrō* hanging lantern		16	打敷 *uchishiki* decorative cloth/antependium
3	ご本尊 *go-honzon* icon		17	前机 *maezukue* front stand
4	脇侍 *wakiji* flanking image		18	過去帳 *kakochō* ancestral book
5	仏像台 *butsuzōdai* Buddhist icon stand		19	マッチ消 *matchi-keshi* match box
6	輪灯 *rintō* oil lamp		20	線香立 *senkōtate* incense holder
7	位牌 *ihai* ancestral tablet		21	前香炉 *maekōro* front incense brazier/censer
8	段盛 *danmori* offering stand		22	経本 *kyōhon* sutra book
9	茶湯器 *chatōki* tea offering vessel		23	数珠 *juzu* prayer beads
10	仏飯器 *buppanki* rice offering vessel		24	蝋燭消 *rōsoku-keshi* candle extinguisher
11	常花 *jōka* eternal golden flower		25	木魚 *mokugyo* fish glockenspiel
12	燭台 *shokudai* candlestick		26	お経 *o-kyō* sutras
13	香炉 *kōro* incense brazier/censer		27	霊供膳 *reikuzen* spirit offering tray
14	花瓶 *kebyō* flower vase		28	鈴 *rin* bell

the teachings of Buddha" (2013, 49–50). Alternatively, an influential *butsudan* industry guide describes incense as food for Buddha and the ancestors (BKSSK 2015, 658). Indeed, theories of incense's symbolic and sensorial significance are particularly rich, given its long association with the purification of corpses and the protection of the newly dead from malevolent influences.

A further level should be added to these three tiers: *hōgu* (法具), or ritual tools that are regularly touched by the living, sit outside or below the *butsudan*. These include a bronze bell or singing bowl (figure 1.2, item 28) and a wooden fish-shaped glockenspiel (item 25), both used in sutra recitation; strings of *juzu* (数珠) or prayer beads; sutra books; and other paraphernalia. These items sit directly on the tatami mat or a small dais in front of *butsudan*, forming part of a wider ecosystem of sentimental and ritual goods that extends into the domestic space. Inge Daniels (2010b), in her pioneering ethnography of the Japanese home, positions *butsudan* as just one of several focal points in a sacred domestic landscape, which also includes display areas in formal alcoves, the entrance hall, kitchen, and atop the television or piano. In particular, *butsudan* are often positioned in relation to, but separate from, the home's *kamidana* (神棚), or Shinto shrine (Nakamaki 1983, 2003). It is therefore difficult, and perhaps imprudent, for scholars to draw strict boundaries of sacred space around *butsudan*.

There is a further variety of objects that do not find their way into official diagrams or descriptions of *butsudan*, including silk banners, spent matches, cremated remains, work pay slips, amulets from festivals, and candle stubs. The total composition varies greatly from home to home, as do the principles governing its arrangement; some people follow family tradition, some meticulously follow a guide provided by clergy, and some maintain the arrangement first installed by the *butsudan* store. Layers of ritual goods and household detritus often build up at the altar over generations. Last year, when cleaning his family's *butsudan* in preparation for a formal service, my husband found an enamel pin worn at his high-school entrance ceremony buried deep in the ash of an incense brazier. Nobody knows quite how it got there. Similarly, in chapter 4, I describe how *butsudan* become a kind of catchall space for items that are difficult to dispose of, from old teeth to tarot cards and holiday souvenirs. None of these items are sanctioned or feature in *butsudan* guidebooks. Nor is their addition considered particularly sacrilegious. Even pious owners can create unorthodox altar configurations. Mitsume-san, who has worked in the industry for many decades, told me of one unusual altar, belonging to a Shingon family, that included more than thirty tiny dishes of water placed as offerings to different historical ancestors.

An even more expansive account of the *butsudan* assemblage might include the universe of forces and sensations that coalesce there: kneeling human bodies, strains of sutras, smoke, ghosts, grief. I use the term "assemblage" here and throughout with reference to its archaeological etymology, as a "collection of things and their relations" (Wise 2011, 92). Wise argues that "the elements that make up an assemblage also include the *qualities* present . . . and the affects and effectivity of the assemblage: that is, not just what it *is*, but what it *can do*" (2011, 92, original emphasis). Perhaps most importantly, this usage of "assemblage" conveys a transient temporal quality. *Butsudan* are not timeless; they come together at a particular moment, expand or retract with life events, and may one day fall apart. An assemblage at times "seems structural," but it is "inherently unstable and infused with movement and change" (Marcus and Saka 2016, 102).

Birgit Meyer's work on "sensational forms" provides a useful addition to this framing of *butsudan* from the perspective of material religion. Meyer describes sensational forms as "relatively fixed, authorized modes of invoking and organizing access to the transcendental" (2006, 9). This concept directs attention to the aesthetic and sensorial dimensions of *butsudan* as structuring how they make the sacred tangible. And *butsudan* provide a particularly rich multisensory interface, encompassing sound (bell and sutras), taste (offerings of food), smell (incense, flowers), touch (prayer beads), and sight (icons, candles). Sensational forms do not just make the transcendent present and palpable, they can also generate action, provoking people to adopt particular dispositions (Meyer 2006, 13; 2012, 26), for example, kneeling on tatami mat floors or joining one's hands in prayer. As we shall see throughout this book, transforming the sensational form of *butsudan* has implications for the embodied practice of being with the dead.

Powerful ideas circulate in the industry and popular media that contribute to this ordering of the sensational form of *butsudan*. For industry insiders, one important source of standards is the *Guidance on Buddhist Altars and Buddhist Goods* (BKSSK 2015). Cracking open its 888 pages, one finds chapters full of detailed diagrams visualizing each instrument and its position on the altar, as well as variations across different Buddhist schools, geographical regions, and configurations of domestic space. I often found well-thumbed copies of the guide in the corners of *butsudan* artisan studios or retail offices. It is also the primary text examined in the two-hour test for *butsudan* retail workers seeking certification as a "Buddhist ceremonies coordinator." In contrast, for *butsudan* consumers, etiquette guides and "conduct literature" (Bardsley and Miller 2011), online resources, pamphlets distributed by temples, and conversations with retail store employees appear to be the main source of information about standards for *butsudan* form. As I consider in chapter 3, this level of codification diverges from descriptions of the improvised nature of domestic altars around the world (see Turner 1999). Rarely did the *butsudan* I encountered conform entirely to the standards set out in these guides. But equally, I heard frequent fierce debate and worry about what *butsudan* should or should not be. One powerful way in which *butsudan* are ordered is through the circulation of competing narratives about their history and function.

Abundant histories

Butsudan are syncretic artifacts, representing a synthesis of distinct traditions that have converged through time. Exactly how these traditions came together, their national origins, and the relative weight of each as reflected in contemporary *butsudan* is contentious. Indeed, the national origins of ancestor veneration and *butsudan* ritual in Japan has historically been an academic battleground for broader ideological debates about religion and Japanese ethnic identity (Smith 1974, 79).[7] These debates gain volatility when they intersect with theories of Japanese cultural exceptionalism, particularly in the tradition of *Nihonjinron* (日本人論), with its tendencies to essentialize an ethnic-nationalist character. In the late nineteenth and early twentieth century, when Shintoism was promoted as a tool of national cohesion, attempts were made to align ancestor worship with an imperial ideology that positioned the emperor as the ultimate head and original ancestor of a national family (Takeda 1976, 130–32). This association meaningfully stunted the academic study of ancestor worship, as during this period it was "strictly taboo to make scientific studies of ancestor worship (except for purposes of advocating the ideology)" (Takeda 1976, 132–33; Kretschmer 2000a, 5–7). Hozumi Nobushige's manuscript *Ancestor Worship and Japanese Law* (1901) represents an early attempt to analyze ancestor worship as a national ethic codified in the civil law and to detail its multireligiosity (Nobushige describes how the dead were encountered as either *kami* or *hotoke*—deities or buddhas). Appeals to an essential Japanese spirit continue to shape descriptive accounts of religious practice, particularly those produced within and for the Buddhist goods industry (e.g., Kobori 2017).

Early Japanese-language research into ancestor veneration focused on collating detailed descriptions of regional variation and theorizing the practice's origins. This body of work is shaped by the overwhelming influence of Yanagita Kunio (柳田国男). Yanagita, the founding father of the Japanese discipline of folkloristics (民俗学 *minzokugaku*), has had a marked, if under-realized, influence on Japanese anthropology (Kuwayama 2004, 14). Vlastos argues that Yanagita "invented *the tradition* of Japanese tradition by claiming that Japan's preservation of its original culture made Japan unique among modern nations" (1998, 12, original emphasis). Much Japanese scholarship on ancestor veneration in the post–World War II period can be read as a response to Yanagita.

Yanagita's magnum opus, *Senzo no hanashi* (先祖の話 *Concerning the Ancestors*) (1946), draws a direct line between the practice of making seasonal offerings to the ancestors at "spirit shelves," *tamadana* (魂棚) or *bondana* (盆棚), during the Yayoi period (300 BCE–250 CE) of Japanese history and contemporary *butsudan* practice. He does so through historical reconstructions and comparison of the rites of O-bon (an ostensibly Confucian/Buddhist celebration) and rites of the New Year (an ostensibly Shinto or folk religion celebration). This allows him to forward an argument about the original identity of ancestors as tutelary deities of villages or clans (氏神 *ujigami*), mountain gods, and field gods (Ooms 1967, 204). Yanagita provides, however, very little empirical evidence to support his argument (Kuwayama 2004, 14); subsequent folklorists have attempted to bolster his claims but have also criticized and amended the model (e.g., Hirayama 1949; Takeda 1953). In this regard, Yanagita's work must be understood within the context of its production. Completed in the last months of World War II, *Senzo no hanashi* was heavily influenced by the earlier school of *kokugaku* (国学), or nativist studies, which sought to uncover and preserve the origins of Japanese culture (Bokhoven 2005, 10; Mayer and Ishiwara 1970). Proponents of this school, like famed eighteenth-century scholar Hirata Atsutane, held Confucianism (and to a lesser extent Buddhism) responsible for what they saw as the corruption of native ancestor worship (Kirby 1910).

Many scholars diverge significantly from Yanagita's nativist stance. Takeda Chōshū acknowledges the possible identification of ancestors with tutelary deities but also recognizes the significant contributions of Buddhism:

> This is not so much the influence of Buddhism on the Japanese ancestor worship as the metamorphosis of Buddhism in the course of its interaction with the indigenous folk faith. (1976, 122–23)

Buddhism came to Japan around the sixth century. One origin story, set out in *The Chronicles of Japan* (日本書紀 *Nihon Shoki*), describes a gift of religious art from the Kingdom of Baekje (located in modern-day southwest Korea). Scholars also identify earlier envoys from continental Asia (Deal and Ruppert 2015, 13–18). Buddhism first gained popularity among the elite classes, and their possessions, including the seventh-century Buddhist shrine known as *tamamushi* (玉虫) and Lady Tachibana's shrine (both now held at Hōryū-ji [法隆寺], Nara), are identified as early possible antecedents of *butsudan* (Hirayama 1949, 60; Rambelli 2010, 64). An oft-cited passage of *The Chronicles of Japan* describes an edict issued by the Emperor Tenmu (天武天皇) around 685 CE regarding the creation of Buddhist shrines:

> In every house a Buddhist shrine should be provided, and an image of Buddha with Buddhist scriptures placed there. Worship and offerings of food [are to be] made at these shrines.[8]

John Nelson describes how Tenmu faced a series of "weird omens" indicating an imbalance of spiritual forces, including strong earthquakes, vertical rainbows, and sparrows with three legs, and thus may have turned to the foreign cult and its reputed powers to secure his rule (2008, 309). The historical impact of Tenmu's edict on the proliferation of *butsudan* has been challenged, however, on the grounds that the language refers to "public buildings" and not commoners' residences (Rambelli 2010, 71)..

Architecturally, strong candidates for early *butsudan* are private Buddhist halls (持仏堂 *jibutsudō*) belonging to the aristocratic classes of the Heian era (794–1185). Takeda Chōshū (1953) and Hirayama Toshijirō (1959) have separately argued that over time these external structures moved inside the domestic complex, becoming rooms dedicated to Buddhist ritual and ancestor veneration (仏間 *butsuma*) and eventually, during the Meiji period (1868–1912), smaller cabinets placed inside a room (仏壇 *butsudan*). Within the Tōgudo Buddhist Hall (東求堂) of the Ginkaku-ji temple, constructed in 1486, there is evidence of a shelf containing ancestral tablets or *ihai*, erected apart from the main Buddhist image. This style of architecture was adopted by many Zen Buddhist temples after the Edo period, and the *ihaidana* were also built into houses. Although the *butsudan* sold today are generally freestanding units, altars arranged on shelves built into wall alcoves (仕込み仏壇 *shikomi butsudan* or 造り付け仏壇 *tsukuritsuke butsudan*) are not uncommon in certain regions. In summary, the *Guidance on Buddhist Altars and Buddhist Goods* offers up three objects: personal Buddhist halls (持仏堂 *jibutsudō*), ancestral tablet shelves (位牌棚 *ihaidana*), and spirit shelves (魂棚 *tamadana*), with their respective origins in Buddhist, Confucian, and Shinto/folk traditions, as the main historical influences that converge within the form of contemporary *butsudan* (BKSSK 2015, 176).

These narratives and debates remain vital within the contemporary industry, where they are deployed as evidence of an essential, if now threatened, component of Japanese national identity. In my conversations with *butsudan* retailers and clergy, this was often expressed as a natural inclination for Japanese people to join hands before an altar, rather than as a particular set of teachings. An industry publication by Kobori Kenichi, entitled *Japan's Pride: A Non-Religious Attitude*,[9] describes *butsudan* as modeling "a feeling of gratitude to one's antecedents" that is "shared by all Japanese" (2017, 1). This statement affirms a wider trend in popular culture of recasting ancestor worship not as a religion but as "common sense for all Japanese" (Dorman 2007, 34). This occurs both through suppression of its foreign origins and through emphasizing the power of Japanese culture to localize and remake foreign elements. In her work on Japanese modernity, Ivy describes how "Japan is literally unimaginable outside its positioning vis-à-vis the West," having been "as a *nation-state* . . . instaurated in response to the threat of domination by European and American powers in the mid-nineteenth century" (1995, 4). However, in the world of religious retailing, China is the earlier and more pertinent foil, and continues to loom large as much *butsudan* manufacture has moved off-shore.

Overt public appeals to *butsudan*'s Buddhist origins are often more subtle. One notable reference to a Buddhist imaginary appears in a share-holders' report for Hasegawa Butsudan (2005), which supports the quality of the altars it manufactured in Myanmar via an appeal to a shared, trans-national Buddhist identity. More explicitly, Takimoto Bukkōdō in Osaka runs events in the local community to celebrate Buddhist holidays, which include having employees dress up in Buddha costumes and distribute sweets to children. The store's public Facebook page also makes overtures to Buddhism, with one post describing it as "the only religion that was not spread through violence." As will become apparent, aligning oneself with or main-taining distance from religious institutions is for *butsudan* retailers a strate-gic move, accompanied by risk and reward. Companies may publicize their Buddhist credentials by marketing historic acts of devotion, such as large donations, artistic productions, or sutra readings. Perhaps the most direct example of this I encountered was at Ōgoshi Butsudan, where their five-story, pagoda-shaped showroom features a twenty-meter-high painting of Amida. In the showroom there is a hand-painted mural depicting the death of the Buddha surrounded by his followers, several of whom appear in the likeness of the Ōgoshi chairman, his wife, and his son.

Most scholars of Japanese material religion give a more judicious ac-count, which recognizes the multifaceted origins of the *butsudan* tradition. Jeroen Bokhoven (2005), for example, suggests that the *butsudan* arose out of the confluence of (at least) five different historical events: (1) the enforce-ment of the temple-parishioner system (檀家制度 *danka seido*, or 寺請制度 *terauke seido*); (2) the introduction of *ihai* from China; (3) the travels of roaming spiritual teachers, or *hijiri* (聖), throughout Japan; (4) the religious fervor of Jōdo Shinshū followers; and (5) the development of the *butsudan* industry. Of these, the *danka* system and the industry are most pertinent for this investigation.

The *danka* system had a dramatic influence on social, political, and reli-gious life in Japan, including the diffusion of *butsudan*. As enforced by the Tokugawa Shogunate in 1638, it legally formalized a long-term affiliation be-tween households and temples, such that Buddhism came to function as a semigovernmental institution (Takeda 1976, 129). Each household was re-quired to register with a mainstream Buddhist temple, which allowed the Tokugawa government to suppress the spread of Christianity and radical

Buddhist schools (Hur 2007, 9). The *danka* system also strengthened popular consciousness of the household unit (Bokhoven 2005, 28). Rambelli describes how temples were required to certify that their patrons visited a temple frequently, owned prayer beads, enshrined a Buddha image, and made offerings to that image regularly (2010, 73). Indeed, although the term *butsudan* is now written with two characters meaning "Buddha" (仏 *butsu*) and "shelf" (壇 *dan*), the original character for *dan* was 檀, derived from the word for "patron" (檀家 *danka*) (Rambelli 2010, 64). Finally, the *danka* system made temples responsible for the performance of funerals for patrons, helping to establish Japanese Buddhism as "funerary Buddhism" (葬式仏教 *sōshiki bukkyō*).[10]

The Meiji Restoration (1868) brought modernization and the end of the feudal era, but the subsequent Meiji Civil Code (1896) still enshrined "ancestor worship" (先祖崇拝 *senzo sūhai*) as a national ethic (Takeda 1976, 132). It codified the position of the patrilineal household and the duties of the household head (usually the eldest male) toward their ancestors. In particular, the code put forth that "the *ie* (and therefore, ancestral rites) exists in perpetuity and must never be allowed to lapse" (Takeda 1976, 129). After World War II, a reformed civil code made inheritance laws more egalitarian, shifting from primogeniture (the eldest son as sole heir) inheritance to an equal distribution among all siblings, at least on paper, if not always in practice (Kawano 2010, 38). But this did not extend to "ceremonial assets," including the *butsudan* and grave, which cannot be easily divided and distributed. While the *danka* and the household have been significantly weakened, they retain power today, if not as lived reality then, at the very least, as powerful ideal (Rowe 2011, 4; Boret 2014, 62–65).

The emergence and development of the *butsudan* industry are far less studied and understood. Its origins are generally traced to *busshi* (仏師), or Buddhist sculptors, who specialized in constructing temple halls for elites (Bokhoven 2005, 30–33). Such artisans congregated around Kyoto, which established itself as a center for traditional crafts, and the industry slowly expanded to meet popular demand. Published in 1690, the *Illustrated Compendium of People and Their Professional Status* (人倫訓蒙図彙 *jinrin kunmō zui*) lists more than twenty-five categories of artisans related to religious goods, including makers of *ihai* and temple carpenters (Rambelli 2017, 9; BKSSK 2015, 157). Similarly, the *Guidance on Buddhist Altars and Buddhist Goods* reproduces drawings of retailers of ritual instruments for altars that originally appeared in late seventeenth-century Kyoto periodicals such as the *Kyōto Suzume Atooi* (BKSSK 2015, 154–55). One of the first recorded uses of the term "*butsudan* store" (仏壇屋 *butsudanya*) also dates to this period (BKSSK 2015, 155), suggesting a significant popularization of altars.

As even this brief foray into the history and form of *butsudan* reveals, these artifacts bring together diverse material and symbolic traditions into seemingly fragile and fluid assemblages. What is often omitted by these official histories, and further hidden from the customer's view, is the labor that goes into making *butsudan*. Altar craftsmanship has not been the subject of sustained study (cf. Araki 2005), and its embodied traditions are rarely transcribed or transmitted textually. But in the act of crafting, the history and present of *butsudan* form converge, with significant consequences for how people encounter the dead in the everyday.

MAKING

In my mind, President Yamashita's *butsudan* (plate 3) is always paired with another altar, of equally impressive artisanal skill and regional style. I encountered the latter in the garage of a *butsudan* maker in Toyama Prefecture, where it was stashed behind a motorcycle. Decorated in the same Jōdo Shinshū style, the altar features an intricate set of internal folding doors constructed from batons and mesh and embroidered with gold thread. The gold leaf applied throughout is so thin that it reveals the texture of the underlying wood grain. The altar came into the care of Kawasaki-san, artisan and heir to a local *butsudan* company, when a customer downsized to a smaller model and could not locate a relative willing to inherit it. Impressed by its rare decorative techniques, Kawasaki does not wish to dismantle it, but he lacks the time and finances required to fully restore it. Perhaps he will strip it for parts. For now, it sits in the garage, where it has been stored for over five years; as I discuss in chapter 4, objects like altars are difficult to dispose of. The ongoing vanishing of the *butsudan* tradition creates cumbersome remains, and it is among these remains that artisans like Kawasaki now live and work.

Kawasaki is first and foremost a *butsudan* joiner, a trade he inherited from his father, but he also works with lacquer and gold leaf. He is humorously nihilistic about the future of the industry, commenting at regular intervals throughout our meetings that "it's all over" (もう終わり *mō owari*). For his generation of *butsudan* artisans, on the cusp of taking over the family business, the economic outlook is grim. Between 1990 and 2000, the domestic religious goods manufacturing industry experienced declines of 25 percent in the number of firms and 40 percent in the number of workers (Araki 2005, 100).

On my first visit to his workshop, Kawasaki joked that he would much rather discuss the motorcycle, which he is also restoring, than discuss the altar. Above the garage his studio is filled with curling strips of wood, a large drying rack where *butsudan* parts are arranged, and, somewhat inexplicably, an unplugged television, dumped in the middle of the floor. It is uncomfortably warm, but the windows are shut tight to avoid gold leaf flying in the breeze and to preserve the *urushi* (漆), or lacquer. Kawasaki describes *urushi*, made from sap of the tree *Toxicodendron vernicifluum*, as a living being (生き物 *ikimono*) that responds to temperature and humidity. It is a little more than just stifling, as raw *urushi* lets off fumes that have been known to produce a mild allergic reaction or itching. In Kawasaki's workshop, different colors and qualities of *urushi* are stored in rice bowls with squares of plastic wrap covering the surface to prevent a skin from forming.

Kawasaki began working with *urushi* and gold leaf to supplement his income from joinery and because his family company could no longer source the artisans required to complete *butsudan* restoration projects. The crafting of *butsudan* is a collaborative undertaking, bringing together specialist artisans from throughout a region, or throughout Japan, or sometimes, overseas. As the market has contracted, many artisans have taken on multiple crafts or transitioned into retailing. This is the origin of prominent firms like Ōgoshi Butsudan in Toyama and Ikeda Butsudan in Kanazawa, which both began as joiners. Some of the smaller *butsudan* stores lining the streets in Kawasaki's town are staffed at irregular hours by retired artisans, whose children work office jobs in neighboring cities, but the majority are closed. Kawasaki estimates there are only about ten local makers left. Although the regional style favors grandiose golden altars in the Jōdo Shinshū tradition, many consumers now purchase inexpensive models online or from Tokyo-based retailers.

Perhaps because of its perceived conflict with the modern world, anthropologists have exhibited renewed interest in craft over the last two decades. Luckman and Thomas describe "a zeitgeist moment of popularity as part of 'turn toward the tactile' . . . in the digital age" (2018, 1). Craft reemerges after topics like material culture and technology, traditionally associated with anthropology's roots in the ethnographic museum and concomitant models of cultural evolution, "broke under the weight of anthropology's need in the 1990s onwards to speak to the contemporary, urban, and cosmopolitan" (DeNicola and Wilkinson-Weber 2016, 1). Scholars today assert that craft is "fully contemporary" but also describe tensions resulting from clashes with the temporalities and geographies of a capitalist world system (DeNicola and Wilkinson-Weber 2016, 2). As of 2019, more than 80 percent of all *butsudan* sold in Japan are imported from overseas, overwhelmingly from China and Southeast Asia (although as a total percentage of sales, this number has fallen slightly post-COVID disruptions).[11] In Japan, *butsudan* artisans often struggle to communicate the value of their craft across the commodity chain to consumers. Further, they are confronted by rival value systems centered on ideas of regionalism and cosmopolitan interior design, which shape the cultural heritage discourse, on the one hand, and the contemporary altar market, on the other. These discourses can constrain artisans' ability to adapt and continue practice.

Making altars, training senses

Itō Butsudan is the first altar workshop I ever visited, accompanied by Tamara Kohn and Daisuke Uriu, back in 2016. Located in the suburban outskirts of Saitama, Kantō, it appears, from the outside, nondescript, until one is hit by the acrid scent of wood varnish. Itō-san manufactures the wooden frames and interior structures of Tokyo-style *karaki butsudan*. Entering the store, we were greeted by President Itō, a second-generation artisan who has been making *butsudan* for nearly fifty years. He is distinguished by his round face, spectacles, and rough, calloused hands.

The walls of the front office are almost invisible behind layers of order forms, calendars, and promotional materials. A few *butsudan* are arranged around the room: damaged altars awaiting repair and one or two new models ready for delivery. Next door, I hear dry wood being sanded. Two workers sit cross-legged on layers of newspaper, surrounded by *butsudan* parts (figure 1.3). They wear white masks to lessen their inhalation of wood dust particles. Their work appears engaging; beside them, a tray with untouched cups of green tea perches precariously on a stack of *butsudan* drawers wrapped in last month's sports section.

The company used to make grand *karaki butsudan*, one to two meters tall, from rosewood and ebony. Today, compact versions, about fifty centimeters square, with more subdued decorative features are popular. As rosewood and ebony have become expensive and their import restricted, Itō has increasingly favored teak from Indonesia, which he praises for providing a smooth finish with few knots. Each wooden piece is cut using machine tools, then sanded. The frame is slotted together without the use of nails or adhesives, and veneers of a more expensive wood are applied over the teak. The surface is finished by hand with at least ten repetitions of staining and sanding to achieve a rich color; a natural oil was once favored, but today Itō applies a synthetic compound that stains rather than varnishes the wood. In total, three people work over the span of several weeks to construct a single *butsudan* frame.

One of my first questions to Itō seems both to confuse and get to the heart of his practice: who designs *butsudan*? I had assumed, rather naïvely, that there must be templates mandated by different Buddhist schools, a single

Figure 1.3. Sanding Tokyo-style *butsudan*, Tokyo, 2016.

artist for each model, or perhaps a past artisan whose designs continue to be emulated. Itō's eventual reply, after the question goes through several clarifications, is that "*butsudan* don't have a design [デザイン *dezain*], they just have a form [型 *kata*]." That is, there is no fixed model but, instead, a way of making, which has emerged across generations of artisans. The concept of *kata* is essential to understanding both the transmission and transformation of Japanese traditional arts, including performance arts such as Noh and martial arts like karate (e.g., Cox 2007; Hendry 2000; Yamada Shōji 2002). In these traditions, the creativity and distinction of individual artisans emerges not from unrestricted artistic freedom but from subtle amendments that add to the *kata* without destroying it (Yamada Shōji 2002, 167).[12] At Itō Butsudan, the in-house *kata* is materialized in long boards of timber that line the factory walls. Markings in pencil and ink down the boards give them the appearance of rulers. In-house style is distinguished by the tiniest of details, like the angle of joins—Itō describes his as "like the point of a katana [sword]"—and the gradient curve of the lip of the frame on the face of the altar. This exact curve is reproduced on the company's single pair of electric saw blades, which hang on the workshop wall. At other locations, such as Kawasaki's factory, the style is recorded in charcoal diagrams on paper, passed down from his grandfather.

To illustrate the character of Tokyo *butsudan*, Itō begins assembling a collection of freshly sanded parts. His apprentice places both shoulders inside the *butsudan* frame and flexes, slightly spreading its width. Together, he and Itō knock at the joints with the butt of their hands, which eventually enables Itō to insert a series of decorative carvings and two drawers into the frame. The wood, Itō explains, slowly hardens over time as it dries out and thus occasionally *butsudan* have to be forced back into their original shape (plate 4). Here he has used teak, but heavy woods like ebony and rosewood are even more prone to warping. In the moment, it strikes me that I have never seen anyone so confident in their physical interactions with *butsudan* and indeed, so rough in their use of force. After finally fitting the drawers into the frame, Itō demonstrates what he calls the "magic trick" of Tokyo *butsudan* and his craft: one drawer, when closed, fits so snugly into the frame that the other drawer is naturally forced open. He continues dramatically pushing the drawers in and out, explaining that, "it's only because it's a perfect fit that we are able to do this." Perhaps I fail to give a sufficiently impressed reaction, because he looks at me ruefully and shakes his head, "You don't get this? *This* is my job" (これが仕事なんだ *kore ga shigoto nanda*). It is not the first time, nor will it be the last, that a *butsudan* artisan accuses me of not being able to see, hear, feel, or smell something important.

Although markings on wood and paper condense the house style, they cannot be read in isolation from the enskillment of artisans' senses. *Kata* are embodied via continuous repetition. Joy Hendry suggests that repetition is valued by artisans "as the most appropriate method of acquiring artistic, and other (such as technological) skills" (2000, 179). In a similar vein, Cristina Grasseni's concept of "skilled visions" describes an interactive process of enculturated learning that equips the body with certain modes of sight in coordination with other senses, with artifacts and images acting as powerful generators of sense and cognition (2007, 6). Grasseni repositions vision within the context of other sensory attunements, whereby a skilled look is coordinated with skilled movement and skilled touch. She describes practitioners' attempts to blend the powerful systems of visual representation that set design standards with the embodied skills of apprenticeship. In the case of *butsudan*, these standards are set by diagrams like those in the *Guidance on Buddhist Altars and Buddhist Goods* and, increasingly, in retailers' marketing materials. For artisans, the visual appearance of altars is only one facet of their making. Indeed, in many cases, the quality of raw materials and artisanship can only be judged through smell or sound or touch, for example, in sensing tiny variations in wood grain.

For Shimatani-san, the sixth-generation owner of a company manufacturing brass bells (お鈴 *orin*), crafting requires that sound and sight be refined in combination. Entering his workshop in suburban Toyama, I am greeted by a soundscape very different from the dry wood sanding of Itō's factory. Given the importance of precise pitch in his profession, I am surprised at the level of noise. Sets of double doors throughout the facility muffle sound transmission between different spaces, but still I hear a German cuckoo clock that chimes every half hour, slamming doors, and the constant drone of hammering metal. Amid this cacophony, individual bells are welded together from strips of brass, then beaten by hand with a hammer and tuned. Skilled hearing, it becomes apparent, is as much about ignoring extraneous elements of the soundscape as it is about letting sound in.

The tuning of *orin* occurs incrementally: the artisan beats each section of the bell's rim with a small hammer, then tests the effect on its tone. A roundish shape slowly emerges, but the impact of each strike is too infinitesimally small to judge by sight alone and so must be continuously tested by ear. Shimatani explains that there are three components to the sound of bells: *kan*, *otsu*, and *mon*. *Kan* are the vibrations that disappear quickly; before tuning, the waveform of bells is only *kan*, rapid and close together. *Otsu* are the middle waves, more subtle and difficult to hear, and finally, *mon* are the lower, slower waves that move through the sound as a whole. Cheap bells have only *kan*, but *mon* is the factor by which you judge a quality bell. As Shimatani explains these patterns, he raises and lowers his hand rapidly in front of his chest to demonstrate *kan*, and then stretches down to the floor and above his head for *mon*. Once again, the crafting of *butsudan* strikes me as far less formulaic than I first imagined it might be. I had expected that bells were tuned to a particular pitch, perhaps varying between Buddhist schools. Instead, Shimatani talks about drawing out the best timbre that exists inside each bell, just as later, a Buddhist sculptor would describe his practice to me as "releasing the Buddha from the tree."

The tuning of bells is gradual. Like *butsudan* frames, bells harden with time and manipulation. Smaller bells are more difficult to make, as they soon become brittle and then must be reheated; making a good bell is about knowing when to stop. What, then, is a good sound? Shimatani pauses before replying:

> A good sound? Well . . . there is no true good or perfect sound. Everything depends on the taste of the maker, or on their *sense*, which is felt in one's body, in one's chest.

The "sense" to which Shimatani refers is neither immediate nor natural but is gained over many years of tutelage. Shimatani's own apprenticeship lasted for fifteen years. For the first five years, he was only permitted to sit by his grandfather's side, listening. The next ten years he spent tuning bells with a small hammer and anvil, each time checked by a master. It was not until he had worked for two to three years on his own that he finally reached a degree of mastery. In this manner, both the object and the artisan are tuned through the process of crafting bells. Richard Sennett describes the intimate relationship between the body of the artisan, their tools, and the materials. His focus is on the hands, as "intelligent" tools capable of precise attunement to the level of prehension (grasping); "the body molded to fit the material world" (2008, 149–55). Applying this to altar making, the "*butsudan*-artisan" can be read as an entangled assemblage that emerges through the process of crafting. Calluses build up on artisans' hands just as layers of lacquer and gold accrue on altars.

This *butsudan*-artisan is an increasingly vulnerable assemblage, one threatened by automation, offshore manufacture, and consumer demand for cheaper, simpler altars requiring fewer artisanal skills. Globalization has had an unequal impact on Japanese *butsudan* artisans. Large retail companies now manufacture most of their stock overseas, and there are few opportunities for the global marketing or export of domestic *butsudan* craft. Sennett makes a plea for protecting these fragile assemblages from the pressures of global capitalism. In some cases, Japanese artisans have been able to engage with global economic and aesthetic systems to leverage their position within hierarchies of value operating in Japan. For example, as recounted in Brian Moeran's monograph on potters in southern Japan (1997), artisans were able to tap into a global revivalist movement of folk art and thus elevate their work. For *butsudan* artisans, difficulties of the global marketplace manifest closer to home. Frustrations are directed less toward foreign artisans than to domestic *butsudan* retailers and clergy, who they accuse of failing to communicate the value of their craft. This situation is exacerbated by the contemporary popularity and promotion of "modern *butsudan*."

Making butsudan *modern*

The emergence of modern *butsudan* (現代仏壇 *gendai butsudan*) is perhaps the most visible and significant transformation to *butsudan* manufacture and design in the last few decades. The moniker describes a heterogeneous array of products, broadly characterized by their compact size, minimal ornamentation, and à la mode design. They typically have an open interior (with no miniature temple structure) and an exterior that blends with contemporary furniture. As such, their manufacture is easily automated. The design of modern altars also provides fewer opportunities for the visible demonstration of artisanal skill. Where such skill is involved, it is often too subtle for most laypeople to appreciate. However, "modern *butsudan*" is an umbrella category, that spans high-end models designed by celebrity architects and crafted using expensive raw materials and "cheap but cheerful" altars made from chipboard or even cardboard covered in paper printed to mimic wood grain. These materials open altars up to an expanded range of colors and together with plastic (rather than bronze) candles, incense holders, and vases, make *butsudan* cheaper, easier to repair, and easier to clean.

Since the 1990s, modern *butsudan* have been positively received in urban areas, surpassing sales of traditional altars. According to the 2018 industry-wide survey conducted by Shūkyō Kōgeisha, the Religious Craft Association, stores in central Tokyo report that, on average, 80 percent of sales are of modern altars (2019, 6–7). In contrast, for Ōgoshi Butsudan, trading in the more rural areas of Toyama and Ishikawa, modern altars account for approximately 20 percent of sales. The difference is most likely due to more spacious homes in the region, the prominence of Jōdo Shinshū populations, and higher levels of religious participation among the local, older population (see Roemer 2009, 316). Modern *butsudan* were developed by the industry in response both to consumer demand and to declining sales. Modern *butsudan* are generally better suited to the Western-style floor plans of apartments, which might lack a dedicated room or alcove to house religious displays. They are thus heavily marketed to families living in urban areas (Nakamaki 2003, 23–235).

Although *butsudan* are not yet lined up next to flat-pack furniture in Ikea or domestic furniture giant Nitori, the industry is increasingly market-oriented and popularist.[13] The reorientation of the market toward responding to consumer desires and minimalist aesthetics does more than mark a shift in *butsudan* material form; it has implications for the whole production process and the role of artisans within it. My question regarding "who designs *butsudan*" found little purchase when talking to Itō, but it was animatedly taken up by staff at large *butsudan* firms. Companies like Hasegawa convene multiperson product development teams and design *butsudan* in response to multiyear market research surveys. As I describe in chapter 5, these teams also take inspiration from a range of experimental prototypes launched by independent artists, tech entrepreneurs, and global industry trends.

An ongoing partnership between Hasegawa and Japanese furniture designers for the company's "LIVE-ing" collection (リビング・コレクション) exemplifies these high-level changes to how *butsudan* are designed and produced. In late 2017, Hasegawa first launched a product range known as SOLID BOARD JUST that was designed in consultation with Shizuoka furniture maker Karimoku Kaguya.[14] The altars are approximately fifty centimeters square and manufactured entirely in Japan (a rarity for modern *butsudan*) using imported walnut and oak. They are constructed so as to blend seamlessly with the existing product ranges sold by Karimoku, including a 70-by-60-centimeter double-door storage cupboard that acts as a stand. This design facilitates easy coordination with other furniture in high-use and high-visibility areas of the home. According to the Hasegawa website (October 2019), the range was designed to "increase opportunities for communing with the dead in modern everyday life," by removing the "gloomy" (暗い *kurai*) associations surrounding *butsudan*. Indeed, online customer testimonials praise the product for its "very bright atmosphere, cute feeling," and "natural warmth." The suite of products is luxurious, costing upward of 460,000 yen per set (altar and stand), but this figure pales in comparison to the cost of custom-made artisan models. Such was the initial demand for SOLID BOARD JUST, that within six months of release the company's production line was at full capacity. In total, Hasegawa sold approximately twenty-seven thousand *butsudan* in 2017/2018, and about 60 percent of those were part of the collaboration with Karimoku (Kamakura Shinsho 2018). The product continues to grace the front page of the Hasegawa website and has inspired further collaborations with furniture designers. Hasegawa also periodically updates the product line, tailoring new designs to address feedback gathered from in-store interactions with customers. In this way, ready-made *butsudan* designs that are carefully calibrated toward consumer demands have proved extremely successful.

Perhaps unsurprisingly, artisans are among those most critical voices of contemporary *butsudan* design and manufacture. In Itō's workshop, furniture-style *butsudan* were often met with skepticism, if not scorn. Much sighing and shaking of heads was involved in our discussion of the topic. Yagiken Butsudan, having fully embraced overseas automated manufacture and secular furniture-style designs (家具調 *kaguchō*), is particularly infamous within the industry. Indeed, substantial bad blood between Yagiken and other *butsudan* retailers meant that my engagement with the former had to be limited. Itō is rather definitive in his pronouncement that these altars "are just made to mimic the shape of *butsudan*. They are not the real thing." He also makes altars for national *butsudan* chains but clearly distinguishes the *butsudan* he crafts from mass-produced altars of similar size and ornamentation. In the company of artisans, then, "furniture" (家具 *kagu*) can be a derogatory term.

The exact qualities of what makes a "real" *butsudan* can be difficult to discern. For example, modern *butsudan* typically lack the hourglass-shaped raised wooden platform known as *shumidan* (須弥壇) (figure 1.4) upon which the icon is placed, and for Itō, if there is no *shumidan*, then there is no *butsudan*:

> The meaning of the *butsudan* is a miniature temple, right? If that's true then what is the point/meaning of furniture *butsudan*? Young people today will look at those *butsudan* and think "aahhh what a lovely design" [デザイン], but you can't put the ancestral tablets in there. That shouldn't be done.

Looking back, I am surprised by the degree of Buddhist orthodoxy in Itō's comments. I had not previously observed any sign that he viewed them as sacred objects, at least in their various stages of assembly in the workshop. This is true of all artisans I spoke to, with the exception, perhaps, of some *busshi*, for whom carving Buddhist statues is part of a daily meditative practice. As I talked more with Itō about modern *butsudan*, it became clear that it was not just the decline of religiously marked altars—their shift from reliquary to furniture—that drew disapproval. It was also something about the manufacturing process and the lack of physical effort involved therein:

> Other *butsudan* makers you will visit have huge factories and lots of machines, they are completely different to this operation. You can't call them artisans, they don't do a lot of handicraft [手仕事 *teshigoto*]. Even if they make it by hand, they don't do the small details because it's bothersome. . . . The one in Shizuoka, you just put the wood into the machine and *ba~~*, out pops the *butsudan* at the other end.

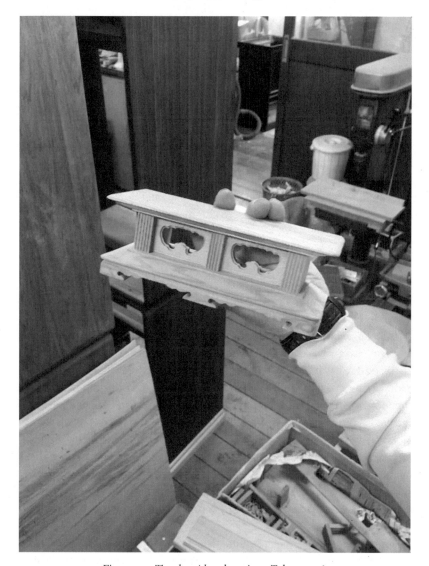

Figure 1.4. The *shumidan* altar piece. Tokyo, 2016.

In light of this comment, one additional reading of the significance of the *shumidan* emerges: these ornaments are too intricate to be machinable and so speak to the necessity of hand carving in making altars. Many artisans I spoke with similarly invoked a connection between skilled hands and wood over time, rather than specific religious or symbolic features, when speaking of the form of true *butsudan*.

These qualities of a real or good *butsudan* are difficult to communicate to consumers, who often walk into retail stores with little to no understanding of *butsudan*, let alone the artisan tradition behind them. Although certain patrons like President Yamashita still invest in artisanal *butsudan*, the value of handicraft cannot compete on a broad scale with the low prices created by overseas and automated manufacture or the cosmopolitan allure of newer designs. As I describe in the next chapter, modern *butsudan* are sold through branded images of a contemporary family lifestyle. These packaged designs communicate differential value and create choice for knowledge-poor consumers. The qualities of hands and time are more difficult to discern or market in the final products. Salespeople sometimes resort to offering customers a sample of wood or lacquerware to examine, but the systems that codify traditional *butsudan* do not do well to communicate artisans' skill.

Making butsudan *traditional*

Like all craft traditions that enter a heritage context, the parameters that define artisanal *butsudan* production have become more and more tightly drawn. In Japan, the official category of "traditional handicraft" (伝統工芸品 *dentō kōgeihin*) is a product of Meiji era invention and debate (Murata 2015, 10; Satō 2011). As defined by the Ministry of Economy, Trade and Industry, traditional handicraft must (a) be used in everyday life; (b) be handmade; (c) involve skills and raw materials practiced and transmitted for over a hundred years; and (d) be established as an industry in a specific region. Certified artisans must have a minimum of twelve years of experience and undergo an examination of skill from peers. But certification is also a political process. Eades et al. note that the "the forces of globalisation mean that the rules themselves have to be flexible in wording, in interpretation, and in enforcement" or no artisans would qualify (2000, 179). Leeway is given in many areas, such as the machining of certain elements before they are finished by hand.

Domestic, if not regional, production is the number-one signifier of value communicated to consumers in *butsudan* stores, advertisements, and price tags. For example, the Japanese Religious Goods Association certifies that *butsudan* adhere to regional production standards.[15] But this is not what is always most valued about *butsudan* by artisans. Itō, for example, appears less concerned with the overseas production of altars than with the automation of the manufacture process. He tells me that when *butsudan* workshops were first established in China, many companies sent over Japanese master craftspeople to train local apprentices. These artisan traditions have since flourished and reached an extremely high standard. Indeed, I often heard praise for Chinese artisans and their commitment to hundreds of hours of intricate handicraft that would be impossible in Japan today. Itō's ire is thus largely directed domestically to *butsudan* retailers and Buddhist priests who he feels are "not doing their job" to teach younger generations the importance of *butsudan*.

One sad corollary of location-based *butsudan* certification systems is that when one artisan retires or dies, an entire style of *butsudan* can be lost. For this reason, President Yamashita's *butsudan*, although decorated in the Mikawa style, is not technically a Mikawa Butsudan. Almost no regions are now able to complete entire *butsudan* exclusively (Araki 2005, 2). There is perhaps only one working artisan in Kanazawa able to produce the *ranma* (欄間), a carved transom or altar crosspiece, in that regional style. At over seventy years old, he has no apprentice in training; when he dies, the tradition of Kanazawa *butsudan* will die with him. Even if somebody could complete a (rapid) apprenticeship, it would be rather unfair, as there is slim livelihood to be made from carving in contemporary Japan. Even as Itō, like many other *butsudan* artisans I visited, proudly showed off the thick calluses that covered his palms, he seemed to acknowledge that he was on the losing side of a battle: "It's an interesting job, but how are you supposed to go on?"

Some younger artisans have sought to adapt their skills to the manufacture and marketing of modern *butsudan*. Others have transitioned into new industries such as home décor and jewelry, producing everything from lacquered sake bottles to bespoke doorbells. A few have even begun making products for the burgeoning New Age or spiritualist market, which has come to rival organized religion in contemporary Japan. In Kyoto, I met the sixth-generation owner of a Buddhist prayer beads company that had recently started making healing crystal or "power stone" (パワーストン) bracelets, largely targeted at young professional women with an interest in tarot, astrology, or alternative therapies. Many younger artisans are tech-savvy and try to circumvent retailers to reach new customers directly, even launching their products on crowdfunding sites like Kickstarter.

In comparison to his colleagues in bronze casting, Kawasaki has yet to find an obvious lateral move. He is part of the Takaoka *densan* (伝産), or "traditional industry," collective, which during his father's generation had about 250 members. Today, there are around fifty. Upon hearing about my research, *densan* members jokingly asked me to advise Kawasaki how best to rebrand. They had been able to take advantage of Takaoka's regional fame for bronze casting and so move into new markets. However, there are far more famous Japanese regions for lacquer and gold leaf, and Kawasaki has found it difficult to compete. Further, for those trained in crafts inextricably and exclusively tied to *butsudan*, such as the architecture of miniature temple roofs, a new career in the arts is all the more challenging.

Despite a bleak outlook for the future of his industry, Kawasaki is unwilling to produce the furniture-style altars that are now popular. Although much of the literature on crafts in the contemporary age emphasizes artisans' flexibility and adaptability, refusing to compromise, even if it means one's craft tradition will decline, is also a powerful move. One day, a man walked into Kawasaki's workshop asking to purchase a modern *butsudan*. Kawasaki directed the customer to stores in the city or online, as he does not stock these altars. The man was insistent and pointed to a small cabinet in the corner of the workshop. And so, as Kawasaki tells it, this was the moment that he sold his television stand as a "modern *butsudan*." Whether or not this story is entirely true (I have my doubts), the image it conjures, of a highly skilled artisan with a golden *butsudan* gathering dust behind a motorcycle who sold his household furniture as a modern altar, illustrates some of the wryer ironies of contemporary religious retailing in Japan. For now, Kawasaki remains in the *butsudan* business, but his television now sits in the middle of his floor.

As Joylon Thomas argues (2015), narratives of decline can be powerful discursive tools, intentionally deployed to generate popular support, advocate for reform, or align religious practice with the politics of the day. On the one hand, decline motivates a salvationist ethos, to define and protect Japan's traditional crafts before they disappear. This is carried out through detailed cataloging of altar forms, legal protections, and certification systems. On the other hand, decline motivates efforts to reinvent altars for a modern consumer and globalized marketplace, as part of a wider, pragmatic religious revivalism movement in Japan (what John Nelson dubs "experimental Buddhism" [2013]). The effect of both moves is to distill ideas about what *butsudan* were, are, and could be. However, not all ideas or values are equally empowered or circulated. Artisans face particular difficulties in translating their embodied skill of crafting *butsudan* into a sign of quality and economic value that can be communicated to customers during the retail experience.

Across different stages in the lifecourse, I will continue to encounter passionate laments and resigned eulogies about the state of *butsudan* artisanship and Japan's domestic craft traditions. Whether or not this mourning is shared by a general populace is less certain. There is a huge gap in knowledge and familiarity between *butsudan* artisans and consumers, the latter being largely unaware of the history, religious symbolism, and artisan tradition of *butsudan*. Given this ignorance, why do (at least some) consumers continue to invest many millions of yen in *butsudan*? What do they value about altars? For this, we must look to the retail encounter.

[CHAPTER 2]

Retail

Two men walk into Hasegawa Ginza, the flagship location for Japan's largest and only publicly traded *butsudan* company, and make their way upstairs to the display of *ihai* (位牌 ancestral tablets). The three-story showroom is located in Tokyo's most fashionable shopping district, nestled between Harry Windsor and Armani. From the outside, I think it resembles a jewelry box, with yards of woven gold thread suspended before floor-to-ceiling windows. Inside, female staff dressed in identical black suits and black ruffled shirts position themselves strategically around the showroom floor, accompanying individual customers upstairs to where rows of *butsudan*, *ihai*, and *butsugu* (Buddhist goods) line the walls (figure 2.1). Their black outfits mimic the formal mourning wear (喪服 *mofuku*) commonly worn at funerals. Members of the management team, all men impeccably dressed in three-piece suits, occasionally join the women on the floor to cover busy periods or to facilitate the commission of a grave. Behind the scenes, in an office no larger than a broom cupboard, team members write up quotes for new *butsudan*, manage online inquiries, and prepare tea.

The two men—the senior dressed in a suit, the junior in jeans—stare at the rows of *ihai* for several moments, quietly conjecturing about differences in quality and size. Matsumoto-san, a petite woman in her sixties and one of my mentors at the store, steps in to offer counsel and I follow behind. As it transpires, their mission today is urgent. The mother died three weeks ago and with her forty-nine-day service approaching, they have yet to purchase an *ihai*, which acts as the vessel for the spirit of the deceased in this ceremony. Matsumoto explains that at least ten days are required to complete the etching of the *ihai*, and thus the order must be placed today. After several minutes of hedged questioning, Matsumoto discovers that the men are in fact brothers, not husband and son, as I had presumed. She sympathizes aloud with the older man, who, at thirty years of age, has just taken guardianship of his younger brother and has no living relatives to help him through the process of performing his mother's death rites. Staring at the *ihai*, the

Figure 2.1. Showroom at Hasegawa Butsudan, in Tokyo's Ginza. Image courtesy of Hasegawa Co. Ltd., 2022.

older brother expresses reservations at the prices (ranging from 12,000 to upward of 175,000 yen), which he notes are far higher than at other stores he has visited. Matsumoto apologizes and tries to explain their value, describing the high-end materials and artisanship that have gone into their manufacture. These *ihai* are "sturdy" (しっかり *shikkari*); they give a comforting sense of solidity and are unlikely to topple over during an earthquake. She further explains that *ihai* is a one-time purchase, something to retain forever. As "the last thing you can do for the dead," it is worth making an investment.

The *ihai* display at Hasegawa is wedged between modern *butsudan* models decorated with sets of *butsugu* and icons. Matsumoto inquires gently, does the family own a *butsudan*? Are they planning to purchase one? Do they know which style? Confusion reigns. The men have a temporary altar set up in the living room to house their mother's urn. The urn is likely to remain there for some time, as the family has not yet established a grave. The older brother retrieves a folded packet of papers from his pocket that describe the orthodox progression of *kuyō* rites. His family belongs to the Nichiren school of Buddhism, a fact he discovered only after his mother's death. The entire process appears somewhat baffling, and Matsumoto, catching on, proceeds to give a simplified explanation of the role of *ihai* and *butsudan* in death rites. She then leads the brothers around the showroom, pointing out the features of different compact *butsudan* that could easily be placed in a modern living room. The younger brother follows behind, alternately surveying the *butsudan* and glancing at his phone, and very occasionally voicing his approval or objection to a certain model. He perks up when invited to strike the range of brass bells on display and is praised by Matsumoto for the adept performance. After lengthy discussion, the older brother sighs, "Okay, but today at least, we need to decide on an *ihai*." That task appears to require more time, as the pair thank Matsumoto, take her business card, and promise to return by evening.

The knowledge about *butsudan*, or lack thereof, demonstrated by this pair is not atypical of the contemporary customer I witnessed during my time working in *butsudan* stores. Indeed, popular disinterest in or ignorance about Buddhist teachings and ritual practice is an oft-remarked feature of Japanese religious life, particularly among younger generations, who might encounter *butsudan* and Buddhism for the first time upon a death in the family (Nelson 2008, 308).[1] The stage of the *butsudan* sales floor thus reveals an expertise gap indicative of a transformation in the transmission of ritual knowledge. Inge Daniels suggests that with growing numbers of people residing in nuclear families and urban areas with neolocal communities, rather than in multigenerational households, "ritual knowledge, no longer transferred through the extended family or the local community, became the preserve of commercial companies" (2010b, 85; also Suzuki H. 2013a, 10; Himonya 1994, 65–66). Despite widespread ignorance about the histories, religious meanings, and in some cases, practical uses of *butsudan*, it is notable that many people do still choose to invest substantial financial resources in their purchase. This puzzle of motivation is one that has captured the attention of scholars of Japanese religion more broadly. Ian Reader and George Tanabe famously describe Japanese religious life as driven by practical action and ritual habits aimed at securing "worldly benefits" in one's lifetime, and argue that Japanese religious practice shows that "human understanding is not a prerequisite for ritual to have power and effect" (1998, 127). Steven Heine suggests that we should also pay attention to the psychological effects, particularly the calm or peace of mind (安心 *anshin*) that rituals produce (2012, 177–83). As I will describe, both considerations appear pertinent in contemporary altar purchases, although, where the ancestors can no longer be relied upon to deliver the immediate, practical benefits of inheritance, the latter motivation is perhaps more germane.

As I note in the introduction, until recently, scholarly analysis of Buddhist economies cross-culturally has tended to focus on networks of patronage and donation that emanate from and support temples. In contrast, the activity of religious third actors has been largely overlooked. But these companies play a central role in facilitating and indeed shaping the everyday practice of Buddhism. Altar artisans and merchants were influential in disseminating *butsudan* across early modern Japan (Bokhoven 2005, 30). Today, they are some of the most publicly accessible agents of Buddhism, particularly in urban areas. As we shall see, sales negotiations are a key opportunity for retail staff to communicate their knowledge about *butsudan* to customers and for customers to ask questions in an atmosphere that is far more relaxed and informal than are interactions with clergy. Retailing is thus a key site at which the contemporary form and practice of *butsudan* is established.

The dynamics of death-related consumption cross-culturally make retail an interesting site for thinking about the lifecycle of necromaterials. A similar level of naïveté is observed among consumers engaging with the US and Australian funeral industries (Arnold et al. 2018, 101–2). The vast majority of consumers purchase funeral products and services on an "at-need" basis, that is, immediately after a death, and often cannot perform research and comparison (Sanders 2012, 267). Timelines set out by the ritual process, the decay of the body, or the availability of public services (e.g., the crematorium) can place additional pressures on the purchase of certain items. Indeed, funeral customers often exemplify the "impulse buyer" (Mitford 1963). In Japan, this purchasing pattern largely holds true, despite the growing trend toward preplanning one's own funeral and disposition. The interpersonal stakes surrounding funeral purchases after a recent bereavement also complicate this process, provoking family disputes with social, moral, and soteriological consequences. Finally, funerals and memorials tend to be one off purchases; extended relations between companies and consumers are rare, or might be rebuffed, as I describe in this chapter. This makes the retail encounter a potentially potent site of sociality and meaning-making.

Anthropology has tended to cast production and consumption in an antagonistic relationship, wherein consumption contests the alienation and coercion of commodities, appropriating and thus transforming market messages into individuated meaning (Suzuki 2000, 204–5). But in her ethnography of Japanese funeral homes, Hikaru Suzuki shows how an "interdependency between companies and consumers" might give rise to ritual practice (2000, 204). This chapter, which describes the process of negotiating a *butsudan* sale, similarly shows production, consumption, and disposal to be interrelated processes via which contemporary *butsudan* practice emerges. This is not to say that retailers and customers always agree. There are frequently disputes and capitulations, spoken and unspoken, on the showroom floor. Selecting the right altar is a difficult task. It means weighing up of the needs of the dead, the tastes of the living, practical considerations, aesthetics, and the marketing powers of salespeople. Through retail, people struggle with the messiness of investment and divestment from relations with the dead. Still, many people do invest, often because of a difficult-to-articulate, at times visceral desire to *do something for the dead*, whatever that may be.

SALES

Customer typologies and motivations

O-butsudan no Hasegawa (お仏壇のはせがわ) began as a single storefront in Nogota, Fukuoka, in 1929, and is now *the* premier Japanese *butsudan* chain, with a nationwide chain with 130 stores, 1,190 staff, and annual sales of twenty billion yen.[2] Like many larger *butsudan* firms, Hasegawa has pursued a strategy of franchising and investment diversification, as well as actively rebranding itself as a consultancy service and "one-stop shop" for products across the entire funeral and memorial process. My internship with Hasegawa, negotiated over several months and a series of personal introductions, begins at the corporate headquarters with instruction from famed (former) president Hasegawa Fusao on his personal religious-corporate philosophy. After a last-minute purchase of appropriate mourning wear, I am released onto the Ginza showroom floor to observe the everyday work of *butsudan* retail. This is where I spend most of my internship, learning from sales interactions and preparing the signature blend of cherry blossom tea for customers.

My internship begins on a freezing Saturday morning, which turns out to be the coldest day of the Heisei era (1989–2019). Upstairs, five different client groups are being guided through displays of the company's modern *butsudan* range (figure 2.2). Below, the ground floor is arrayed with boxes of candles and incense, prayer beads, and seasonal objets d'art. This floor attracts a steady stream of nearby office workers and well-dressed middle-aged women, who order formally wrapped boxes of incense, this being the obligatory gift for the recently bereaved. Customarily, such gifts are placed on a temporary funerary altar and burned throughout the day as an offering to the deceased. During the COVID-19 pandemic, incense companies saw a marked uptick in sales, as the practice of sending incense was embraced as an alternative to visiting the bereaved household. Staff treat incense customers with efficiency, deploying their extensive knowledge of the appropriate cost and quantity of incense to send, depending on the customer's relationship to the dead.[3] Hasegawa Ginza is a rarity among *butsudan* stores in that its location within the famous high-end shopping district also attracts

Figure 2.2. The range of modern *butsudan* on display at Hasegawa Butsudan,
Tokyo, 2018

foreign tourists. Most tourists peek in the windows and then walk on. Some
enter to peruse incense and objets d'art, but mostly quickly depart when
faced with a wall of unfamiliar ritual implements.

Being able to "read" customers as they walk into the store and accurately
assess their family situation, inclination to purchase, and even preferred
style of altar is a valuable skill within *butsudan* retail. Factors like age, gender, and style of dress all contribute to customer typologies that staff build
up through years of experience. These typologies allow one to individually
tailor the sales experience, for example by deploying certain staff, and to op-
timize the chances of a sale. Customers who do not fit these models neatly,
such as the two young men at the beginning of this chapter, can thus present a challenge.

Industry-wide and nationwide information on exactly who makes up the
contemporary *butsudan* consumer base, their motivations for purchase, and
the timing of purchases, is difficult to obtain. One factor contributing to
this blind spot is some customers' expressed desire for relative anonym-
ity and transactional finality in dealings with *butsudan* stores and temples.

According to after-purchase surveys conducted by Kamakura Shinsho, who runs the largest *butsudan* comparison website, *e-butsudan*, the most common *butsudan* customer is in their fifties, followed by people in their forties.[4] A recent bereavement is the single most significant factor motivating the purchase of a new *butsudan*. Although "there is no set timing," *e-butsudan* identifies the top four situations in which customers using the consumer advisory site make a purchase:

1. After the funeral and before the forty-nine-day ceremony
2. Before the first O-bon festival after a death in the family
3. In preparation for one's own death
4. When moving to a new house

For those who stress the strictly Buddhist dimensions of *butsudan*, the strong association between *butsudan* purchases and recent bereavement might be concerning. While industry-led marketing campaigns promoting *kuyō* as a contemporary moral value often endorse "living together with an altar" and encourage newly married couples to purchase *butsudan* when they move into a home, the link between *butsudan* and death appears unshakable. Indeed, some feel that purchasing a *butsudan* prematurely may even invite death into one's family (Fukuhara 1997, 92). In addition to being recently bereaved, the vast majority of customers I observed purchasing *butsudan* were members of branch families (分家 *bunke*) who, upon a death in the immediate family, find themselves without an established altar or grave. Orders from head households (本家 *honke*), whether for entirely new *butsudan* to replace old ones or for restoration of existing *butsudan*, tend to be more financially valuable but are far less common, as people tend to hold on to *butsudan* for several generations.[5] Heine estimates that approximately a third of the altars sold today are purchased by first-time buyers and the rest are replacements or upgrades (2012, 168). A key factor limiting new *butsudan* sales is thus market saturation; with fewer children being born and fewer people getting married, there are fewer new family branches that do not already have an altar.

A less common motivation for the purchase of *butsudan* is conversion, particularly to a new religious movement. In Japan, the term "new religion" (新宗教 *shinshūkyō*) describes a range of organizations, most of which emerged in the nineteenth and twentieth centuries that are broadly characterized by charismatic leaders, high levels of syncretism, and proselytization.[6] New religions often develop idiosyncratic forms of *butsudan* practice. For example, Sōka Gakkai (創価学会), an offshoot of Nichiren Buddhism and arguably Japan's most successful new religion, teaches that *butsudan* are solely tools for veneration of the Lotus Sutra mantra and not the dead or the ancestors.[7] Conversely, some new religious movements elevate the role of ancestor veneration and suppress its Buddhist dimensions (e.g., Lebra 1976; Kerner 1976). In some cases, conversion can require dramatic changes to *butsudan*. For example, an early movement within Sōka Gakkai encouraged new converts to discard or destroy their old *butsudan* and shrines, and this has contributed to a marked separation between the mainstream *butsudan* industry and this organization. Many *butsudan* retailers I spoke with chose not to stock altars for new religious movements, both because they lacked the specialist knowledge required to advise customers on their purchase and because they were wary of negative public associations with these movements.

Returning to the question of customer typologies, although the *e-butsudan* site does not collect data on the gender of clients, I observed that the second floor of Hasegawa was often occupied by women, alone or in multigenerational groups. In Japan and elsewhere, women tend to outlive their partners and take on the burden of memorial care work for both sides of the family (Tobin and Goggin 2013). I was told by multiple *butsudan* salespeople that in Japan, women hold the purse strings when it comes to decisions about home décor, including altars, despite ancestral veneration being the nominal responsibility of the eldest son. As I discuss further in the next chapter on the practice of domestic rites, the care for *butsudan* has been one of the most important spiritual duties for women in modern Japan (see also Obinata 1990; Danely 2008, 219–20; Starling 2019). Sales negotiations at Hasegawa Ginza are also often led by female staff. The company has an official policy of recruiting staff who have previous experience in the funeral industry (Hasegawa 2005, 3) and, in my experience, an informal policy of hiring personable women who can offer a "sympathetic ear" to the bereaved. In contrast, male management staff were deployed to address eldest sons or when an air of authority was deemed necessary. My status as a foreign researcher granted me access to after-work drinks with the male management team. However, I spent most of my time at Hasegawa with mostly female sales staff, who worked hard to communicate to customers the importance of *butsudan* and of people's obligations to the dead.

The matter of en *(bonds)*

The concept of bonds, or *en* (縁), being "connections, both concrete and mysterious" (Rowe 2011, 45), is crucial to understanding the motivations of people who purchase altars in Japan today. *En* extend between moral persons both living and dead, human and nonhuman. Indeed, this moral universe can include religious artifacts, like the *butsudan*, and even sentimental items, like wristwatches. The concept of *en* has roots in the Buddhist teaching of dependent-origination (Jp. 縁起 *engi*; Sk. *Pratītyasamutpāda*), whereby all things in the universe arise in dependence upon other things. As such, any phenomenon can "become a cause" or bring about action in another's life (Rowe 2011, 46–47; Reader 1991, 47–48). In common usage, *en* is a polysemous term deployed in a variety of contexts, but it retains this sense as "the relational conditions of a person's life" (Starling 2019, 92). In everyday parlance, two people who appear to have been destined to meet might be described as "having *en*." Indeed, my interest in *butsudan* was occasionally attributed to my *en* by people within the industry, in that both my marriage to a first-born son from a temple family and the recent death of my father made it clear, in retrospect, that this was the research I would inevitably complete.

Mark Rowe (2011) describes how, in the context of Japan's changing family and religious structures, many people now approach death in possession of few or vulnerable *en* with the living. Without descendants or other kin to perform *kuyō*, one risks becoming a "bondless buddha" (無縁仏 *muenbotoke*) who wanders pitifully between the worlds. As I explore in detail in the following chapter, *kuyō* should be distinguished from popular metaphors relating to memorialization or commemoration in English. Fear of becoming *muenbotoke* cannot be collapsed with a fear of being forgotten, because *kuyō* prescribes physical acts of caring for the dead, especially through the regular making of offerings. As several ethnographies attest, a fear of dying *muen* (bondless) is well-founded in contemporary Japan, given new demographic and financial realities (Allison 2018; Boret 2014; Kawano 2014; Kim 2016; Uriu et al. 2018). Rowe (2011) thus suggests that fear of becoming *muenbotoke* is a key force driving innovation in the Buddhist death-care sector, born out in the many new products and services launched as alternatives to conventional altars and graves.

Fear of dying *muen* clearly motivated at least one category of customers at Hasegawa, who are also notable for their purchase of *butsudan* outside a period of immediate bereavement. A number of affluent elderly couples dressed in sweaters and blazers came in seeking to "downsize" their current *butsudan* to a sleek modern model. During the period of my fieldwork, this was a financially attractive option, as under Hasegawa's winter sales campaign, the removal and disposal of the old altar (often a substantial cost) was included free with new purchases. These customers were sometimes accompanied by their children, but more often than not they came alone. In conversations with sales staff, they expressed a conviction that bequeathing fashionable, compact altars would increase the chances of their descendants agreeing to inherit them, and thus secure their continued welfare after death. This kind of preplanning speaks to a wider discourse that has emerged in the Japanese death space in recent years, of people not wanting to become a burden or *mendō* (面倒) on their children, either in old age or in death (Kawano 2010, 6). Allison describes the practice of "managing the details of one's dead remains while still alive," which has grown in popularity in recent years, with people creating "new forms . . . of relatedness . . . around the crucible of death" (2018, 181–202; 2023). These forms of relatedness often draw on horizontal social ties (including friends) or commercial relationships (including *butsudan* store employees), rather than vertical kinship structures.

The prospect of dying *muen* is a concern for many facing death, but for most *butsudan* customers I found instead that the all-too-present weight of bonds caused the greatest concern. *En* can become a burden for the living, particularly those unsure of how to act or what to do to resolve their obligations. Eiko, an artist and part-timer in her late twenties, was weeks into the process of researching a *butsudan* purchase when we first met. Eiko's father had died some months earlier, succumbing to an aggressive form of throat cancer. As Eiko and I chatted, I heard lots of echoes of my father's story, and we shared a few moments in a busy coffee shop, surrounded by happy faces who did not appear to understand the turn in our conversation. Like the two men who arrived at Hasegawa to purchase *ihai*, Eiko expressed a strong but ambiguous desire to *buy something* (何かを買わなければいけない) for her father. Whether this was the full retinue of an *ihai*, grave, and *butsudan* or a more minimalist ensemble, my initial questioning about whether she might not purchase an altar at all was met with discomfort: "I'm not really sure what to get, but we have to get something." Not making a purchase in response to the death was not an option for Eiko. Rowe acknowledges that "the only thing worse than becoming *muen* oneself, my informants consistently told me, is to be the one who allows this fate to befall the family ancestors" (2011, 47).

One way to understand this "pull" is through the uncomfortable sensation generated by an unfulfilled obligation to reciprocate gifts received from one's predecessor or ancestors, be they material, financial, or emotional. There is, then, a powerful obligation to reciprocate, à la the exchange theory of Marcel Mauss (1925). Summarizing the intergenerational relations of this model, Kawano suggest that "younger generations are morally obligated to transform their family dead into benevolent ancestors through many years of material and social investment" (2014, 6). We can see this reciprocity at work when (occasionally) a large financial inheritance is the clear motivator behind purchasing a new altar, such as President Yamashita's *butsudan*, described in chapter 1. An unexpected windfall such as winning a prize or the lottery, or being promoted at work, might also be attributed to one's *en*, understood as the underlying conditions that bring about a certain fate, and thus seen as grounds for a *butsudan* purchase. Commonly, however, the gifts one receives from the dead, if any, are far less concrete and enumerable.[8] Further, I do not want to suggest that this sense of obligation is naturally arising or universally felt across Japan. Concerted public marketing campaigns espouse the moral values of performing *kuyō*, making offerings, and purchasing *butsudan*. Perhaps the most famous commercial for Hasegawa Butsudan, which has run periodically on national television for at least twenty years, features a close-up shot of a young girl who stumbles over the words, "placing my hands together [手を合わせる *te o awaseru*] brings me happiness." This body disposition, as a symbol of one's gratitude to the dead, is a motif deployed in a number of similar campaigns.

There is value in exploring the affective dimensions of *en*. Eiko's discomfort at the prospect of not purchasing an altar manifested in her body as she spoke, in the form of a recoiling torso and inclined head, and I saw like expressions in many other people I spoke to about purchasing *butsudan*. It is similar to the difficult-to-articulate discomfort I describe in chapter 4, which arises in relation to the dumping of old *butsudan* or abandoned tombstones on the roadside rather than investing in the ritual process for their desacralization and disposal. In his ethnography, Rowe first uses the term "thirst" to describe the demands of the Japanese dead, who desire offerings of incense, food, and "most of all . . . conversation, visits by family and updates on our goings on . . . for attention and remembrance" (2011, 2). Intentionally or not, I think "thirst" is a particularly apt metaphor, because it speaks to the visceral nature of the interdependence of the living and the dead. Purchasing a *butsudan* or performing a rite can slake this thirst, generating a feeling of security or peace of mind.

This affective dimension is notably absent from earlier accounts of ancestor veneration in Japan. For example, Herman Ooms (1967, 1976), informed by the symbolic-structuralist anthropology of his time, describes how the living socialize the dead into ancestors over a series of multigenerational rites in one's family of orientation, rites that directly mirror the upbringing of children into adults in one's family of procreation. Oom's model appears to endorse the long-running theorization of ancestor worship as driven by kinship structures. The question of whether ancestor worship (or veneration) should be understood primarily as a form of religious belief or as a projection of kinship relations was raised by Edward Burnett Tylor and has been debated by anthropologists since (Fortes 1976, 1–2). Earlier scholars of Japanese religion expressed a desire to keep "emotional ties with individuals who died in recent memory . . . analytically separate from ancestor worship," largely to maintain the latter as a category for cross-cultural religious comparisons (Plath 1964, 301). The array of actions performed at *butsudan* thus get separated out, at least analytically, into distinct categories of Buddhist practice, ancestor veneration, and mourning the recent dead. Scholars' continued commitment to this distinction appears in several opening disclaimers (e.g., Smith 1974, 128; Suzuki H. 2013a, 16). However, it is a division less clearly realized in the actual ethnography. And it does not ring true for my own experiences, in which the function of rites performed at the *butsudan* is ambiguous at best. We should be wary, also, of erecting a division between emotion and structure on the topic of death (Toulson and Newby 2019, 7). Indeed, as a powerful force within both death ritual and death consumerism, *en* demonstrate the dependent-origination of kinship structures, belief, and emotion.

Studies of bereavement have similarly addressed the question of "bonds" between the living and the dead, although they ascribe slightly different meanings to this term. For much of the twentieth century, models of bereavement in Western psychology, influenced by Freud, prescribed detachment as a necessary stage in the process of mourning the dead. Correspondingly, ongoing relations with the dead were thought to be indicative of an unhealthy condition of grief (Field 2006, 738–39). In work that sought to depathologize and reorient psychology's approach to grief, Dennis Klass, Phyllis Silverman, and Steven Nickman (1996) developed the (now mainstream) theory of "continuing bonds." This paradigm suggests that ongoing necrosocial relations can be "an integral part of successful adaptation to bereavement" (Field 2006, 739).

Attempts to connect psychological studies of bonds with studies of *en* in religious studies or anthropology have largely been led by scholars of the former. Early in this discourse, Yamamoto et al. (1969) critiqued this medical model of continuing bonds by suggesting that mourning and its timeline are culturally relative. Three decades later, Klass had fully embraced the suggestion, acknowledging the importance of culture and presenting Japanese ancestor veneration as a particular system of "ritual, supported by a sophisticated theory, by which the living manage their bonds with the dead" (1996, 279; also Klass 2001).

The primary distinction between continuing bonds and *en*, as described by Klass, is the dependency operating in this relationship in Japan. Klass invokes Doi's (1973) classic notion of *amae* (甘え), or dependence (usually between parents and children), to explain the relation between the living and the dead in Japan and contrasts this with the cultural value of personal autonomy in the United States (1996, 285–86). Not only do *en* carry moral weight, they form a causal link between the living and the dead. Further, *en* appear to have a more ambiguous valence than continuing bonds. *En* might become burdensome to the living, and although Japanese ancestors are primarily cast as benevolent, there is at least the potential for the dead, when poorly treated, to do harm or become a negative cause in someone's life (Maeda 1976, 137). This negative potential does not appear to immediately motivate a severing of *en*. Indeed, there are taboos around the act and language of severing or cutting (切る *kiru*) within the domain of death. Enomoto-san from Takimoto Bukkōdō once told me that cutting anything in front of a customer has great potential to cause offense. He recalls how he once cut some nonslip tape with scissors during an installation job. Although the customer did not express displeasure at the time, the store later received a call of complaint regarding the incident. Responding to *en* correctly involves sustained investment in a measured process of both care and separation, rather than sharp break. This work requires specific ritual tools, and thus, for many, the purchase of *butsudan*.

Selecting an altar

Most sales negotiations at Hasegawa begin with staff attempting to clarify the personal circumstances behind a customer's visit. This can be tricky business, requiring restrained inquiries to avoid offense. Occasionally, purchases pass from initial inquiry to altar installation without staff ever uncovering exactly who has died. Most conversations are devoted to more practical considerations, often beginning with the question of size. According to Kamakura Shinsho, between 2015 and 2018 the most important factor people identified when purchasing an altar shifted from "value (for money)" (28 percent of respondents in 2015) to "a size that fits within my residence" (50 percent in 2018). In both years, "design" was the second most important factor. Very few homes in Japan's sprawling metropoles are now built with the dedicated alcove and tatami mat sitting room that traditionally housed *butsudan*, and thus compact designs that fit into Western floorplans are favored.[9] This is a matter not simply of available domestic space but also of shifting priorities for the utilization of this space; many urban families do manage to fit large televisions into their tiny apartments. Accompanying a decline in *tatami* flooring has been a decline in the embodied practice of kneeling for extended periods of time (Tei 2009). Hasegawa Ginza thus specializes in smaller, lighter altars that can be placed on a platform or desk to raise the altar above eye level from the position of a chair, alleviating the need for kneeling. There are also several popular designs that include a small stool built into the bottom drawer of the altar.

Once the parameter of size has been established, conversations turn to the interconnected issues of style and cost. *Butsudan* are exempt from inheritance tax, but they are a still a significant investment. In cities, the average cost for a new *butsudan* is between 150,000 and 250,000 yen, exclusive of the *go-honzon* (icon), *ihai*, and *butsugu*, which can almost double the cost. The nationwide average cost for a new *butsudan* is 340,000 yen (Kamakura Shinsho 2018). Located in Japan's most exclusive shopping district, Hasegawa Ginza specializes in fashionable altar designs that appeal to status-conscious clientele. Many newer models are created in collaboration with famous furniture companies and designers. Further exclusive features, such as Yakusugi cedar, domestic Japanese manufacture, or specialist crafting methods (such as nail-free construction) also incur a premium. These features are communicated to customers via labels positioned around the display room, including official certifications and small biographies of the designers. Still, staff may be called upon to justify the value of items, particularly now that customers are wont to "shop around."

The range of altar options available to customers, both in-store and online, is vast. Many customers visiting Hasegawa Ginza have performed at least a modicum of prior research into the variety of altars available (if not their religious meanings or ritual use). *Butsudan* stores advertise in a range of print media, television, local letterboxing campaigns, and posters on public transport. Less conventional methods of public messaging that I have encountered include a YouTube channel run by Takimoto Bukkōdō, which offers guides to *butsudan* ownership and answers customers' frequently asked questions. Other popular sources of information are comparative websites like *e-butsudan*, which advertises its services as arming consumers with the knowledge required to navigate the industry. The site collates customers reviews of over eight thousand stores, operates a 24/7 telephone helpline, and provides customers with discount coupons to use in-store (from which the site receives a commission).

The proliferation of digital resources globally has been described as "undermin[ing] the reflexive non-choice making" that once characterized consumption in the funeral sector (Arnold et al. 2018, 104). In Japan, where families may once have been served by the local *butsudan* maker attached to their affiliated Buddhist temple, it is now far easier to shop around. One should be careful, however, not to conflate consumer choice with consumer agency. Writing on the US, George Sanders suggests that an abundance of options combined with consumers' relative unfamiliarity with available products and the emotional demands of bereavement can in fact "severely limit the survivors' ability and willingness to familiarize themselves with those things" (2012, 267). This uneven set of circumstances means that

Figure 2.3. A promotional image for the "LIVE-ing" range of modern *butsudan* featuring the SOLID BOARD JUST *butsudan*. Image courtesy of Hasegawa Co. Ltd., 2022.

consumers can end up ceding significant agency to salespeople and the brands they present during a purchasing negotiation.

For retailers, consumer ignorance represents both an opportunity and a challenge. For one thing, it means that *butsudan* stores rely heavily on branding to meaningfully communicate the differences between altars and to market their appeal. Where forms of value cultivated by artisans, such as the embodied construction process, sensory qualities, or raw materials, prove difficult to communicate to customers, visually rich brands help position altars within different lifestyles. On their online store, Hasegawa offers two modes to search for *butsudan*. Advanced search options sort altars by category: (1) "Japanese style," "foreign (Western) style," or "either"; (2) positioned on a stand or on the floor; (3) "traditional design," "modern design," "Japan made," and so on; and (4) size and location of the altar. But the default option presents a collage of photographs showing different "room atmospheres" (お部屋の雰囲気 *o-heya no funiki*) (figure 2.3). The images almost evoke an Ikea catalog in positioning furniture within visual lifestyle narratives.

In her ethnography of Ikea, Pauline Garvey states that through this characteristic style of display in stores and in catalogs, "designed objects and environments conflate Ikea with normative domesticity" (2017, 1–2). In a similar manner, Hasegawa's brands project aspirational visions of domestic family life. Perhaps most importantly, they depict *butsudan* and all that it represents as anchoring, rather than contradicting, modern living. Each product line has a name, from "Marron" and "Nordly," invoking Romantic and Scandinavian aesthetics in Western-style altars, to "Kisaragi" and "Seoto" for Japanese designs. The brands also sort *butsugu* (altar goods) into distinct "mix-and-match" sets that can be combined with different altars to form a package deal. Very few customers now purchase *butsugu* individually, so most new *butsudan* have a uniform appearance, one that has often been curated by retailers. Marketing thus does heavy lifting in the presentation of *butsudan* today.

This focus on design and cost is far removed from the naïve impression of religious retailing I had formed before fieldwork. Writing a decade previously, Nelson states that a "standard sales tactic directs potential customers to the altar approved by the family's denomination, even to the point of hinting that divine retribution (罰 *batchi*, 祟り *tatari*) has been reported for those deviating from the norms" (2008, 314). I, however, never witnessed such explicit appeals to Buddhist ethics or orthodoxy. Customers do tend to purchase the icon and decorative goods belonging to their family's Buddhist school but largely, I think, because they do not know or question what other options are available. A limited number of customers across the stores where I worked exhibited a strong religious consciousness. One challenging day at Hasegawa began with greeting a couple from Osaka, who spent several puzzling moments with Kitahama, a senior salesperson, trying to determine their family's affiliation based on a conflicting set of vague recollections about the altar in their hometown. The altar in question appeared to have design elements associated with both Nichiren and Jōdo Shinshū schools, and the couple had to return the next day with a photograph before the *butsudan* could be identified (it was Shingon). For most, religious affiliation appears to be just another parameter used to narrow down altar choice. This pragmatic approach is a noted feature of Japanese religious life. Anthropologist Tadao Umesao (1973) was one of the first to propose conceptualizing Japanese people's relation to religion as that of consumer to producer. Hirochika Nakamaki extends this idea by comparing religion in Japan to the act of purchasing whitegoods; most people buy and own products from an array of makers (Sony, Mitsubishi, Panasonic, etc.), but a few exhibit brand loyalty, purchasing different brands only when something is on sale (2003, 12–13). In a similar fashion, religion is not irrelevant to contemporary *butsudan* retailing, it is simply weighed up against other priorities and concerns.

Finally, as *butsudan* are (ideally) objects bequeathed across multiple generations, striking the right balance can involve extensive family debate. Eiko spent two weeks visiting *butsudan* stores in Tokyo and Kyoto with her mother and older sister, gathering catalogs, narrowing down contenders, and trying to reach a decision that would please all family members. Eiko told me that that her mother thought deeply about the afterlife and spirits and so "wants to arrange it as conscientiously [丁寧 *teinei*] as possible." Her paternal grandfather also expressed strong opinions about how to proceed. As Eiko's father was the eldest son and died in unfortunate circumstances, her grandparents had arranged multiple ritual services in recompense for his "bad death." As Eiko's family belongs to one of the smaller branches of Jōdo Shinshū, Takada (高田派), both arranging these services and sourcing a *butsudan* had been difficult. When the family last traveled to Kyoto, they were advised to improvise an altar from the more popular Jōdo Shinshū styles. For her father's part, after learning of his terminal diagnosis, he never acknowledged his death and thus left very little instruction. He also had a difficult relationship with his parents and was not very interested in Buddhism. Eiko related:

> The *jikka* [実家, parents' home] is very strong, but its maybe just a show. . . . Still, it's not an easy item to purchase—you can't just throw it away. We will eventually inherit the *butsudan* when my grandparents die, so it's something that we need to have everyone agree upon.

The future fate or disposal of *butsudan*, as objects that travel through time beyond human lives and deaths, can thus factor into purchase. The necessity for negotiation with older generations can result in more conservative choices. But not wanting to inherit the burden of an elaborate golden altar, Eiko continued to search for a suitable compromise. The family eventually settled on a golden *butsudan* that was constructed in two parts, of which the bottom stand could be removed to make a more compact model for Eiko's generation to inherit. Given the negotiations required to balance these considerations, extended periods of deliberation are not unusual for *butsudan* retailing.

Closing a sale

When I announced my proposed course of fieldwork, a senior colleague in Japan Studies expressed her rather visceral distaste for the industry. She recounted how, soon after her mother-in-law's death, the family posted a notice of mourning, only to have *butsudan* companies start cold-calling

Outside of the industry, such impressions of the insidious, profiteering character of *butsudan* retailing are certainly strong. The industry is gently ridiculed in Juzu Itami's famous film *The Funeral* (お葬式 *O-sōshiki*). In the 1984 film, after the sudden death of their father, a family takes on the expensive, stressful task of organizing a Buddhist funeral. To compensate for their ignorance, family members consume instructional books and rely on the advice of industry professionals, sometimes to the detriment of their wallets and, it appears, their sanity.

The funeral industry worldwide is frequently accused of profiteering and funeral directors often imagined as "slick salespeople and opportunists" (Hyland and Morse 1995, 454; also Bailey 2010, 208–9). Writing on the UK, Brian Parsons (2003) outlines a number of reasons for such critiques: the dominance of a few large brands means consumers feel they lack choice; the amount of backstage activity involved in mortuary work appears inscrutable; and finally, many customers of the funeral sector are in a "state of distress." In 2010, consumer complaints about the Japanese industry prompted a government-led review and, ultimately, the establishment of the Butsudan Fair Trade Convention (仏壇公正取引協議会 *butsudan kōsei torihiki kyōgikai*). Today the convention enforces regulations concerning accurate public display of information about altar price, materials, and country of manufacture, as well as the provision of aftercare and warrantees. It has not, however, saved the industry from public critique.

Retail practice has perhaps become more transparent, but it is still highly competitive. Pressure to make sales and shift merchandise was palpable at all the stores where I worked or interviewed. Hasegawa Ginza had a system of daily targets and rewards. When 100,000 yen worth of products were sold, the manager bought each employee a choux pastry. When the total reached 250,000 yen, it was an individual cake slice from the local upmarket department store. On truly extraordinary days, a whole cake was ordered from a famous French patisserie. Each evening after closing, the staff assembled downstairs to receive their "just desserts," hear the latest messages from the head office, review the day's sales, and plan for the coming season. The meetings also allowed staff to keep track of recent bereavements and potential clients as they passed through the various stages in the purchasing process. I was sometimes invited to leave before these meetings, but sometimes found myself in the middle of forthright review from the regional manager. On one occasion, the store was participating in a campaign for Higan (彼岸), a Buddhist observance around the spring and autumnal equinoxes, which required every staff member to phone up their previous clients to inform them of the new sales deal. However, as we neared the end of the month, it became apparent that the tactic had not proved successful. The manager was clearly frustrated: "What are you doing? Are you actually making the calls? Because this is your job, and this is the worst result for us as the flagship store—the worst." The silence that followed was painful, and the mood only lifted when the conversation turned to more operational issues. Over the next few days, staff expressed discomfort, revealing that many felt ill at ease contacting past customers, especially those who had already made significant purchases.

Fostering close relations and making personal appeals are crucial to the work of *butsudan* store employees. Workers at Hasegawa are a mixture of company employees and part-timers, with varying degrees of commitment to and interest in the *butsudan* tradition. The average age of Hasegawa's employees is 41.5 years old and their average length of service is 13.9 years (LIMO 2019). Hasegawa implements regular exams for its staff, quizzing them monthly on the details of newly released altar models and aspects of Buddhist theology. At most stores where I worked, however, after a two-week induction, training was primarily conducted on-the-job. When I asked Shimoyamada-san, the Ginza store manager, what he values most in new workers, he suggested empathy or an ability to "get close to" (寄り添う *yorisō*) others. The president of Takimoto Bukkōdo once explained to me that of course the company only hires "kind people," but the process of doing the job itself "makes one kind." For him, everyday parts of the job, including gazing at the Buddha and joining one's hands in prayer before altars effectively "softens one's heart." This explanation is broadly in line with Arlie Hochschild's description of affective labor, whereby aligning oneself with the "feeling rules" that govern the emotional labor of the profession, also known as "deep acting," is more than just a Goffmanesque presentation and might actually bring about "a change of heart" in the performer (1979, 38). *Butsudan* retailing both cultivates and covets this "getting close" skill.

One further actor needs to be factored into this work: the dead. On several occasions, the ultimate beneficiary of commerce and care in *butsudan* retail was explicitly described to me as the dead. Consideration is given not just to their tastes but also their personal welfare. One reason the aforementioned regional manager pushes his sales team is, in his words, because it encourages customers to "perform the best *kuyō* they can, so the dead can be at ease." For him, it is salespeople's duty to inform customers of the meaning of Buddhist rites and encourage their regular performance. Building on the approach of Hochschild (1979), a number of works have considered the caring labor performed by funeral industry staff in the West (e.g., Bailey 2010; Howarth 1996; Hyland and Morse 1995). Howarth (1996, 28–33) describes the many meanings of "care" in the Western funeral industry and argues that the ultimate goal of caring for bereaved customers is achieved in proxy, through acts of care for the dead. Similarly, Bailey sets out how UK funeral directors care by "advising bereaved people in 'doing the right thing' by instructing 'proper' treatment and presentation of the corpse and arranging a 'fitting' send off" (2010, 217). Many funeral arrangers, she concludes, interpret their emotional labor as being for the benefit of the bereaved. In contrast, *butsudan* retailers conceptualize *butsudan* purchase and the performance of *kuyō* as benefiting the dead, and only secondarily the bereaved. On occasion, industry professionals and clergy may even bypass the bereaved family's wishes to perform acts of *kuyō* for the dead, including priests visiting the family home and *butsudan* uninvited and unannounced during O-bon and making and enshrining an *ihai* for the deceased in a temple. In contrast, the concept of "grief care" (グリーフケア) for the bereaved only recently entered the industry lexicon; quite literally, it appeared in a new section toward the end of the *Guidance on Buddhist Altars and Buddhist Goods*, fourth edition.

The relation between investment in material artifacts and quality of care for the dead appears reasonably direct. During my time at Takimoto Bukkōdō in Osaka, our team was about to depart on a delivery when a call came in from a local funeral company. A customer was looking for the cheapest *butsudan* available, so Enomoto, who had answered the call, pulled out the store's catalog to compare prices. The most basic model was approximately 100,000 yen. Anything smaller, he explained, would be a reliquary that could fit only the *ihai* or the icon but not both, and would be far too small to house *butsugu*. His passing mention of a reliquary evidently received a positive response as he went on to search for an even smaller model. He found two altars, sixteen and twenty centimeters tall, that cost 18,000 and 36,000 yen respectively. In parting, however, he cautioned the funeral company against recommending these models. He explained:

> Of course, there are cheaper ones online. Of course. And I can't say for myself whether they are good or bad. But we try to sell real *butsudan* in this store. Otherwise, what is the point. People should buy as good as a *butsudan* as they can afford, or else it's a little impolite (失礼 *shitsurei*) to the dead.

Regarding people who are unable to afford a *butsudan*, one Hasegawa salesperson suggested to me that if somebody has a sincere heart, even a cardboard box will suffice: "That becomes a *butsudan*. It's the same meaning, as long as it generates the same feelings." As I describe in chapter 1, the sensational form of *butsudan* can extend beyond the artifact to include people's embodied response toward it. At the same time, however, retail companies place great importance on the quality of raw materials, manufacture location, and skill of artisanship when promoting and selling their goods. Further, particularly majestic and lavishly decorated *butsudan* are praised for their power to generate an embodied response, to make you join your hands in prayer. *Kuyō* can occur without lavish *butsudan*, but the industry is eager to promote them as powerful generators of this orientation to the dead.

INSTALLATION

Delivering new *butsudan* and installing them in people's homes is a process in which the affective labor of *butsudan* retail staff is performed and their ideas about *butsudan* come into contact with customers' domestic religious practices. Private and public, official and unofficial ideas about the dead and how to engage with them collide, and the parties must reach consensus, whether or not this consensus lasts after the workers leave. Many stores now rely on nationwide distribution services like Yamato Transport to deliver *butsudan*. In this case, the altars are installed by the families themselves, with help from local clergy, guidebooks, and, in my experience, a healthy dose of googling. Some retailers, however, including Takimoto Bukkōdo, provide a full installation service. In these encounters, customers ask questions and learn *butsudan* practice from staff, and staff, in educating them, attempt to form good (ideally lasting) bonds with customers. But as we shall see, not all customers wish to engage in such "sticky" relationships, and some now pursue more transactional, terminal means to resolve their obligations to the dead.

Takimoto Bukkōdo is located in Moriguchi City, a northeastern suburb of Osaka, and is the first company where I undertook fieldwork, starting in mid-2017. Its highly energetic, effervescent third-generation president, Takimoto-san, tells me he is glad I started my fieldwork with his company, given its "Osaka nature." With approximately half the population of Tokyo, Osaka is considered Japan's second city, historically populated by the merchant classes and closely tied to Japan's comedy scene. Despite the population gap, President Takimoto estimates that approximately equal numbers of *butsudan* are sold in Osaka and Tokyo each year. He attributes this to the many family-run businesses in the region and the continuing practice of passing agricultural land down through generations, which fosters a sense of indebtedness toward the ancestors. Osaka also has relatively higher numbers of Jōdo Shinshū followers, and Takimoto specializes in golden altars to service this community. Given this customer base, Takimoto must cultivate good relations with local temples as well as customers. I spent many hours driving around the Kansai countryside with the team, calling on temples with business cards, catalogs, and small gifts in an effort to build rapport. In contrast, stores like Hasegawa, which services a more religiously diverse and secular customer base, are less frequently called to answer to temples.

At Takimoto, I joined the delivery team, which works out of the central headquarters, ferrying *butsudan* purchased from any of Takimoto's eleven display stores to customers throughout Kansai. The team consists of four characters: Enomoto, a kindly junior colleague and former pet-shop worker; Kobayashi, an ex-*manzai* comedian and experienced member of the team;[10] Mitsume, an industry veteran who largely handles interactions with temples; and Tan, a "strong and silent" type, who drinks sweetened coffee throughout the day and then crushes the cans in his fist as he drives. Before delivery, *butsudan* are disassembled and wrapped for transport. If the *go-honzon* (icon) is a hanging scroll, it is attached to the back of the altar using tacks covered in silk brocade before we leave the store. Tan explains that some clients object to seeing holes being made in the icon—even its silk binding—and so this process is completed at the shop. Installing the *go-honzon* in front of customers can be nerve-racking, as a slip might be interpreted as bad luck and cause offense. Enomoto recounts that he was incredibly nervous on his first solo delivery, as there is so much information to memorize and so much that can go wrong, particularly when customers and priests have idiosyncratic ideas about what is and is not acceptable.

Delivery One

Outside a customer's house, the Takimoto workers cover a *butsudan* in navy quilted blankets so as to protect it from scratches and shield it from prying neighbors' eyes. Some customers wish to keep their purchase, and all it communicates about religious affiliation or recent bereavement, private. Deliveries to apartment blocks can involve navigating multiple flights of stairs or narrow lifts. Often, the most grandiose altars are delivered to traditional houses in affluent areas that have high-walled gardens surrounded by tiny one-way streets that must be delicately navigated by the store van. On other occasions, we install altars between televisions, pianos, and desks (see figures 2.4, 2.5).

Today's delivery is of a high-quality modern/traditional fusion altar to Mori-san, a widow in her seventies. It occurs on an auspicious day on the Japanese calendar, known as *taian no hi* (大安の日).[11] A temporary altar is set up in the front room with a smiling photograph, a large pile of incense and sweets, and two urns. The smaller urn contains the *nodobotoke* (喉仏) or "throat-buddha," the hyoid or tongue bone, which is religiously significant

Figure 2.4. The Takimoto Bukkōdō team installing a golden *butsudan*.

because it is thought to resemble a seated Buddha. The family is affiliated with Jōdoshū (Pure Land) Buddhism, and at her late husband's bequest, the *nodobotoke* will spend a year enshrined at the school's head temple in Kyoto. The larger urn contains the other cremains, which will eventually be interred in the ancestral grave. Our delivery team—Tan, Enomoto, and I—kneel to give greetings to the deceased by lighting incense, striking the bell, and joining our hands together. Occasionally, customers appear uncomfortable

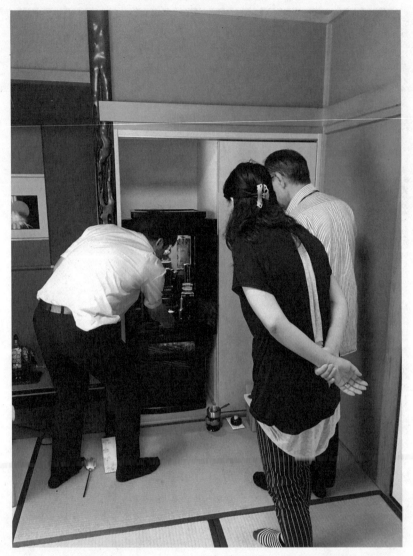

Figure 2.5. Tan (of Takimoto Bukkōdō) explains the features of a new modern *butsudan* as the family looks on. Kansai, 2017.

with these greetings and linger awkwardly in the background, but Mori-san eagerly joins.

We move the temporary altar aside to make room for the *butsudan*, which is made of dark walnut and approximately a meter and a half tall by 70 centimeters wide. Mori-san renovated the room by installing tatami mats and building a dedicated alcove. She had thought about buying a smaller altar, she tells us, but Enomoto reassures her that many people regret such purchases, as *ihai* and other accruements soon pile up and the tight space proves difficult to clean. Sometimes, *butsudan* require labored maneuvering to fit them into tight alcoves (figure 2.4). After installing the altar frame, we lay out each of the *butsugu* on the floor. Enomoto unwraps each element from its paper and foam coverings and places it in the altar, starting from the top tier and working downward. I note that these *butsugu* are made from high-quality materials and represent the full set of altar trappings, including a cushion, three different forms of bell, two candlesticks, and two flower vases. The richness of these ornaments, despite their relatively modern design, suggest to me that the Mori family are devoted. That Mori-san's husband was a very committed Buddhist is further evidenced by the grand scroll (掛け軸 *kakejiku*) that hangs next to the *butsudan*, which he received after completing a pilgrimage visiting temples on foot. He had died one month earlier but secured a grave in a prime location almost a decade ago and left meticulous instructions for his wife about his posthumous care. As we unwrap and position each *butsugu*, Mori-san asks detailed questions about its meaning and use. How often should I change the flowers? What type of incense is best?

Mori-san is busy preparing for a combined forty-nine-day ceremony, consecration rite or "eye-opening ceremony" (開眼式 *kaigenshiki*) for the new altar and *ihai*, and ash interment ceremony, all scheduled for the day after tomorrow. Combining these (usually distinct) events into a single day is rather unusual and, the team gently warns, potentially exhausting. It is, however, becoming more common, Enomoto notes, as people find it difficult to take several days off work and want to minimize the costs of calling a priest multiple times. This explanation, given for my benefit, opens a floodgate of inquiries from Mori-san about correct conduct on the day. The presiding priest has told her, rather opaquely, that his services will cost "as much as you feel" (気持ちに *kimochi ni*). Enomoto translates this into approximately 100,000 yen for the *butsudan* rites, 100,000 yen for the interment ceremony, and 10,000 yen for transportation costs. He presents her with several of the company's preprinted white envelopes, labeled in a calligraphic font, to be used for each of these fees.

In this manner, *butsudan* stores often act as intermediaries between priests and customers, filling in gaps in ritual knowledge and setting expectations so that rites run smoothly. Despite the variety and experimentation involved in *butsudan* practice, people's concern for "doing the right thing" is palpable. Enomoto reflects that one of the most difficult and persistent parts of his job is relieving customers' fears about doing something wrong and thereby offending priests or the dead:

> I often just want to say, "You don't have to worry about x or y. You don't have to mind so much, and do whatever makes you feel comfortable." But if the customer asks, then I need to explain to them what the correct process is.

But "correct practice" is contested, and *butsudan* store workers must often accommodate competing opinions. One common strategy is to say, "This is what many people do . . ."—gently instructing while allowing room for personal variation. Throughout the workday, customers would ring Takimoto and Hasegawa with inquiries about the correct placement, decoration, and ritual practice for *butsudan*. Matsumoto-san, at Hasegawa, spent over thirty minutes on the phone with one young woman who had recently been berated by a local priest for having placed the altar in the same room as a Shinto shrine. Matsumoto-san explained that the location was entirely acceptable, as long as the two icons were not facing one another. "Young priests these days don't know enough about altars," she later sighed. "They are not specialists." Nonetheless, she ultimately counseled the woman to follow her priest's directions. Indeed, retailers frequently defer to Buddhist priests, even when they believe they know better.

Equally, retailers must heed the "customer is always right" doctrine of business, and thus can find themselves caught between two masters. During home visits, my coworkers at times demonstrated extreme deference to both customers and clergy. I was instructed, for example, to kneel *beside* floor cushions until directly invited by the host to sit on them. Similarly, offers of tea or sweets should be refused several times; after several refusals, one could drink the tea but should consume the sweets only if the host absolutely insisted. This directive also had a practical aspect; on long days spent making deliveries, workers may be offered mountains of cake and tea.

Other manners apply when visiting temples, including bowing when entering or exiting the main hall, always wearing a string of prayer beads around your wrist, and carrying a more formal string of beads for use in prayer. Such customs may appear antiquated, but they help present workers as upstanding Buddhists and thus soften accusations of profiteering, at least from temples. Upholding some standards can be physically challenging, especially in the height of summer. The men on the team often wore white hand towels wrapped around their necks to soak up the sweat that poured from their foreheads when lifting heavy altars, and everyone on the team favored moisture-wicking short-sleeve business shirts. By the time the installation of Mori-san's altar was complete, my legs, which had been folded beneath me in the formal kneeling position, had lost all feeling and balls of sweat slowly dripped down my back. I had to surreptitiously grab at my feet and hook my numb toes beneath my heels to restore blood flow while pretending to clean away boxes. The pain seemed justified, however, when I saw Mori-san gaze toward the photograph of her late husband and say, "See love, I've made you a splendid house" (立派なお家 *rippana o-uchi*). In the car on the way back, I commented that the husband's photo made him seem kind. Enomoto, however, worried that he had left such exacting instructions for the memorial. Enomoto is more moved by the figure of Mori, who followed these instructions exactly and at great expense. With her eldest son living away in Tokyo, will Mori-san ever receive similar favor?

Delivery Two

Not all installation jobs result in warm connections. One memorable encounter from my time at Takimoto concluded with our team leaving the altar in pieces on the floor. That morning, Kobayashi-san and I drive for almost two hours to the outer suburbs of southeast Osaka, where Takimoto's most distant outlet is located. We load up our cargo and set off to a local house with a modern Shingon *butsudan*. Arriving at row of brutalist-style units in a rather rundown state, we are greeted by a gentleman in his seventies. Our conversation does not proceed smoothly. His beloved pet bird roams free around the house, perching on his shoulder and dropping guano on the floor. At several points during our conversation, his answers to our inquiries seem non sequiturs. At first, I chalk this up to my deficits in Japanese, my Hiroshima accent, or the client's Osaka dialect. However, Kobayashi too is confused, and it soon becomes apparent that the customer might not be able to hear us well.

Beyond the cluttered living room and messy kitchen, a modest formal sitting room holds a large temporary altar, set up with the photograph of the man's youthful-looking wife, who was ten years his junior. The room is overflowing with sweets and flowers, which spill out of vases of all shapes and sizes placed on every available surface. We begin unpacking the *butsugu* but are soon told to leave them as is. Kobayashi expresses his reservations, explaining that this design includes quite a few complicated glass shelves that need to be professionally installed, but the customer insists that the local priest and his eldest son will manage. Kobayashi reluctantly acquiesces. He later states that this occasionally happens when the person's house is disorderly:

It often happens when the wife has died. The husband does not want us to enter because he suddenly realizes that he does not know how to look after the house.

[...]

Usually we don't hear from them again, especially if they are strong enough themselves or have somebody around to lift it for them. I once carried an altar over the sleeping figure of an ill grandmother to position it in the home of hoarder. I don't think customers understand that we've seen it all.

Before we take our leave, the customer inquires after the number of flower vases included in the set. The *butsudan* the client ordered customarily comes with *mitsugusoku* (三具足), that is, one vase, one candlestick, and one incense brazier. Kobayashi quickly reassures the man that another vase will be delivered promptly, free of charge. In our parting conversation, the customer, almost talking to himself, laments that "I was supposed to go first, I am so much older." There is silence in the car on the drive back. It is not the most difficult or emotionally trying circumstance in which Kobayashi has made a delivery. But he worries what will happen to this client, with nobody to care for him but his bird, and now the responsibility of caring for his wife in death. Men of that generation, Kobayashi notes, do not generally do well in such circumstances.

For some customers, refusing help from *butsudan* staff appears to be more of a strategic move. More than one prospective customer browsing *butsudan* rebuffed staff's advances, refusing to accept a business card or tea or to give their name. Carolyn Stevens describes business cards in Japan as an extension of a moral person ensuring continued favor in the future (2011, 17). By bucking the obligation to receive, customers also refuse the social relations that come with such a gift, pushing the interaction into the transactional realm. For example, one middle-aged man, clearly in the midst of serious deliberations, visited Hasegawa Ginza three times in the course of one week. Each time, he positioned himself in front of the wall of modern altars, staring intensely, and feverishly waved away any staff who approached. Puzzled by this behavior, the team wondered if he was considering another altar at "that place down the street" (Yagiken) or had an online model in mind. For those wishing to circumvent the social niceties of *butsudan* stores altogether, online services offered by Amazon, Rakuten, and Aeon (Japan's largest supermarket chain) remove the need for face-to-face interactions entirely. In 2018, online purchases accounted for less than 1 percent of total *butsudan* sales (Kamakura Shinsho 2018), but as in other sectors, COVID-19 significantly bolstered these numbers.

The desire to minimize the financial and social obligations generated by ritual consumption surrounding death is not limited to the purchases of a new *butsudan* or grave. *Kazokusō* (家族葬), or micro funeral services attended only by family members, have risen sharply in popularity in recent years. Indeed, approximately half of funerals in 2021 were *kazokusō*, according to estimates from Kamakura Shinsho (Yokoyama 2022). Family-only funerals cost less time and money for the bereaved, and also avoid conventional practices of (cash) gift exchange between the bereaved family and attendees. These examples suggest at least some people have a desire to follow convention and "do right" by the dead, while entering into as few additional obligations as possible. For retail workers, this new reality can be a challenge to navigate sensitively and successfully; we never did hear from the business card–refusing customer again.

Some, such as President Yamashita (chapter 1), continue to cultivate deep financial and social bonds with temples and local businesses via acts of patronage that generate social capital from the living and the dead. For those like Mori-san (above), these ties can be a source of comfort and reassurance that they are doing the right thing. Many customers spend hours in a *butsudan* store, drinking tea and asking clarifying questions about their ritual responsibilities. For these people, investing in bonds with *butsudan* stores appears, if not desirable, then at least necessary. In this way, *butsudan* stores have become a major site for the transmission of ritual knowledge and the promotion of ritual observance, often communicated through appeals to the aesthetics of altar brands associated with a cosmopolitan, modern lifestyle. For many, however, it appears that transactional exchanges have become more desirable, as evidenced by customers refusing to engage with staff and the growing popularity of online ordering.

In the next chapter, "Practice," I examine what happens to *butsudan* after they enter the home. How does the form and meaning of altars, modeled in catalogs and by *butsudan* employees during the sales process, hold up to the everyday practice and interpretations of laypeople? Who takes care of altars and the dead, and what kind of relations does this practice generate?

CHAPTER 3

Practice

Every summer, Sensōji (浅草寺), a Buddhist temple in Asakusa, Tokyo, holds a public "lantern memorial rite" (万霊燈籠供養会 *banrei tōrō kuyōe*) to venerate the masses of abandoned or neglected dead. Lanterns painted with the posthumous names of the dead are arranged along wooden racks in the temple's main hall (figure 3.1). A team of helpers dart around, ensuring the lanterns remain illuminated throughout the evening. In the forecourt, a special temporary altar known as a *segakidana* (施餓鬼棚) is arranged with offerings of fruit, flowers, water, and incense. *Segaki*, or "feeding the hungry ghosts," is a practice of caring for and pacifying wandering spirits who lack the ties that bind them to the living. It extends as well to spirits in an even more dire situation, the starving ghosts, or *gaki* (Jp. 餓鬼; Sk. *Preta*), who have fallen deeper down the karmic hierarchy (Smith 1974, 41–43). Prominent figures in medieval Japanese literature and contemporary popular culture, *gaki* might be spirits of jealous or greedy people, who, as punishment for their moral vices, become struck with an insatiable hunger for material things that they can never satiate (Osterfeld Li 2012, 176). At the main altar at Sensōji, a large black *ihai* with the inscription "abundant spirits" (万霊 *banrei*) or "All Souls" is positioned in front of the Buddha icon. The dead take precedence tonight.

It is not just the unvenerated dead who are beneficiaries of this service. Recently bereaved people also pay to dedicate paper lanterns to their dead. Some donate an additional fee to sit within the inner sanctum of the temple and experience the ceremony, which is presided over by twelve priests and includes chanted sutras and recitation of the names of the dead. The tropical humidity of a Tokyo summer begins to take its toll on me as the sutras drone on, but my interest is piqued by a formally dressed woman standing close by, who holds a large photo album open at chest height. From my position, I can just peek inside to see a formal funeral photograph (遺影 *iei*) of a young man dressed in a black *kimono*. The woman appears to be angling the image so that it is directly in line with the main altar, perhaps so as to better

Figure 3.1. Lanterns are lit in the forecourt of Sensōji, Asakusa, 2018.

receive the benefits of the rite. As the ceremony winds down, the priests, dressed in colorful silk robes, file out into the main hall. Anticipation builds and guards press the crowd back from the center of the room. The priests briefly address the *segakidana* and then throw petal-shaped paper cutouts in an array of bright colors into the air. After what seems to me the absolute minimum of a respectful pause, the crowd rush the stage, scrambling to pick up the petals, which serve as powerful charms.

When the scramble for petals dies down, my friend Laura and I head to the rear of the temple, where the paper lanterns are being piled onto a huge bonfire. Attendants from the temple light small fires at each corner of the arena, and handfuls of pine prayer tablets (塔婆 *tōba*) are periodically added throughout the ceremony to feed the flames. Jostling for space beneath our transparent PVC umbrellas, Laura and I position ourselves beside the arena, located between the temple hall and the brightly illuminated amusement park next door; O-bon is a rare public holiday in Japan and seasonal festivals are in full swing. As the main bonfire is finally lit, an impeccably dressed elderly woman asks if she may lean on the handrail before me. We strike up a conversation. With very little prompting, she begins to explain that she has been attending *segaki* at Asakusa for about nine years, ever since her husband died. His ancestral tomb is located in Shizuoka Prefecture, simply too far to visit over O-bon and New Year's, so she comes here instead. She describes her husband as a kind and conscientious person, well loved by the local community. When she asks why I am attending, I explain my research and, in solidarity, tell her about my father. After a few moments of silence, she launches into a cascade of thoughts:

> So, I come here and watch the lanterns being burnt, and I feel safer, at ease. Sometimes, when I go home, I feel a little bit lonely, because I am going home to an empty house. But I come here and I look at the smoke rising from the bonfire and I realize that I am not alone, that we are all together, because we are all returning to the sky with the other souls of the dead—and they are not alone. . . . Your father is definitely there also.

The burning lanterns launch a stream of smoke into the air, accompanied by an occasional smoldering fragment that dances its way into looming rain clouds. The lanterns, made of Japanese rice paper, pine, and wax, burn rapidly. As they do, priests chant the mantra of Fudō Myōō (不動明王; Sk. *Acala*), a fierce-looking protective deity who is often depicted as cloaked in flames. The strains of the sutra mix with squeals of joy and terror that drift across the temple from the Ferris wheel at the amusement park next door. Soon after the service ends, the woman departs with a parting greeting of "I'm in your debt."

As I too turn home, I am struck by a strange sense of affinity with these two women, the one holding the young man's photograph and the one watching the bonfire, and an appreciation for the work they do for their dead. As the *segaki* rite shows, there is something to be done for the dead in Japan, more than just remembrance or "keeping them in your heart"—a phrase I am familiar with from Australian funeral rites. These women have found meaningful ways of engaging with the formal Buddhist ceremonies, and so often it is women who do this work. In this chapter, I look in more detail at *kuyō* as a popular rite performed for the dead, such that *butsudan*, graves, lanterns, photographs, and other objects become sites for affirming, as well as disentangling, the bonds that tie people together.

More specifically, this chapter examines *butsudan* in the home. What does the encounter between bodies and *butsudan* in everyday settings tell us about the texture of contemporary necrosociality? Scholars of Japan have proposed fundamental shifts in the ontological status of the dead as well as people's relationship to them, for example, with "ancestors" being replaced by "beloved antecedents" (Suzuki 1998). But do these shifts play out in domestic practice? Behind closed doors and often away from the authority of priests or the industry, the home is where many idiosyncratic, improvised meanings and practices surrounding *butsudan* manifest.

Past ethnographies of Japanese domestic life have hinted at the diverse array of engagements with *butsudan*. These include descriptions of daily offerings made to the dead and ancestors (Danely 2014; Daniels 2010b, 81–85; Dore 1958, 312–29, 427–30), the recitation of sutras and veneration of Buddha (Bokhoven 2005; Starling 2019), deploying the authority of ancestors enshrined in the altar to discipline wayward children and report good news (Hamabata 1990, 79–80),[1] and the practice of first offering gifts received by the family to the ancestors by placing them at the altar (Daniels 2010b, 84). Quantitative surveys have shown declines not only in rates of ownership and new purchases of *butsudan* but in the frequency of people's engagement with altars in the home (Reader 2011, 240–41; 2012, 22–23; Ishii 2007, 78). Dore's touchstone ethnography of a Tokyo ward (1958) found that almost 90 percent of households that possessed *butsudan* conducted regular rites at them. Decades later, Ishii's compilation of surveys administered by Kokugakuin University showed a decline in the already much lower percentage of households where daily rites occurred, from 30.6 percent to 25.9 percent, between 1999 and 2004 (2007, 78). Survey data hints at the changing shape of people's interactions with *butsudan* but does not capture their texture or quality. Further, my experiences suggest that scholars should be wary of a simple equation between *butsudan* practice and shifting patterns of necrosociality or belief. Competing ideas about altars coexist within households, generations, and individuals. I thus follow Angelika Kretschmer's guidance to approach the practice of *kuyō* "as a puzzle, collecting as many pieces as possible and trying to piece them together, albeit at the same time keeping in mind that the puzzle cannot be completed" (2000a, 21).

After the lantern ceremony, my companion Laura, a literature scholar, remarked on the apparent ease of ethnographic data collection, given the woman's unprompted loquaciousness. I could only laugh. As noted in the introduction, *butsudan* present significant problems of access to ethnographers, borne out in the paucity of their study to date. Working at altar retailers provided me with extraordinary access to their customer base within the confines of sales transactions, but my relationship with the store also made it difficult to approach customers for follow-up interviews.[2] Further, as Bokhoven discovered in his survey of modern *butsudan* practice, informants often prepare for visits by cleaning the altar or even buying new *butsugu*, thereby obscuring the "regular state" of altars in daily use (2005, 5). The ethnographic case studies that form the backbone of this chapter are thus drawn from personal networks and fieldwork relationships built up over time through a continuous negotiation of access.

Before I launch into the narratives, it is necessary to set forth how relations between the living and the dead in Japan have been framed hitherto. In particular, I want to critically assess how distinctions—or lack thereof—between terms like worship, veneration, and memorialization have been used to forward arguments about the changing texture of necrosocial relations. While a sojourn into linguistic particularities might appear unexpected in a work on material culture, I think it a necessary first step to understanding the cultural particularities of a Japanese necrosocial world, and to avoid imposing assumed truths embedded in a theoretical vocabulary derived from Western cosmology.

DEATH WITHOUT MEMORIALISM?

The nature of relations between the living and the dead has been of ongoing concern to anthropologists from the earliest days of the discipline. Beginning my work in Japan, I was struck by the proliferation of terms used to describe this relationship, each in varied patterns of use by scholars, clergy, retailers, and laypeople. This rich vocabulary includes *tsuitō* (追悼; mourning), *tsuioku* (追憶) and *tsuisō* (追想; recollection, reminiscence), *sūhai* (崇拝; worship, adoration, reverence), *kinen* (記念; commemoration, celebration, anniversary), *irei* (慰霊; consoling the spirits of the dead), *aitō* (哀悼; condolence, tribute, lament), *tsuizen* (追善; mass for the dead, Buddhist service), and of course, *kuyō*. However, there is often a lack of clarity about which Japanese term, if any, scholars are referring to when writing in English. These terms and the distinctions between them are important to Japanese scholars, as revelatory of subtle differences in how the ontological status of the dead and their relationship to the living are conceptualized. For example, cultural studies scholar Naitō Rieko points out that "mourning"

(追悼 *tsuitō*) does not imply the existence of a soul or spirit, whereas this idea is central within the meanings of "venerate" (供養 *kuyō*) and "comfort the spirit" (慰霊 *irei*) (2013, 45). Contrastively, within the semantic field of the term "memorialize" (記念 *kinen*), she argues, reflection (回想 *kaisō*) on an individual's life is key (2013, 45). Naitō describes *kuyō* as the "more practical" and prevalent term in Japan today (2013, 46).

Let us focus on *kuyō*, which I have broadly described as a practice of care, and which describes a complex interweaving of absencing and presencing the dead played out through material goods like *butsudan*. The first character (供), derived from the verb "to offer," is collocated with terms like "serve (a meal)" or "submit." The second character (養) means "foster," "rear," or "bring up." The term is ultimately derived from the Vedic ritual of (Sk.) *pūjanā*, a practice of making offerings to important teachers, deities, or a temple community that generates good karma. In contemporary Japanese, however, the term is almost exclusively used in the context of funerals, occasionally as part of a longer phrase, *tsuizen kuyō* (追善供養) or "Buddhist service for the dead" (Shintani 2007, 172). But *kuyō* is polysemous and slippery. Several Japanese scholars give it a much broader reading, one that exceeds Buddhist thought (Naitō 2013, 47; Nagano 2015, 214). This resonates with the expansive approach taken by Kretschmer in her study of *kuyō* in Buddhist, Shinto, and nonreligious settings as "probably the most frequently observed religious rites in contemporary Japan" (2000a, 1). Daisuke Uriu, a scholar of thano-technological design, considers *kuyō* to be Japan's dominant orientation toward the dead and is convinced of its endurance beyond vast social and technological change (see chapter 5). He once told me that "*kuyō* is the religion of the Japanese people, not Buddhism."

In the same spirit, *kuyō* has been used to sketch out a wider Japanese cosmology distinct from Western or Christian metaphysics. Nagano Hironori argues that the Western equivalent of *kuyō* is *kugi* (供犠), meaning "sacrifice" (2015, 218–19).[3] He further draws on the work of Nakamura Ikuo (2010), who distinguishes between Christian/European "sacrifice" or "killing culture," which involves killing (but not consuming) animals offered to the gods, and a Buddhist/Asian *kuyō* or "eating culture," in which people eat the animals they sacrifice to the gods. The former, Nagano argues, is anthropocentric, placing humans on a level above animals, whereas the latter emphasizes interspecies communality and is motivated by a desire to lessen feelings of guilt arising from the consumption of an equal. This, Nagano suggests, helps explain historical *kuyō* rites for whales (see Itoh 2018), more contemporary rites for animals used in scientific experiments (see Asquith 1986), and, more recently, *kuyō* for domestic pets (see Ambros 2012). As I describe in chapter 4, the performance of *kuyō* for nonhuman persons, including *butsudan*, has been invoked as evidence of a less human-centered cosmology operating in Japan. For example, social theorists Casper Bruun Jensen and Anders Blok (2013) use *kuyō* as an anchor for their model of Japan's "never modern" modern cosmology in the manner of Bruno Latour (1991). They suggest that *kuyō* reveals "a vivid sense of the pragmatic interplay of human and non-human agencies, in terms of their mutual fertility and—eventually—killing" (2013, 102).

Given the weight ascribed to the term by many, translating *kuyō* and the activities it describes is a monumental task. Looking at the direct English glosses scholars have used, we observe great variety: "a service for the dead" (Ooms 1967, 229), "placation, tendance" or "reverence" (Plath 1964, 300), "pray for" (Smith 1974, 128); "offerings and memorialism (of the ancestors)" (Suzuki 1998, 185), "consolation and pacification . . . of the deceased" (Suzuki 2000, 163); "rites of separation" (Kretschmer 2000a, 379); "an offering of nourishment" (Foulk 2008, 63); "a memorial service" (Reider 2009, 247); "memorial rite" or "memorial ritual" (Wilson 2009, 4; Rambelli 2010, 70); "sponsoring religious services" or "giving offerings" (Repp 2010, 51); "repentance" (Heine 2012, 173); "an activity involving prayer, worship, and offerings" (Guth 2014, 172); and "(making a symbolic sacrifice) performs loss in order to transform it (into mourning/memorial)" (Danely 2014, 26). One of the most enduring renderings of *kuyō* revolves around Robert J. Smith's distinction between 崇拝 (*sūhai*), or "worship," as "praying to the dead" who are notable or powerful figures and 供養 (*kuyō*) as "praying for the dead" who are reliant on the living for care (1974, 128). It should be noted that while some scholars use glosses like "memorial" without comment, many point to the inadequacy of this translation and the importance of context (see, for example, Ambros 2012; Repp 2010, 51; Irizarry 2022, 187–88).

Many translations incorporate the language of "memorial." Memorialization has proved a powerful tool for studies of death and material culture in anthropology and beyond. An excellent example of its deployment is found in Elizabeth Hallam and Jenny Hockey's *Death, Memory and Material Culture*:

> We trace connections between the crises of death and the formation of memory . . . and here we find concepts of death and memory intimately bound together. Indeed, we witness death acting as a deep incentive to remember and the process of dying can give licence to intense phases of memory making with all of its attendant material complexity—from the

disposal of the corpse to the repeated act of returning to the graveside with flowers. (2001, 3)

In this excerpt, memory functions as the connective tissue between death and stuff; death generates object-making practices, and it is through the operations of memory in these objects that the absent dead become sensorially accessible to the living. Material artifacts, spaces, and words are thus described as "external cultural forms functioning to sustain thoughts and images that are conceived of as part of the internal states of living persons" (Hallam and Hockey 2001, 4).

But memory-based glosses for *kuyō* are increasingly criticized by Japanese scholars such as Shintani Takanori as arbitrary and inaccurate, and guilty of uncritically reproducing a Western cosmology (2007, 174–76). More broadly, a focus on memory as the interface between the living and the dead has been defined and critiqued as "memorialism" (メモリアリズム),[4] "commemoration doctrine" (記念主義 *kinen shugi*), or "reminiscence doctrine" (追憶主義 *tsuioku shugi*) (Naitō 2013, 48). Naitō, in conversation with philosopher Watanabe Manabe, defines this paradigm as follows:

Rather than veneration (供養), comforting the spirit (慰霊), and mourning (追悼), the idea that drives funerary rites and memorials is the importance of *purely remembering the individual* . . . the act of remembering is located in the heart of the bereaved . . . and thus belief is bestowed by the act of remembrance alone. (2013, 47–48, emphasis added)

Naitō describes memorialism as markedly more secular than Buddhist or Christian modes of relating to the dead. This is not to say that memorialism does not exist in contemporary Japan, but rather to distinguish it conceptually from *kuyō* (2013, 50).

If not memory, then what? Although it does not receive the attention given to memory, the relation of exchange has provided fertile grounds for the anthropological study of death ritual. In their rich comparative study, Barraud et al. champion this approach in framing the divide between the living and the dead as "not insuperable barriers, but rather loci of relations of exchange" (1994, 122). Questions of inheritance, the intergenerational transfer of wealth, and relations of obligation and reciprocity have been key concerns in studies of death in societies across Africa (e.g., Metcalf and Huntington 1991, 13; Goody 1962) and Asia (e.g., Ahern 1973; Williams and Ladwig 2012). Operating in the lineage of Marcel Mauss's approach to exchange as a *fait social total* (1925), these studies connect death rites to broader secular

and spiritual economies. In Melanesia, mortuary exchanges have been analyzed as elements in a much wider system of prestations.[5] Further, ethnographies of ancestor worship and Buddhist death rites across East Asia are replete with descriptions of "feeding the dead" as a practice of both obligation
and care (for a recent example, see Wu 2018).

There are indications of a turn in the tide in English-language theorization of *kuyō*, driven in part by rich contemporary ethnographies of its practice. The connection between *kuyō* and sacrifice is rarely preserved in English, but Jason Danely captures this deeper reading in his suggestion that
kuyō operates as a "symbolic sacrifice" following the "logic of exchange"
(2014, 26). For Danely it is also a transformative process, one that makes
"loss" into "mourning/memorial" (2014, 26). Recent work by Joshua Irizarry
(2022) similarly returns to the etymology of *kuyō* to describe this practice
as one of nourishing or raising the dead via concrete offerings. Irizarry's
reading evokes work by Ooms (1967) on the double domestic cycle, which
parallels the maturation of the household dead with the rearing of children.
What is not necessarily captured in the language of nourishment, however,
is the intended separation once the dead are matured (but see Kretschmer
2000a, 379). As I describe in chapters 4 and 5, dead spirits who linger on
and necromaterials that take up space in the home can, like the adolescent
who never moves out, become burdensome to the living. It is for this reason
that I want to keep both nourishment and separation in mind when thinking about *kuyō*.

The distinctions scholars draw, or do not draw, between *kuyō* and memorialization are interesting not just as reminders of the difficulties of translation, or as a cautionary tale against Anglocentrism. As I explore below,
different terms have been deployed as touchstones to describe changes to
everyday practices of relating to the dead, or to explain a decline in *butsudan*
ownership. Rather than falling cleanly into one or another of these categories, the following encounters are full of complex emotions and uncertain-
ties in the midst of concerted efforts to do well by the dead. Indeed, altars
should be noted for their ability to hold together a multiplicity of different
engagements in a single space.

FORMAL RITES

My first week of fieldwork is heavy with personal obligation, as I attend a *hōji*
(法事), a Buddhist service marking the first anniversary of the death of my
husband's grandmother, on his paternal Matsuura line. The *hōji* is a formal
ceremony conducted by a priest, who explains that it is to "pray for the happiness in the next world [冥福 *meifuku*] of the deceased." This event is slated

for the family home in Chiyoda, a village in mountainous North Hiroshima. Daisuke's paternal grandfather, now widowed, recently moved in. Ninety-seven years old, he has a full head of bright white hair that sticks straight up as if electrified. Every morning, he walks down two flights of stairs to the living room, where he settles at the low heated table. There, his days are spent watching television and snacking, mostly on red meat and carbs; he stopped eating vegetables at ninety.

Around him, preparations for his late wife's *hōji* are in full swing, and I am enlisted to help out, half out of family obligation and half because everyone agrees that this is excellent data. Historically, Hiroshima has been a stronghold for followers of Jōdo Shinshū. This affiliation is reflected in the style of almost every *butsudan* I visit over the next two weeks, thanks to the grand tour of neighborhood altars organized by my mother-in-law. However, Daisuke's grandfather was born into a Sōtō Zen temple family, who still train at the famous Eiheiji Temple in Fukui (Daisuke's grandfather, lower in the succession order, left to become a businessman). The upcoming service will thus be performed by family, namely, Daisuke's second cousin, who runs a temple on an island in Hiroshima Bay, and his famed mentor, who will travel from Eiheiji especially.

The frequency of such visits by priests to people's homes varies widely, largely dependent on the strength of ties between the household and the temple, the recency of a death, and the piety of the deceased and the bereaved. Some priests make seasonal visits to give offerings and prayers at their parishioners' *butsudan* during O-bon and Higan (another Buddhist festival held for three days before and after the spring and autumnal equinoxes). Others only come when requested (and paid for), such as on special death anniversaries. In some of the more religious areas I visited, such as throughout Ishikawa Prefecture, it is not uncommon for parishioners to host brief *kuyō* rites at the altar on a monthly basis (月参り *tsukimairi*). Indeed, I met several families who left their doors open so the priest could come and go as they please, visiting the *butsudan* without disturbing the residents. For priests, a strong personal relationship with the deceased can motivate visits even when the bereaved are less enthusiastic. Contrastively, *butsudan* stores in Tokyo frequently have to mediate for customers who wish to avoid priests' visits altogether.

The presence of high-ranking priests marks the Matsuura *hōji* as a special event, warranting preparations from the whole community. The most pressing task is the altar. As the patrilineal altar is still located in the grandfather's former home in Hiroshima City, the family decides to use the temporary cardboard altar (*saidan*) supplied by the crematorium, draped in a white tablecloth and somewhat precariously hoisted onto two garden benches to give it the proper height (plate 5). Before the *hōji*, the *saidan* sat in the grandfather's sleeping quarters, next to his futon. It houses his late wife's photograph, her cremains, some fruit, and flowers. Before the family eats in the morning and evening, somebody takes freshly cooked rice and offers it in a small bowl at the altar, accompanied by the strike of a bell. Sometimes, they forget. Very rarely, when rice is not part of the family meal, microwaveable packets are used. To prepare the altar, *butsugu* (figure 3.2) are unpacked, carefully dusted, and arranged. Some have been retrieved from the city, some borrowed from an altar on Daisuke's maternal side (despite its being Jōdo Shinshū). This improvised bricolage departs rather sharply from the craft implements described in chapter 1, or the designer sets sold by Hasegawa (chapter 2). Daisuke's father has received detailed instructions on how to prepare the altar for this event from both the funeral company and the family temple, including precise guidance on the relative height and orientation of each *butsugu*. The family spend most of the morning trying to reproduce the diagram, but Daisuke and his father appear pretty happy with cutting corners. For example, the flowers have begun to brown, but it is deemed wasteful to buy new bouquets.

In place of a Buddhist icon, Daisuke's father hangs a large painted scroll, a gift from Eiheiji, on the wall. He muses, "Didn't we get scolded last time for those two top cords being bent out of shape?" Concern about getting in trouble with Buddhist priests for the subpar state of one's altar, especially on an occasion such as a *hōji*, was something I became all too familiar with during my research. Because of this, one new service offered by some *butsudan* stores is to arrange and clean customers' altars before special occasions. Even retailers' efforts are sometime ineffectual, though, given the idiosyncratic preferences of certain priests. It is notable here that, cross-culturally, domestic altars are often described in opposition to institutional religious spaces, as potentially freer sites of spiritual expression and experimentation, albeit shaped by historic and economic circumstance, the power structures of the home, and personal life experiences (see Romberg 2018, 157). In Japan, by contrast, experimentation has been curtailed by a long history of *butsudan* being used as tools of civic regulation (during the Edo period) and by the continued authority of priests. The proliferation of temple-issued guides on altars as well as independently published "conduct literature" (Bardsley and Miller 2011, 15–16) further speaks to the existence of a strong normative discourse around *butsudan*, whether or not it is taken up by laypeople. Certainly, improvisation does occur, as both altars in this chapter show, but it occurs in conversation with (or defiance of) Buddhist priests and *butsudan* merchants. Eventually, Daisuke's father decides that they will

Figure 3.2. Altar goods boxed for transport and cleaning, Hiroshima, 2017.

ask the Matsuura family priest to fix things up before the senior priest enters the room, so as to avoid a repeat reprimand.

The object that sparks the most debate within the family is the large formal photograph of the dead, known as the *iei* (遺影). At first, Daisuke's father places the *iei* on the top tier beside the newly carved *ihai* for the grandmother and in front of the main scroll. I express some hesitation about this placement, but the image is beloved and so stays there. Rather unusually, Daisuke's grandmother appears in the photograph wearing a knit hat, which Daisuke brought her as a gift from Australia, but the image otherwise conforms to the *iei* style. Irizarry likens this style to a passport photo, "a frontal head shot, cropped from the chest level; gray or blue background" (2014, 162). All other contextualizing features are photoshopped out. Famed scholar of Japanese funeral culture Yamada Shinya (2002) argues that this occurs so that the photography can become a timeless icon of the dead, rather than a snapshot of a moment in their life.

Accessible only to the elites of the Edo period (1603–1868), *iei* became standard at Japanese funerals during the Taishō period (1912–1926), buoyed by the popular spread of photography. Their aesthetics have changed significantly over the ensuing century (Yamada Shinya 2002) and continue to evolve. *Iei* are now often put together quickly and cheaply by the family at a local print shop. Contrastively, the other key vessel of the dead at the altar, the *ihai* (ancestral tablet), is a luxury good that must be specially commissioned. The introduction of photographs into the customary retinue of mortuary artifacts has not been without controversy. Some more conservative Buddhist priests have criticized the focus on photographs in funeral rites as representative of a wider encroachment of mourning the dead on the "true purpose" of *butsudan*—the veneration of Buddha or, at least, the dead in the guise of Buddha (see Taniguchi 2013, 7). Indeed, when Daisuke's family priest arrives, he swiftly moves the *iei* to a small side table so the Buddha may take precedence. The photograph will regain its pride of place when the altar is reassembled the next day in Daisuke's grandfather's bedroom.

Other offerings placed on the altar similarly demonstrate the idiosyncratic nature of altar assemblages, which might be "cleaned up" on formal occasions. On the morning of the *hōji*, Daisuke and I duck out to buy prayer beads (*juzu* 数珠) from the local *butsudan* store. As a reluctant participant in the role of eldest son at the *hōji*, Daisuke has taken some convincing that such items are necessary. In our brief tour of the store, he is shocked to find a coffee-scented candle set in a tiny coffee cup, which he purchases as an offering. Green tea or water is the usual offering at altars, but his grandmother loved black coffee. Daisuke comments that the beer-shaped candle will make a good purchase for his grandfather's future altar. The candles are the first thing he mentions to his family when we get home. His father chuckles, noting that "it doesn't seem very Buddhist." For my part, the most surprising find of the trip was a box of "freeze-dried offerings" retailing for 1,200 yen. Just add water and a lavish array of dishes is ready—"even if the family wants to eat pizza," as the salesperson joked.[6] The reaction of Daisuke's family to this product was surprise mixed with sympathy, both for people with no time to prepare "real" food and for *butsudan* stores, who they judged were now forced by economic circumstance to hawk such wares.

On the morning of the *hōji*, we are greeted by a stream of Matsuura relations, many of whom had traveled from Osaka or Tokyo for the event. Daisuke's second-cousin priest arrives early in the morning, wearing a cardigan and looking like a posh Kichijōji dad dressed for a Sunday picnic with the family. Having studied in San Francisco, he speaks English fluently and relishes the chance to guide me through the day. (His fluent English, sparkling Rolex, and fast car become an ongoing point of humor for Daisuke, who thinks them questionable choices for clergy and teases his family about their "suspect" relation). He fixes the altar and changes into robes before his senior priest arrives, who, already dressed formally, heads straight to the *saidan* to greet the deceased and make even more adjustments. Finally, Daisuke takes his place next to his father and grandfather behind the two priests, and the ceremony begins. The progression of a *hōji* can broadly be described as followers:

1. Greeting by chief mourner
2. Sutra readings
3. Offerings of incense by bereaved family
4. Offerings of incense by other participants
5. Priest's sermon
6. Visit to the grave
7. Meal
8. Parting greetings (and payment)

After a brief greeting, what follows in this case is an extensive recitation of Zen sutras, accompanied by the occasional striking of a wood block and bell, which lasts around thirty minutes. Daisuke's grandfather knows the sutras by heart, but most in the crowd mumble along hesitantly, relying on printed handouts. In Japan, Buddhist sutras are usually composed in transliterated Chinese characters and their meaning is beyond the comprehension of most. Toward the end of the ceremony, an incense brazier is passed across the participants' knees, so that we can add some wood-chip incense to the smoldering pile. When the sutra recitation finishes and the priest's sermon begins, I breathe a sigh of relief. The talk mostly focuses on cultivating a good heart, then winds around to discuss the *kaimyō* (posthumous Buddhist name) given to Daisuke's grandmother, which is noted to reflect her good deeds and kindliness.[7]

Afterward, Daisuke's parents dryly note that the sutra reading was "impressive." My mother-in-law suggests that this is the gift and the burden of being related to Buddhist clergy; they do not shirk on the performance of rites for the dead, despite the incomprehension or exhaustion of the living. This elaborate ceremony is partly due to close family ties and partly to the perceived devotion of Daisuke's grandmother. As in the next case study, however, the enthusiastic performance of these rites is not necessarily predicated on a personal or familial commitment to Buddhism. The same normative force of convention that can motivate one to purchase *butsudan* also leads people to pay for and participate in *hōji*. In many cases, the performance of *kuyō*, its *doing*, seemed to me to be more important to participants than whether or not it was meaningful or even understood by the living. Amico Uriu, a friend and funeral attendant, once told me that the greatest challenge she faces is negotiating between bereaved families who want "short and sweet" sutras at funerals and overzealous priests who want to perform extended recitations. For families without extensive connection to temples, priests can be viewed as "sutra-chanting employees of the funeral companies; in other words, just one ingredient in a set funeral package" (Rowe 2011, 31).

Further, although our familial connection secured a lengthy service, the efficacy of *kuyō* performance does not appear to rely on any personal connection between the living and the dead. This orthopraxic approach to *kuyō* in Japan resonates with traditions of professional mourning in contexts across Asia. As we shall see in subsequent chapters, more and more industry bodies are offering *kuyō* as a professional service. For young Japanese people unable to perform *kuyō* by, for example, traveling to the ancestral grave, a professional ritual proxy can now by hired. And this proxy does not necessarily have to be ordained. During social distancing restrictions related to COVID 19, taxi drivers who found themselves without customers offered a new service, cleaning and making offerings at graves in place of the "locked-down" bereaved. Similarly, for elderly people themselves facing a lonely death, new forms of columbarium or grave advertise the promise of ongoing, collective *kuyō*, performed by the facility's staff or other customers (Rowe 2011; Allison 2023).

There is no grave visit as part of Daisuke's family *hōji*. Instead, the ceremony is followed by a five-course meal. Assembling the altar was a major task, but preparations for the meal lasted weeks. Leading up to the *hōji*, the main conversation among the women—my mother-in-law, her mother, and various neighborhood aunties in this tight-knit rural community—was what kind of food would be appropriate. Daisuke's mother and maternal grandmother run a small café out of the residence and so decided to prepare the meal themselves. This is unusual, as most families hold the service at a temple, columbarium, or funeral home, followed by a visit to a restaurant.

However, with rumors of restaurants charging extra as soon as the word "*hōji*" is mentioned, one of the neighborhood aunties helping to prepare the meal dismisses this option as a "total rip-off."

Gendered Care

During the week of preparations leading up to the *hōji*, I battle through some very strong rural Hiroshima accents to learn from a group of six neighborhood women about how to prepare for a big ritual. The main subject of debate is the menu. Preparing a *hōji* feast demands not only culinary skill, time, and energy, but also specific knowledge about what will be acceptable and appealing. This "food literacy" is described as a key means through which women, as stewards of religion, perform and share Buddhism in contemporary Japan (Kolata and Gilson 2021). In this case, all agree that sushi is the most traditional option, but one older woman, who everyone only half-jokingly calls "master," insists that the first anniversary, unlike ceremonies closer to the death, is not a sad occasion but a celebration, and thus it is appropriate for meat to be served. Somebody suggests tiny hamburgers or pieces of steak—"in any case, something that you can eat with chopsticks." The "master" explains that during her childhood, mourners were prohibited from eating meat both at funerals and later at *hōji*, but such taboos have greatly loosened. The prohibition against taking life (殺生禁断 *sesshō kindan*) is one of the many historical norms around food and death explored in a study by Jane Cobbi. In addition to meat, Cobbi notes that Buddhist foods, or *bukku* (仏供), should exclude the "five pungent roots" (五辛 *goshin*): chives, garlic, onion, leek, and ginger (1995, 202). All of these rules are forgotten in favor of taste at the Matsuura *hōji*. The group finally settles on a menu that includes a European-style entrée of fat-marbled beef and roasted vegetables, followed by a Japanese-style tray arranged with tiny dishes of broiled vegetables, pickled clams, and grilled fish, each simmered in broth or dressed with a different sauce. *Sekihan* (赤飯), rice cooked with red adzuki beans, is also on the menu as it symbolizes a special occasion (although more usually a happy one). The list is extensive, and some shortcuts are in order. On the morning of the *hōji*, when one of the priests inquires after the tray of dishes to offer to the dead, we discover that the meal is not yet ready. So Daisuke's mother shrewdly reaches for packets of freeze-dried miso and rice.

Despite the cliché that death is "the great leveler," death and dying can articulate, intensify, and transform the gendered dimensions of social life (Broom 2012, 224). In *Women and the Material Culture of Death* (2013), Beth Fowkes Tobin and Maureen Daly Goggin focus on mourning and memorialization, describing the sentimental labor performed by women across cultures and historical periods. In scholarship on Japan, gender is increasingly recognized as a vital dimension driving change in death rituals. Based on fieldwork conducted in Hiroshima in the late 1980s, Obinata argues that ancestor worship was one of the most important domestic tasks for women in premodern Japan, continuing into the contemporary age (1990, 2). Marriage has immediate implications for women's posthumous sociality, as it means the adoption of new ancestors and an (apparent) relinquishment of obligations to one's own parents and ancestors. Jason Danely describes how incoming women are socialized into the household traditions by their mothers-in-law, observing that "veneration of the ancestors [is] an important way of integrating oneself in the family and a possible site of breeding resentment toward the older women of the house" (2008, 219). However, a sharply declining birth rate can leave women shouldering a double burden, responsible for care of the dead on both sides of their family. Women's ties to their family of orientation and their aging parents often persist beyond marriage. In tandem with changing gender expectations, these demographic shifts have resulted in many women challenging the patrilineal grave system and searching for alternatives. These include facilities for single or communal interment outside the household that create new forms of posthumous kin networks (Allison 2023). For example, at Sakura Cemetery, managed by the Ending Centre, new forms of shared grave are marketed as "grave friends," "forest family," and "share houses." The remains of six families are interred in a "share house grave," dispersing the obligation of *kuyō* among multiple sets of potential descendants.

Cross-culturally, studies frequently align domestic altars with women's religious practice and expression. For example, folklorist Kay Turner's study of Mexican-American home altars contrasts women-led domestic spirituality with the "male-determined or dogma-bound" religiosity of the church altar (1999, 7). Alyssa Maldonado-Estrada's vibrant ethnography of a Catholic community in Williamsburg shows how the church remains a vital site for making masculinity, as seen in a myriad of devotional labors, including constructing icons and carrying shrines through public streets during Feasts (2020, 1–3).

In Japan, although care of the ancestors and the altar is ostensibly the responsibility of senior men, in my experience, day-to-day altar practices, such as cleaning and making new offerings, are usually performed by women. Smith (1974, 90–91) suggests that part of this alignment between women and *butsudan* is because food preparation is seen as a "woman's job," and thus offerings fall under women's purview.[8] Danely describes how his informants in Kyoto commonly associated the *butsudan* with women and the *kamidana* (神棚; domestic Shinto shrine), which is involved in rites for prosperity and good fortune, with men (2008, 202). Still, men may perform a prominent role during formal *kuyō* services, especially when priests are present. This resonates with the work of Michelle Rosaldo, who, speaking more globally, describes how "rituals of authority" (1974, 16–19, 28) are often not available to women, even though ritual labor often falls to them.

This division of public and private ritual labor was evidence in the Matsuura household. During lunch, the senior men and priests took up seats at the head of the table, before the altar, but there was no place set at the table for Daisuke's mother or her mother (Daisuke's maternal grandmother), who spent most of the afternoon in the tiny kitchen, sending out plates of delicately arranged food and bottles of beer. As both daughter-in-law and researcher, I scurried back and forth between the "backstage" kitchen and "frontstage" dining room, and felt caught between the two. This threshold demarcating official ritual space and informal domestic space is exactly where Jessica Starling locates her recent ethnography of *bōmori* or temple housewives in the Jōdo Shinshū tradition (2019). Starling argues that, particularly through the labors of women, Japanese religion pierces the formal and informal, institutional and domestic realms. As the central object of domestic religious practice, *butsudan* exemplify just how grounded religion is in the everyday cycles of the house and so, too, in its gendered relations.

In February 2018, just days before I left Japan, Daisuke called to say that his paternal grandfather had passed away. He would later fly to Japan for the forty-nine-day memorial service. He was saddened but also makes a lighthearted comment about the convenient timing of the death, so close on the calendar to his grandmother's that the family will be able to combine future *hōji*. He had once jokingly asked his grandparents not to die between June to August, as he detests humidity and tries to avoid visiting Japan in the summer months. His lightheartedness masks a bigger question about the future performance of death rites within the family, now that they have immediate ancestors to care for. Daisuke and I settled in Australia over a decade ago; as we have no plans to reside in Japan, his family has confronted the question of what to do about the family grave and *butsudan*. For many years, the possible location of a household grave was subject to playful debate: his grandfather wished to be interred at the distant temple where he trained as a priest, his grandmother to be interred closer to the family home. More than once it was teased that whoever died first lost the right to decide. As it stands, both sets of cremains still sit on the not-so-temporary cardboard altar set up Daisuke's parents' home. One recent suggestion by his mother is to leave the remains to the family's temple, where ongoing rites of *kuyō* would be performed for his grandparents along with the other parishioners.

Other more creative options, which I discuss in chapter 5, appear not yet to have reached the family.

Now, on our trips back to Hiroshima, Daisuke runs upstairs to make a quick "goodbye" before we leave the house; in his words, "I'll just go do a *chi~n* [sound of the bell] for my grandparents." I am amused, as Daisuke is perhaps the least pious person I know. He has been lucky to have long-lived grandparents, three of whom met "good deaths" at an old age. The situation is even more remarkable given that all four of his grandparents survived the 1945 nuclear attack on Hiroshima. After the recent deaths of both paternal grandparents, Daisuke moved our yearly trip to Japan from New Years to their joint death anniversaries around March. He now acknowledges that there "might be something that I need to do" for his parents, or at least for the dead. For those who experience death within their nuclear family at a young age, these responsibilities arrive earlier, bringing about a different confrontation with intergenerational change.

INFORMAL OBSERVANCES

I first met Kiki at an anthropology conference in Australia, and she soon became a key informant, friend, and my guide around the Ishikawa Prefecture of Japan. Both in our late twenties as we began research, we each experienced the death of a parent to cancer before starting our PhDs. My discussions with Kiki about her mother's death and associated ritual practice encompassed visits to her home and that of her extended family, Facebook conversations, and regular catch-ups at coffee shops in Kanazawa. Kiki is generous, driven, and meticulous. It strikes me that she applies the same ethnographer's concern for learning and following "the rules of the game" in the field to the observance of her own culture's norms; I was once gently reprimanded for walking in front of her grandfather, as he was the head of her household. Like many of my female friends in Japan, Kiki is a fount of knowledge about social customs, such as the appropriate gift to give to a company president or a friend and what length of skirt or cut of blouse to wear at an interview. At the same time, Kiki often expressed surprise at the extent to which her own family's *kuyō* practice for her mother followed Buddhist customs in the Jōdo Shinshū tradition, considering their general disinterest in religion.

Kiki's mother died suddenly from brain cancer approximately ten years ago. The family received the diagnosis just three months prior and were able to have some discussions about her wishes. When she died, on the tatami mat in the family home, Kiki and her siblings dressed her mother in a white kimono and scattered deep red rose petals around her. At the time, the family possessed neither a *butsudan* nor a grave; their father is a second son, and her mother was the first person in the immediate family to have died. The family decided that one corner of the room where her mother slept and eventually died would be her space in the home. The space atop a large chest of drawers, originally part of the mother's trousseau, now serves as the site for the *kuyō* goods, including a *butsudan* (plate 6).

The purchase of a *butsudan* and grave did not take place immediately. Indeed, Kiki herself delayed the process for many years because "I didn't want my mother's cremains to go somewhere by themselves. I was against it. . . . I had to prepare my heart for it." Kiki reports that a local priest told her that if the cremains are not interred, then the dead cannot *jōbutsu suru* (成仏する), or "become a Buddha" (an interpretation I had not heard before, and which I now suspect was a sales tactic). In the end, the cremains were left in the home for nearly five years, stored atop the altar supplied by the funeral home. As with Daisuke's family, the cardboard *saidan*, intended as a temporary structure, became a valuable resource during extended deliberations regarding investment in more permanent goods for *kuyō*. "Looking back," Kiki reflects, "us holding onto this flimsy structure is kind of hilarious." The *saidan* was set up in the tatami room, where the family comes together to watch television, where her father now sleeps, and where the family could "keep mum company." It was only when another (distant) family member died that Kiki realized the length of their delay, and the cremains were finally interred. After much searching, Kiki's father was able to secure a city-managed grave during a sale, about three years after his wife's death. Unfortunately, it is rather distant from the family home, and although Kiki wants to visit more regularly, "to make sure that my mum is not alone," she is unable to do so.

The altar was acquired some months after her mother's death, purchased online from a retailer in Tokyo. Like Hiroshima, Ishikawa Prefecture is a stronghold of Jōdo Shinshū Buddhism. But Kiki's family did not have the domestic space, finances, or desire to purchase a grand golden altar typical of the school. Their modern altar, approximately thirty centimeters high and twenty centimeters wide, is made from composite chipboard covered in a thin veneer of lacquered wood. It was mass-produced somewhere in Southeast Asia and cost about 50,000 yen. No *ihai* (ancestral tablet) is enshrined in this altar, a fact Kiki seems unsure about before I tell her that's consistent with Jōdo Shinshū practice. There is, however, a small scroll listing her mother's Buddhist name hanging in the altar. Kiki is quick to downplay its importance:

There is one, but it doesn't really have any meaning to me. Well, even if I
say that it doesn't have meaning, it's not just something that we can throw
away, and contained within the *butsudan* there is a Buddha and instruments.

In addition, several artifacts surround the altar and spill out from its sides,
connecting the *butsudan* to a wider ritual space. These include photographs
of Kiki's mother, New Year cards, fruit, sweets, and fresh flowers. Kiki's siblings have taken to purchasing new objects for the altar space whenever they
travel. Kiki once bought back paper flowers from a trip to Toronto, which
now adorn the wall behind the altar.

This evolving mix of photographs and objects invites multiple different
readings. Are they offerings to the dead? A memorial? A display? The varied feelings of people in the household toward this space becomes a key
point in my discussions with Kiki. I first encountered the altar during a stay
with her family. Her father wakes up early to make breakfast, setting aside a
small portion as an offering. Kiki and I then join her father before the altar.
He lights half a stick of incense (a full stick burns too long), takes up prayer
beads, and recites a short passage from an introductory sutra book. The entire process lasts about five minutes. Kiki notes that her relation to the altar
and this practice has changed over time:

> To begin with, I hadn't really learned anything about Buddhism, not
> formally or from my parents. I knew nothing—nothing of the words of
> prayer [*laughter*]. So, when I go before the grave, it's like what should
> I say? "Ah, it's Kiki. Everyone is well. Mom, are you doing well?" It was al-
> ways like that, so when my mom died, I faced toward her, not toward the
> Buddha, and talked, but toward my mom and talked.

Kiki describes the morning routine as simply "placing one's hands together"
(手を合わせる *te o awaseru*). This enigmatic phrase privileges the practice
of *kuyō* but discloses little about the internal thoughts and feelings of those
addressing the altar. It is a phrase that appeared repeatedly in my fieldwork,
spoken by *butsudan* salespeople extolling the moral virtue of home life with
butsudan, by Buddhist priests instructing parishioners on practice, and by
countless laypeople attempting to describe what *butsudan* rites entail.

Holding Kiki's description of her practice in mind, I will next examine
how *butsudan* and grave rites have previously been analyzed as representative of shifting modes of necrosociality. In considering these theories, I
want to make space for ambiguous, embodied ways of being with altars and

resist the temptation to reduce *butsudan* practice to signifiers of a particular necrosocial mode.

Necrosociality in transition

Kiki's focus on her mother can be interpreted as indicative of an emergent mode of necrosociality in Japan, one that is more focused on personal relationships with the dead as significant others than on formal rites performed in relation to ancestors or *hotoke* (buddhas). Changes in Japanese death culture have been analyzed by religious scholars and sociologists across a number of overlapping dimensions (table 3.1). First, scholars have described a shift in the orientation of the living toward the dead. Smith (1974) contrasts "praying for" the dead's welfare and "praying to" the dead for guidance and favor as sequential stages in the rites performed for the dead as they mature. Whether people pray to or for the dead may depend on their social status or whether the dead experienced a good or bad death (as in the case of Eiko's father, chapter 2). Smith thus produces a model of distinct but coexisting modes of necrosociality: "the Japanese have both memorialism and ancestor worship—all in the context of a single domestic altar—by differentiating persons by status and importance in life and then by according them

Table 3.1

Domain	Traditional		Modern		Contemporary or emergent
Orientation of living toward the dead	Praying for (Smith 1974)	→	Praying to (Smith 1974)	→	Memorializing (Naitō 2013)
Rules governing who becomes an ancestor	Unilineal descent		→		Bilateral orientation (Morioka 1984)
	Household centered		→		Family centered (Smith 1974)
Identity of the dead	Deities	→	Buddhas or ancestors	→	Beloved antecedents (Suzuki 1998)
Motivation for ritual practice	Formal/jural		→		Personal (Morioka 1984)
	Rules of affiliation		→		Emotional bond (Duteil-Ogata 2015)
Material culture (Suzuki I. 2013)	Ancestral tablets	→	Funeral portraits (Yamada Shinya 2002)	→	Personal photographs

differential ceremonial treatment" (1974, 146). Naitō prefers a more blended model, suggesting that even within "a traditional mode of *kuyō*," some kind of memorialism exists "from the start" (2013, 9). She points to the focus on the individual deceased in the early stages of Buddhist death rites (for example, in the use of photographs) as evidence of this mixing. For Hikaru Suzuki (1998), Smith's model appears to describe a (broadly chronological) transformation of the orientation of the living toward the deceased. Although she does not always make a clear distinction between ancestor worship and *kuyō*, her work suggests a general transition away from worship and toward memorialism, which "celebrates the deceased's personal life based on the bereaved's love toward the deceased" (1998, 171). Suzuki hints that this shift results from the rejection of Buddhist funeral rites and a growing asymmetry between the living and the dead, such that the ancestors and elderly are no longer seen as guaranteeing the economic security of younger generations (1998, 184).

The next dimension of this transformation concerns who becomes an ancestor or, indeed, whether that category remains relevant. Morioka Kiyomi (1984) suggests that the principles governing ancestors have expanded to include "bilateral relations" rather than just people of "unilineal descent." Smith traces this shift to the disintegration of the household and emergence of the nuclear family as the core kinship unit (1974, 174). Others question whether categories such as "ancestors," "Buddhas" (仏 *hotoke*), and (historically) "tutelary deities" (see Ooms 1967) retain any significance. One way of describing this change is in terms of a shortening of temporal depth, such that less attention is given to "the remote dead" as ancestors (Smith 1974, 223). More strongly, Suzuki suggests that the contemporary dead may never become Buddhas or ancestors because they do not go through Buddhist funeral rites (1998, 180). She argues that the dead in contemporary Japan are instead encountered primarily as "beloved antecedents," remembered for their individual characteristics and personal relationships to the living but not venerated or empowered (2013b, 228).

It is interesting to compare this shift and Tony Walter's (2016) description of the emerging category of "angels" in Western vernacular religion. Walter describes how "once-human angels" have become a popular "meme" within popular death culture, distinguished by, among other qualities, their agency, as they are empowered to "look after those on earth who still need their care and guidance" (2016, 3). The empowerment of the dead as angels appears to move in the opposite direction to Suzuki's suggested disempowerment of the dead in Japan. I have occasionally observed the language of "angels" being used in Japan to describe the dead, but it is usually for rather pragmatic reasons. I spent time with the Irie family, just after they decided to perform

Christian funerary rites for their maternal grandmother, who died at ninety-five in a Jesuit hospice in Kyoto. This was not, the family were quick to assure me, because she or they had converted to Christianity. She was at least nominally a member of Jōdoshū, and when she died a Buddhist priest did approach the family regarding the funeral. However, family members were moved by the compassion shown by the Christian hospice, and in the son's words, "If it's Christianity, then the dead just go *baaaan* up to heaven, it's all complete, and we don't need to worry about calling priests every year." By offering instant salvation, Christianity secures the eternal welfare of the dead as angels in heaven and relieves the living of ongoing responsibility for ritual performance. Similarly, Susan Long describes Christianity as associated with simpler and cheaper funeral rites in Japan, as well as expertise in palliative care and bereavement support (2004, 918).

Suzuki's argument regarding a shift from ancestors/*hotoke* to beloved antecedents only partly resonates with my observations. Certainly, I rarely encountered people talking about their remote ancestors in relation to *butsudan* practice. However, in more rural parts of Japan and among elderly people, who are still largely responsible for tending to *butsudan*, these ideas retain currency (see especially Danely 2014). And within the religious goods industry, ancestor veneration remains a powerful motif of the Japanese character, to be promoted and marketed to younger generations. More than that, I would suggest that in contemporary Japan, the dead are still popularly conceived of as empowered to intervene in the world of the living, most notably through hauntings but also through financial windfalls and luck. This was powerfully illustrated in the wake of the March 2011 earthquake, tsunami, and nuclear disaster, which produced an abundance of restless dead, as well as new ritual actions to pacify them (Dahl 2017, 29–30). But even outside these extraordinary circumstances, the dead still constitute a potential cause in people's life, whether positive or negative, and thus generate that "pull" for the living.

What I want to suggest is that in Japan, the identity of the dead and the living's orientation toward them, made tangible in a retinue of necromaterials, is far more ambiguous and ambivalent than the above categories suggest. What is intriguing about Kiki's family's practice are the multiple layers of manifestations of the dead and the varied manner in which family members interact with them. Kiki's mother is enshrined not only in their home altar but in a larger, more elaborate golden altar in the home of Kiki's maternal grandparents. Over O-bon and New Year's, the extended family gather around, eating soba noodles, laughing, and chatting. They leave the doors to the altar open, so the ancestors can join in the frivolity. The room in which this altar sits is located at the end of the house, away from the kitchen and television, which attract the most foot traffic. In winter, the room takes hours to heat with a kerosene stove, and Kiki's elderly grandparents now find it taxing to kneel on its tatami floors. Enshrined here, the dead receive little regular company. But Kiki's mother can also be found in material traces spread throughout the family residences, in smiling photographs atop the television as well as family trees and photograph albums. Kiki inherited a suitcase of her mother's clothing, including a bright red jacket with embroidered patches that was purchased from America in the 1980s. Its loud colors are conspicuous beside the muted tones of contemporary Japanese women's fashion, but wearing the jacket around her hometown, Kiki says she feels closer to her mother.

Kiki's older sister, who lives with her and her father, chooses not to participate in the daily *butsudan* rite. Kiki is most surprised by her father's uptake of a Buddhist practice and what she perceives to be his adoption of Buddhist modes of relating to his wife. "It seems like my father faces toward the Buddha to perform rites," she says. "It seems like he has been studying this kind of thing." He is a high school teacher and a shy but friendly man who welcomes me into their home and cooks me several delicious meals. Although he had never expressed any discernible interest in Buddhism to Kiki before, he started reciting sutras each morning and evening after his wife died. Not only does he recite them, but he has begun studying their interpretation on the counsel of a local priest, who he says, in a moment of candor, gave him advice on "how best to care for his wife."

Kiki was so surprised by the apparent transformation in her father that she eventually asked him, "Papa, do you believe in God or the supernatural?" and when he replied, "Not at all," they both laughed. This refutation is instructive, because such belief has on occasion been used as a proxy measure for the practice of domestic *butsudan* rites. For example, Ian Reader quotes surveys showing declining belief in the existence of *hotoke* (Buddhas) or a spirit of the dead among university students, which he suggests "has grave implications for the future engagement of the younger generations in Buddhist rituals" (2011, 241). Drawing the opposite causative connection, Suzuki suggests that the adoption of nonreligious funeral rites "undermines the fundamental belief revolving around the production of household ancestors" (1998, 180). Neither Kiki nor her father expressed a strong belief in the existence of spirits or the afterlife. Nor was a Buddhist rite interpreted as what Kiki's mother (also nonreligious) would particularly have desired. Nevertheless, Kiki and her father continue to perform rites daily, thereby adopting Buddhist modes of caring for the dead. As ethnographic attention to the everyday lived experience of Japanese religion so often teaches, one cannot conflate belief, practice, and cosmology, or even assume an alignment between them.

Alongside variations in the family, Kiki's own understanding of her altar practice has evolved. Some months after my initial visit, Kiki messaged me, hoping to clarify how she felt about *butsudan*:

> The daily rite ends very quickly. But I like that moment. It's like, even when I am busy, there is a ritual. Every morning I have time to think about my mother and think. It gives me a chance to breathe deeply. And my father is happy, and it helps build our connection. . . .
>
> So, my father and I share a lot in that moment, it's like we are sharing our thoughts. We don't speak, but everyday we are reminded of . . .
>
> [Hannah: Of your mother?]
>
> Yes, and of her death. I think that's important. Recently, I've lived overseas a lot, and I haven't been able to do that.

Kiki further likened her mother's afterlife to the Japanese song, "I am (in) a thousand winds that blow" (千の風になって *sen no kaze ni natte*), inspired by a line from the popular English language poem "Do not stand at my grave and weep." Kiki tells me that when she stands before the altar, "what I think of is her death." In a way, Kiki's daily confrontation with absence through ritual performance reminds me of the Hyolmo people's processes of creatively making the unmaking of the dead, as described by Robert Desjarlais (2016, 9–10), in the sense that death requires an investment of time, resources, and labor by the living. In Desjarlais's ethnography, the absence of the dead, their departure from the world of the living, is not automatically conferred by (physical) death but is brought about by the ritual works of the living. In Kiki's case, it is not necessarily an encounter with the presence of her mother—as buddha, ancestor, or beloved antecedent—but an encounter with absence that the altar provides.

Returning to the dimensions of transformation in Japanese necrosociality, scholars have also proposed shifting motivations behind posthumous rites. Broadly, this has been styled as a move from "jural" or "formal" duties to "personal" connections (Morioka 1984) or from "rules of affiliation" to "emotional bonds" (Duteil-Ogata 2015, 234–41). The extent of this change is contested. For example, Suzuki argues that "the meaning of one's death has come to depend upon how the living evaluated the deceased's personality, merit, and his or her good deeds" (1998, 184). However, Kretschmer writes that contemporary acts of *kuyō* are "performed not as a result of the consideration that a person 'deserved' to be honoured and cared for . . . ," but in recognition of the *en* that bind the living and the dead (2000a, 51). As I examined in chapter 2, a complex balancing of factors determines how much people invest in postmortem rites, including consideration of the personality and tastes of the deceased and an embodied feeling of discomfort with the prospect of unfulfilled obligations.

Where the internal motivations, beliefs, and cosmology of people engaged in death rites can prove difficult for scholars to access, material culture appears to offer more solid evidence of change. For example, Iwayumi Suzuki (2013) evaluates the growing presence of photographs of the dead within domestic environments as revelatory of wider changes in how Japanese people connect with the dead in daily life. She argues, first, that photographs have come to rival or replace the function of *ihai* at altars, and second, that photos of the living and the dead increasingly share common space in the home (2013, 141). Consistent with this argument, scholars have interpreted the rise of photography in memorial spaces as evidence of more personalized relationships between the living and the dead (Irizarry 2014; Suzuki H. 2013a, 20; Smith 1983, 29–40). More strongly, Naitō argues that new commercial services and technologies are a driving force shaping new modes of necrosociality. She argues that the trend toward memorialization is not just a "simplification" or "personalization" of *kuyō* but the result of commercialization of the funeral sector (2013, 56). This commercialization brought about a proliferation of "remembrance goods" (記念品 *kinenhin*), including photographs, films, and scrapbooks, merging into a wider DIY and craft-décor trend (2013, 49). However, it is easy to read too much symbolic weight into these products. What attention to the lifecourse of *butsudan* reveals is that necromaterials—traditional and new—are as much shaped by limited resources, happenstance, and personal feelings as they are the stable products of deliberate, considered curation.

At the close of the last chapter, I asked how the tradition of *butsudan* holds up in the context of contemporary desires and practices of engagement with the dead. Like the lantern festival at Sensōji, rites for both Kiki's and Daisuke's dead are performed within and against formal Buddhist models of veneration, but the meanings and materialities of these exchanges are not limited to the orthodoxy of Buddhist teachings. Before *butsudan*, people draw on diverse material resources and personal imaginings of the dead, which can skirt, uphold, or coexist with Buddhist rituals and the traditional model of a good death. As in the case of Kiki's father, Buddhist rites and the *butsudan* medium are not necessarily opposed to maintaining personal relations with the dead. Or, as in the case of the photograph of Daisuke's grandmother, Buddhist convention might be selectively followed in certain contexts or for certain audiences and ignored in others.

Plate 1. A golden *butsudan* in the style of the Jōdo Shinshū school. Hiroshima, 2017.

Plate 2. The interior of a *butsudan*, showing the placement of ritual implements and offerings. Ishikawa, 2017.

Plate 3. Yamashita's ornate golden *butsudan*. Toyama Prefecture, 2017.

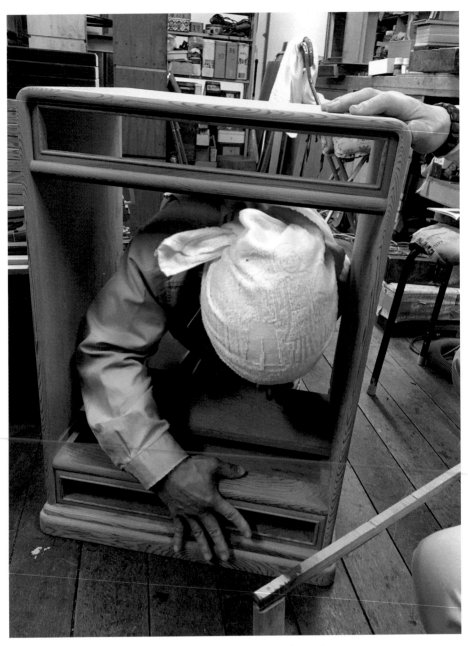

Plate 4. Assembling a handcrafted *butsudan*, Tokyo, 2016.

Plate 5. The altar for the *hōji* for Daisuke's grandmother, Hiroshima, 2017.

Plate 6. The "altar corner" in Kiki's house, Ishikawa Prefecture, 2018.

Plate 7. Priest performing the *tamashii-nuki* rite at a *butsudan*, Osaka, 2017.

Plate 8. Celebrating with the delivery team at Takimoto Bukkōdō, Osaka 2019.

As Hikaru Suzuki (2013b, 228) and others affirm, a generalizable shift from jural/formal/Buddhist "worship" of "ancestors" to personal/emotive/secular "memorialization" of "beloved antecedents" appears well-established in the sociological literature. However, exactly how scholars map these categories onto Japanese-language terms, and the actual embodied practices they denote, is not always so clear. When analyzing *butsudan* rites in the home, I often struggled to classify my own and others' experiences into these categories, or indeed, to see how exclusive categorizations might be sustained. Instead, I encountered a (sometimes uneasy) overlapping of multiple different media for the dead, and multiple, ambiguous orientations toward them. This diversity occurs not only between generations but within them and, further, within an individual's experience of the dead in different spaces or times.

Part of the problem derives from how we tend to interpret *butsudan*, and material religion more generally, as mere reflections of people's changing religious cosmology or social relationship to the dead. From a materially grounded perspective, *butsudan* are better framed as active participants in people's encounters with the dead and, indeed, in an array of other household activities. The presence of personal photographs on altars does not necessarily imply the personalization of death rites, just as the performance of yearly Buddhist rituals does not necessitate a belief in the dead as *hotoke* or ancestors. I have had to resist, then, the temptation to read patterns of addition or absence of items on a *butsudan* or change in altar design as indicative of broader shifts in necrosocial relations, if for no other reason than such conclusions are often actively disavowed by the people I met during fieldwork. As I discuss further in chapter 5, the simple existence of new products and services in the funerary market tells us very little a priori about how people relate to the dead.

In the two narratives in this chapter, *butsudan* act as spaces for connecting with the dead, through the offering of coffee-scented candles and rice cakes, the arduous recitation of sutras, and a daily confrontation of absence. I am less convinced by teleological readings of these acts as aimed at the ontological transformation of the dead (from "*hotoke*" to "ancestor," for example), or symbolic readings of these acts as revelatory of a belief in the continued existence of spirit. If anything, performing *kuyō* appears to provide some form of emotional relief (安心 *anshin*) for the living, as an assurance that one's obligations are fulfilled. But this emotive force cannot be separated from religious and social pressures that dictate what "doing the right thing" looks like. Off the showroom floor and into the home, *butsudan* practice demonstrates a high degree of improvisation and personalization. This is not to deny the role of Buddhist orthodoxy or priests in shaping *butsudan*

rites, nor the influence of gendered power dynamics. Indeed, in comparison to cross-cultural studies of altar practice, *butsudan* show how the domestic sphere and domestic religion are not free from, but tied up in, the
same power dynamics that structure institutional religion (that permeable
threshold works in both directions). By paying ethnographic attention to
how formal rites and informal observances around the *butsudan* are played
out in the everyday, we can acknowledge the capacity of *butsudan* to give
space to the contradictions and subtleties of exchanges between the living
and the dead.

CHAPTER 4

Disposal

The call of the cicadas is unimaginably loud at the place where graves and *butsudan* go to die. It is late summer of 2022 and I am in a clearing of a bamboo forest, deep in the mountains above Fukuyama city. Stretching out before me are headstones of different shapes and sizes, all taken from abandoned or unwanted graves (無縁墓 *muenbaka*) (figure 4.1). Some are old and eroded with rounded edges and worn markings. Others are made of newer marble with clear-cut laser engravings of a family name. Dotted across the landscape are statues of Buddha or *Jizo Bosatsu*, the occasional stone monument for a decorated soldier, and one for a beloved family dog (figure 4.2).

This is the "grave of the graves" (お墓の墓 *o-haka no haka*), a mountain refuge where abandoned or unwanted headstones are collected and receive ongoing rites of *kuyō* from a local priest. The stockpiling of abandoned or excess graves in mounds, known as *muendzuka* (無縁塚), is a common strategy in cemeteries across Japan, but the scale of this ruinous landscape makes it exceptional. Alighting from the car at the bottom of the allotment, I slowly ascend the mountainside on foot, passing a forklift, a dedicated space for making offerings, a collection of old, boarded-up *butsudan*, and a fire pit, to reach the summit. Stretching out across the vista are tens of thousands of headstones. In remote aerial footage (Yagi 2019), the collection forms an artificial landscape, like a flowing river with undulating waves and troughs, all formed from the material remnants of the abandoned dead.

Japanese graves are made of multiple stone slabs that fit together to delineate and protect the space of interments. But only the top headstone, which carries the family name, known as the *saoishi* (棹石), is sent to the grave of the graves. There is also the occasional *reihyō* (霊標) stone, which lists the individual Buddhist names of all of those interred. The *saoishi* represent a huge variety of styles from different regions and eras—flat top, rounded, prismatic, *ihai* style, picture frame style, and so on. There are even a few horizontal "western headstones" (洋型墓石 *yōgata boseki*), likely only erected in recent years before ending their short life here.

Figure 4.1. The view of the "grave of the graves" from the peak, Fukuyama, 2022.

The headstones arrive in Fukuyama from all across the country. They are carried on trucks from as far as Kansai and Chūbu, sometimes in loads of five hundred stones in a single delivery during the peak grave-visiting seasons (Yagi 2019). Usually, after the necessary rituals of desacralization, gravestones are ground down into a fine gravel for use in construction projects. Indeed, that is the likely fate of all those stones that supported the *sao-ishi* collected here. But for some families or Buddhist clergy, such recycling

Figure 4.2. A Buddha in the grave of the graves, Fukuyama, 2022.

practices prove uncomfortable or distasteful, and so they opt to send headstones to this resting place. There is also some public disquiet about the profane afterlives of unwanted or abandoned graves. A cemetery in Kobe that I
visited faced public backlash following rumors that a winding road outside
its property was paved with crushed gravestones. A number of car accidents
had recently occurred on that section of road, and stories circulated that it
was haunted. The dead were pulling the living into the bitumen to join them.

Collected in this mountain refuge, the dead appear to experience a more restful repose. The site is managed by Fudōin, of the Tendai Jimon school, and cared for by head priest Mishima. Fudōin is a small but seemingly lively rural temple, offering a diverse set of newer Buddhist services alongside this site: they manage a pet cemetery and hold *kuyō* rites for pets and for *mizuko* (aborted, miscarried, or stillborn fetuses). The temple established the grave refuge in 2001 upon hearing from other priests troubled by the many abandoned graves in their care (Yagi 2019). Mishima performs *kuyō* rites before the gravestones, reading sutras and offering incense and flowers. At regular intervals, old or abandoned *butsudan, tōba* (塔婆; wooden grave tablets), and other religious detritus made of wood or paper are incinerated as part of this rite. As Paulina Kolata argues, even undesirable excesses can be "generative of new meanings and structures of care" (2022, 1), and for temples like Fudōin, in possession of large plots of land, the ability to absorb sacred waste can be a promising new business venture. At a cost of 2,500 yen per headstone or 6,000 yen per ton of stone, business appears to be booming. But despite the careful curation of this space and Mishima's ritual observances, each time I visit, I suspect that the living are fighting a losing battle against the rising number of abandoned dead. The headstones are neatly arranged, but weeds and bamboo shoots rise into the sky. In rare shady patches, moss has begun to colonize the tops of older headstones. Nature is slowly swallowing the stones.

It is difficult to describe the pathos of this place, the mix of sadness and awe I feel when standing in the midst of thousands of abandoned graves. In many respects, this place should not exist, these headstones should not exist. The Posthumous Security Assurance System (Himonya 1994, 64–65) is designed to continue in an unending chain of generations via which graves and *butsudan* are inherited. Instead, this place discloses the immense scale of necromaterial abandonment in contemporary Japan. Here lies one set of ruins of the decimation of the household. And so even with continued performances of *kuyō* by priests, the dead do not appear to be entirely pacified. On my last visit, my mother-in-law and aunt refused to get out of the car to inspect the site or to take photographs. My mother-in-law explained that "as Japanese people, we worry that spirit(s) might be captured in the image."

Of course, the haunting reality of abandoned gravestones and extinguished households is not immediately apparent to most, given the location of this refuge deep in the mountainside. In 2022, I rattled off apologies to my travel companions as I directed the car along mountain paths, passing rubbish incinerators, pet crematoria, and dairy farms. There was barely a centimeter of space on either side of the car's tires as we followed the GPS, and then handwritten signs, and finally, when both failed us, satellite vision to locate the hoard (which is visible from space). There is an abundance of care evident in the handling and arrangement of these stones into neat rows. But like other forms of powerful, troubling remains—like the human body—the realities of the disposal and material afterlife are often hidden from public view. As Tamara Kohn (2021) articulates in her work on US prison systems, rot, mold, and other forms of neglect or decay are allowed to flourish, or even encouraged, in spaces outside of public visibility.

Graves and *butsudan* represent an interesting addendum to that category of things known as "sacred waste." As typically conceived by scholars, sacred waste describes the unintentional by-products of active ritual practice, the consumable and transient debris generated by religious experiences or the creation of artifacts (Stengs 2014; Wirtz 2009). It is the wine left over at the end of communion or the charred remains of an incinerated offering. Sacred waste might also be conceived of as "exhausted objects" that have been degraded through physical wear and tear (Rambelli 2007, 7). *Butsudan* do sometimes fit this latter category, having a projected consumer lifecycle of approximately sixty years before they need to be repaired or replaced (Hasegawa 2005, 11). *Butsudan* can fall apart over time and from lack of care, becoming dusty and rickety, or musty and damp. Their hard wood and dark corners shelter infestations of mice or cockroaches, and determined termites sometimes find their way behind the thick layers of lacquer to consume the wood from the inside (figure 4.3). Writing on Korea, Laurel Kendall calls the inevitability of decay "the basic problem of material religion" (2017, 861), in that material forms allow ideas of the transcendent to become comprehensible and transmissible, but this also makes the transcendent vulnerable to the vagaries of time and circumstance. However, at the refuge in Fukuyama, crumbling graves and *butsudan* are far outnumbered by new, pristine examples. These objects have not been worn down through use but, instead, have suffered a kind of "social death" (Daniels 2009) as a result of *dis*use. Put another way, the stuff has not degraded, the socioreligious practices that once animated it have. Abandoned or unwanted *butsudan* and graves have thus diverged from their intended lifecourse.

Where do unwanted *butsudan* and graves go? What motivates people to jettison them? And who is responsible for the work of disposal? The mountain refuge of Fukuyama, after all, gathers only a small percentage of Japan's necromaterial waste. At first, investigating this stage of the *butsudan* lifecourse proved incredibly challenging. The topic of waste, particularly sacred waste, generates feelings of discomfort. As discard studies scholar and anthropologist Joshua Reno reminds us, nobody likes a researcher sorting through their bins (2016, 7). My interest in *butsudan* disposal first emerged during my internship with Takimoto Bukkōdō in Osaka, where

Figure 4.3. Insect damage on a *butsudan* tendered for restoration. Toyama, 2018.

daily operations for the delivery team also included the collection and sort-ing of unwanted Buddhist goods. This work is increasingly common, with an estimated seventy to eighty thousand unneeded *butsudan* tendered for removal each year across Japan (Sumida Kotato, personal communica-tion, October 2022). But still, my colleagues often dodged my questions about the afterlife of a particular altar or religious object. This caution is perhaps understandable, given the importance placed on public reputation and highly publicized rumors of improper disposal over the past few years. Such rumors range from temples reselling spent religious goods to television companies for use in commercials (Gygi 2022), to recycling companies abandoning gravestones on public land (Kotani 2014), and even individuals "forgetting" urns of cremated remains on public transport (Mainichi Shimbun 2017). Whether or not these events are true or common, their circulation via national media outlets speaks to the high stakes involved in handling religious goods. Put simply, even though *butsudan* and graves are unwanted, excess, or abandoned, it does not follow that they are powerless or inert.

Disposal is not the termination of the *butsudan* lifecourse. It is a process through which *butsudan* are valued or rejected and their sensational form holds together or falls apart. In tracing the social biography of things, ethnographies of contemporary consumer culture have tended to focus on production or consumption, with processes of discard, disposal, and recycling comparatively neglected. In her study of the waste generated by Cuban ritual practice, Kristina Wirtz posits the origins of this oversight in the dual character of waste, as "simultaneously capable of humility and dangerous potency" (2009, 477). That is, waste is both banal and abject. Wirtz reflects that she sometimes "allowed notions of propriety, in which one does not go digging into trash, least of all spiritually charged trash, to overcome any curiosity I should have felt" (2009, 479). Ultimately, a careful balance of curiosity and propriety was required for me to investigate the disposal of *butsudan*. Even then, some aspects of their contemporary afterlives remain opaque.

CARING FOR SACRED WASTE

On my first *butsudan* disposal job, the Takimoto team is called to a small residence in a tired 1980s apartment block in downtown Osaka. We are there to collect a modestly sized Jōdo Shinshū altar decorated with black lacquer and gold leaf. I approach the job with anticipation, as a rare opportunity to discuss *butsudan* with those actively choosing to divest from this tradition. However, it soon becomes apparent that an interview is not in the cards. Entering the cramped hallway, we are greeted by the Ono family, a couple in their midforties, who sit in *seiza* (formal kneeling) beside the *butsudan* for the duration of our fifteen-minute stay, silently surveying our work. Tan, Kobayashi, and I kneel before the altar and fold our hands in prayer for a few moments. The couple hesitantly inform us that the altar has already been desacralized by a local priest. We hastily dismantle the altar, attempting to hide billowing dust and any excremental evidence of a cockroach infestation. Each piece is immediately transported out of the apartment to the walkway, where it can be further broken down out of the owners' sight. I get the distinct impression, later confirmed, that unlike installation jobs, when we often sit drinking tea with customers, we are to complete these jobs as quickly and silently as possible.

The couple nod politely as Kobayashi comments on the beautiful fabric dust coverings that adorn the altar doors, which appear to have been handmade. On to the rubbish pile they go. The customers decline our offer to leave behind some of the smaller items, such as sutra books and prayer beads. Indeed, in addition to the *butsudan* and *butsugu*, they tender several boxes of ritual consumables (like incense) and sentimental objects (like dolls) for disposal. During parting greetings, circumspect inquiries finally reveal that the husband's mother, who once cared for the altar, has recently died. As the couple have no interest in continuing the practice and are in desperate need of more space in the apartment, they have decided to dispose of the altar.

The sentiments and circumstances of this job are not atypical. Often, disposal of *butsudan* follows a major life event. While a death in the family motivates some people to purchase new *butsudan*, it can also trigger their removal, as part of a regular downsizing of inherited domestic goods. The prospect of moving or renovating a home might also prompt disposal, as might new purchases or commissions, as was the case with President Yamashita (chapter 1). Even when they are built into walls, religious goods cannot usually be left behind, as their presence significantly reduces the resale value of a home. Ancestral graves might also be moved (墓引っ越し *hakahikkoshi*) to be closer to living descendants, or closed down entirely (墓じまい *hakajimai*). In either case, while upgrading to larger, more elaborate styles of grave or altar is uncommon, downsizing has boomed. The size, shape, weight, and design of *butsudan* makes them difficult objects to retain in contemporary apartment dwellings. Large, traditional altars can also raise concerns during natural disasters, particularly earthquakes. These fears are not unfounded, as *butsudan* workers routinely spend the days following an earthquake visiting customers to rearrange their altars and assess damage. As such, when disposal is coupled with a new purchase, the change is more often to a compact, modern altar.

Knowing what to do with unwanted *butsudan* is a challenge. If people are unfamiliar with the rites of *butsudan* use, then they are certainly confused by *butsudan* disposal. Online advice services and household manuals are replete with stylized images of people who are *komatteru* (困っている; "troubled" or "bothered"), with arms folded, brows furrowed and beaded with sweat, as they contemplate the fate of their unwanted graves and *butsudan*.[1] Inge Daniels artfully describes objects in Japanese homes that generate such difficult feelings as "troublesome things" (2010b, 197). Troublesome things take up space in the home and might be unwanted, but they often cannot be easily disposed of for both moral and practical reasons. The anxiety generated by the disposal of unwanted spiritual goods can manifest, as Fabio Gygi has written, in "a desire for orthopraxy" (2019, 8): to follow a manual and "do the right thing." In these cases, people turn to temples, and more and more frequently, commercial operators.

In the car between jobs, a senior colleague at Takimoto, Mitsume-san, reminisces with me about how the disposal of *butsudan* used to be handled, "back in my day." Approaching age seventy, he has worked around the industry for more than forty years and is a proponent of a rigorous health regime that includes walking two hours each morning and eating three lemons whole (as yet his regime does not preclude abundant smoking). Mitsume tells me that only a few generations ago, old *butsudan* were disposed of by families directly, who took them to greenspace allotments to be burned, sometimes with the assistance of a priest. Today, these services are almost entirely outsourced to commercial entities, as with many elements of Japanese ritual and funerary practice. The disposal of religious waste has become one of the key services *butsudan* retailers now provide to both temples and customers. During my internship, waste collection was often used as a reason for visiting temples regularly to build relationships and as a "free gift" that might earn reciprocal favor, such as the introduction of a new customer.

Within the sector, the process of disposal is colloquially referred to as *kuyō*. The word is used to label boxes of old altar goods that accumulate in stores, or euphemistically to designate something that is bound for the bin. Some *butsudan* companies do not oversee the process directly. For example, Ōgoshi Butsudan in Toyama, which in 2017 received only about 150 disposal requests annually (most connected to new altar purchases), directs these items to a specialist waste collection company after making sure that customers have organized the proper rites with a local temple. Hasegawa Butsudan in Tokyo accepts *butsudan* frames and *butsugu* from customers but delegates their collection to a nationwide freight company. Hasegawa staff gently decline ancestral tablets and icons, directing customers to temples for the disposal of these items. As the manager at Hasegawa Ginza explained, "They are things with a soul, and we are just a *butsudan* store."

The overall structure of the disposal process for *butsudan* largely mirrors the disposal of the human dead. It begins with purification rites, then disassembly, and then finally, incineration. The heart of this procedure, ritual purification, is a formal ceremony performed by a priest to remove the spirit from the icon, ancestral tablets, and *butsudan* more generally. The rite is known as *tamashii-nuki* (魂抜き; "spirit removal"), *hakken kuyō* (撥遣供養; "expulsion ceremony"), *heigan kuyo* (閉眼供養; "eye-closing ceremony"), or *senbutsu hōyō* (遷仏法要; "transfer ceremony") within Jōdo Shinshū, and varies by Buddhist school, geographic region, and the personal teachings and performance style of the priest.

Halfway through my internship with Takimoto, I attend a *tamashii-nuki* ceremony in the Sōtō Zen tradition (plate 7). Early in the morning, two full cars carrying the Takimoto delivery team drive out to Settsu City in Osaka, stopping on the way to collect the attending priest, Amaoka-san. Amaoka is both studious and playful. In the car on the way over he regales me with stories of nights out drinking with Kobayashi. The car turns amid rows of single-story, low-slung units made from stucco-clad plaster board. We enter a house in a state of organized disarray, where a married couple are in the process of organizing their deceased grandmother's belongings. A lavish tray of tropical fruit (an expensive offering in Japan) is arranged between packing boxes before a substantial solid-wood *karaki butsudan* in the center of the living room. Our team members arrange ourselves in front of the altar behind the family. The *tamashii-nuki* lasts approximately thirty minutes. Amaoka begins by purifying the room, *butsudan*, and assembled guests by taking a small glass of water, dipping a leaf into it, raising the leaf to the crown of his head, dipping it into the water once more, and finally flicking it around the room and over the altar. Amaoka then leads the crowd in recitations of the Heart Sutra. At the culmination of the ceremony, he takes up his *juzu* (数珠; prayer beads) and, addressing the *go-honzon* and then the *ihai*, entreats the spirits to recede in a loud, clear voice, making circular motions with his hands.

Later, I compliment Amaoka on his performance and he smiles. He animatedly describes his dramatic use of a long brush made from horsehair, which is flicked around before the *go-honzon* and *ihai* to "inject" the spirits into these icons during other rites. It is important, he reflects, to add some flair to one's performance, so that people less well-tutored in the rites' religious meaning can comprehend their value (and continue to pay him to perform). After the ritual ends, the team step in to disassemble the altar, starting by removing the *go-honzon* and *ihai*, and then wrapping the altar frame in blankets for transport. As this happens, the couple thanks Amaoka-san and hands over pre-prepared envelopes marked "offering." Payments for the performance of this rite generally range between 10,000 and 30,000 yen, plus transport costs. As with payment for the rites for new *butsudan*, the cost is often described to customers as "as much as you feel," and so varies widely.

In the car, the team debate the rationale behind *tamashii-nuki* rites. Yes, the ritual purges the spirit from objects, but Kobayashi explains that in doing so, it also "protects people from misfortune [罰 *bachi*]," which can arise from the destruction or mistreatment of sacred things. When pressed for concrete examples of *bachi*, Mitsume tells me of people getting pains in various parts of their body or falling ill due to their neglect of the grave and altar. And then there are the rumors of traffic accidents on a road paved with crushed gravestones. Mostly, however, the concept of *bachi* seems to manifest in a sense of stewardship toward objects and concern for their welfare (even after they leave one's possession). *Butsudan*, I am told, are things "that people have prayed toward for a long time." Having formed such enduring relationships, "it would be wrong not to say thanks," Kobayashi adds. This sense of concern for the consequences of incorrect disposal resonates with David Chidester's warning that "as precarious matter, sacred waste carries an ambivalent electricity" (2014, 239). Chidester recalls the ideas of Roger Caillois, who described the sacred as not merely opposed to the profane, but a "contagious, fleeting, ambiguous, and virulent" force (1939, 139) to be contained through special acts. Put simply, *tamashii-nuki* rites appear to make *butsudan* safe to dispose of.

The thing about things in Japan

Exactly what it is about *butsudan* that makes them sacred and requires ritual disposal is a matter of some debate, tapping into wider questions about Japanese cosmology. The most straightforward reading is that the *go-honzon* and *ihai* function as icons, manifesting the supernatural power of the Buddha, the dead, or the ancestors. The *tamashii-nuki* rite does focus on these objects, but in practice, the numinous quality of *butsudan* is not limited to the *go-honzon* and *ihai* alone. People express conflicting views about exactly what parts of the altar should be treated as sacred. This is especially the case for customers who are inexperienced with *butsudan* ritual but highly motivated to "do the right thing." During the installation of one large gold *butsudan*, a middle-aged, recently widowed customer asked detailed questions about how to clean each implement and how to dispose of consumables like flowers, candle stubs, and incense ash. Enomoto explained to her that candles could be placed with regular burnable domestic waste, and ash could be spread over the garden. However, he ultimately advised that this was something to be worked out within herself, as a "matter of feeling" (気持ちの問題 *kimochi no mondai*). If she felt these items required special treatment, she could take them to a temple for *kuyō*.

Well beyond official Buddhist icons and implements, the space of the *butsudan* itself can become a catchall for difficult-to-dispose-of sentimental objects. This can make the process of disposal akin to a treasure hunt for the team. On various occasions, they have uncovered baby hair, teeth, large sums of cash and pay slips, old wristwatches, wedding rings, war medals, umbilical cords (dried and stored in wooden boxes), and shells collected from the beach on a summer holiday. *Butsudan* stores and commercial disposal services also become recipients of a whole range of spiritual items, such as tarot cards, dream catchers, and Christian crosses. Younger generations who inherit these sentimental hoards with the *butsudan* might know little of their significance and not believe in their power. But at the point of disposal, such objects can rise from a long period of dormancy to become potent. In her study of Cuban ritual waste, Wirtz suggests that "ritual action creates a continuity between ritual offerings and ritual waste that imbues ritual waste with spiritual potency" (2009, 477). But *butsudan* assemblages tendered for disposal in Japan today are often long neglected or abandoned. At the *tamashii-nuki* ceremony described above, Amaoka and the team were given five boxes of figurines, dolls, and other memorabilia that the family had gathered up, hoping that they might also receive *kuyō* and be taken away. As policy, Takimoto Bukkōdo generally accepts the burnable items, but declines more durable items. Still, at times the "gift" of sacred waste is difficult to refuse, particularly if it is tied to a service or sale.

The performance of *kuyō* for objects is often put forth as evidence of the animation or liveliness of nonhuman entities and their moral relations with humans within Japanese cosmology. Since at least the Edo period, rites of *kuyō* have been performed not only for humans, but also for animals (Kretschmer 2000b, 384; Ambros 2012), including whales (Itoh 2018), monkeys used as scientific test subjects (Asquith 1986), and cats whose skin was used in the production of *shamisen* (Nagano 2015), and for domestic tools, including needles, scissors, eyeglasses, and more recently, bras, *tamagotchi* (Kretschmer 2000b), and the robot dog AIBO (Robertson 2018). The list of entities subject to *kuyō* throughout Japanese history is not standard nor stable but open to contestation and change. Notably, during the second half of the twentieth century, Japan experienced a "*kuyō* boom" driven by rapid economic growth, prompting professional organizations to sponsor rites for the tools of their trade as repayment for good fortune (Matsuzaki 1996, 162; Ambros 2012, 7–8). These included scissor *kuyō* rites sponsored by hairdressers and needle *kuyō* sponsored by seamstresses and tattoo artists (Ōsaki 1997). Another example is *mizuko kuyō* (水子供養), or rites for aborted, miscarried, or stillborn fetuses, which rose to particular prominence in the 1990s. Helen Hardacre (1999) has argued that the emergence of *mizuko kuyō* was driven by temples' commercial interests and a "fetocentric" discourse in popular media that targeted women's social anxieties around reproduction (see also LaFleur 1992; Anderson and Martin 1997; Wilson 2009). Thinking about the current moment in Japanese history, we can see how an unexpected excess of hereditary religious artifacts might give rise to *kuyō* aimed at dealing with all the difficult emotions and obligations these objects provoke.

An array of influences and histories are recognizable in analysis of the performance of *kuyō* for nonhuman entities. Guth describes medieval veneration of needles (針供養 *hari kuyō*) as motivated by their perceived "potential to be reborn in other forms" (2014, 181). Rambelli's work explores several strands of Buddhist writing that extend a Buddha nature (仏性 *busshō*) to nonsentient beings.[2] For example, the Tendai teaching *sōmoku jōbutsu* (草木成仏), or "trees become buddhas," suggests that inanimate objects may have a capacity equal to that of humans to receive and transmit dharma and, indeed, to achieve Buddhahood or enlightenment (Rambelli 2007, 12–27).

Shintoism is a second major influence invoked in explanations of *kuyō* for nonsentients. Although primarily associated with Buddhist temples, *kuyō* is sometimes performed by Shinto institutions (historically, the religions are deeply intertwined). Some scholars have described contemporary Japan as animist or "techno-animist" (Allison 2006), whereby the world is populated by nonhuman entities (natural and mechanical) in possession of "spirit."[3] For example, Jensen and Blok (2013) put forward Japanese Shinto-infused techno-animism as a prime example of what Bruno Latour (1993) called for in "symmetrical anthropology," that is, a modern "multi-naturalism" to contrast with the denial of fetishism that characterizes Western modernity.

Tales of *tsukumogami* (付喪神) in texts dating back to the Muromachi period (1336–1573) are further examined as evidence of the historical malleability of the categories of the animate and inanimate in Japanese religious cosmology (Guth 2014; Kretschmer 2000b; Reider 2009). *Tsukumogami* are household objects and tools, such as fans, brooms, and umbrellas, that come to life after years of use by humans. They remain popular figures in contemporary Japanese folktales and animations; it was the umbrella *tsukumogami* that the young girl of the introduction mimicked, as she ran around the graveyard. As independent spirits, *tsukumogami* are inclined to play tricks on people and can even become "venegeful and murderous specters" when "abandoned by the human masters whom they so loyally served" (Reider 2009, 232). *Tsukumogami* thus act as a warning of the potential for objects to cause harm when not properly treated.

Finally, looking to Japanese scholarship, the collective research project of *monogaku* (モノ学) argues that the dominant Japanese cosmology comprises a single category of *mono* (モノ), a term that traverses the senses of "people," "spirits," and "things/matter," the study of which thus encompasses social science, philosophy or religious studies, and natural sciences (Kamata

2009; Shimazono 2009). *Monogaku* further challenges a divide between sacred and profane matter and the treatment of human or nonhuman dead.

In sum, different theoretical framings and historical sources suggest that something is going on with things in Japan, or at least, something distinct from how people interact with things in Western, Protestant cultures, whether or not this is unusual globally. Stories of *tsukumogami*, Buddhist metaphysics, and Shinto rituals provide sources for understanding the cultural history of *kuyō* for nonhuman entities. Less commonly explored are the experiences and feelings of those who participate in *kuyō* today and who rarely reference these sources. As I have written, *butsudan* retailers and customers sometimes describe *kuyō* as a means of giving thanks (感謝 *kansha*) and suggest that it conveys gratitude toward the objects that have served oneself or one's family. Conversely, an altar's attachment to generations of its custodians was sometimes cited as reason why *butsudan* could not be sold secondhand, and why *kuyō* was a necessary part of disposal. Rather than attempt to sustain or prove any ontological proposition about the nature of people and things, I have found it more fruitful to pay ethnographic attention to these expressions of relation between the dead, altars, and those that care for them.

Workers at Takimoto Bukkōdō take pains to ensure that the unwanted *butsudan* they accept have been properly treated. As workers who regularly handle used religious goods, their exposure to potential harms or *bachi* from inappropriate treatment is disproportionately large. Still, I was surprised to discover that even after a *kuyō* rite has been performed, the *go-honzon* and *butsudan* in their care are not always considered "deactivated" or returned to being "just a thing," as some scholars have suggested (e.g., Rambelli 2007, 216). For the employees at Takimoto, at least, *kuyō* is not so definitive. President Takimoto and his team routinely organize additional performances of *kuyō* for *butsudan* and other sacred waste, even when customers assure him it has already been performed. Even more fastidiously, at Takimoto, *go-honzon* are separated out and collected at the company's headquarters, where they receive up to five additional performance of *kuyō*, ranging in formality and feeling.[4] This includes calling upon priests from the company's affiliated temple to perform an additional *tamashii-nuki* ceremony, as well as informal offerings of incense and chanting sutras during the cremation itself. I remember sitting around the office with colleagues one evening after work, trying to think through this puzzle. Takimoto's chairman (and former president) struggled to find the right expression, before offering me the following explanation: "Even if *kuyō* could remove 70 percent or 90 percent of the spirit of the thing, there is still 30 percent left. It's not the same as a new thing."

The chairman's words suggest that the ties that bind people and *butsu-dan* might never be fully removed, only dampened or suppressed. *Kuyō* rites for dead human persons require even more performances, over a period of thirty-three or fifty years after death (depending on the teachings of different Buddhist schools). This sense of extended and repeated practices of disposal resonates with Kevin Hetherington's theorization of disposal more generally as "a continual practice of engaging with making and holding things in a state of absence" (2004, 159). Rather than a single, definitive act of destruction or displacement, *kuyō* requires an ongoing engagement with that which is absent. President Takimoto, who also struggled to explain the apparent superfluity of continuous acts of *kuyō*, finally suggested that they are largely motivated by Japanese people's "problematic feelings" (日本人の気持ちの問題 *nihonjin no kimochi no mondai*). Here, once again, "feelings," or *kimochi*, reign supreme in the negotiation of correct ritual practice. In Japanese, the term *kimochi* encompasses both psychological and physiological sensations. In her ethnography of elderly Japanese people's experiences, Natsumi Morita contends that the term *kimochi* connotes a "deeper existential experience" as opposed to passing emotions (2011, 173). The focus on feelings suggests that *kuyō* operates not on a binary logic of the addition or removal of spirits, but as a kind of ongoing, affective work that acts on the relation between *mono* (human and nonhuman).

One of the joys and challenges of fieldwork in the religious industry in Japan, where there is extensive introspection about the meaning of Japanese culture, is that my research queries were often followed up with long email treatises from my research participants. On my final day at the Osaka store, and after much apparent reflection, President Takimoto handed me a typed page of text, accompanied by a hand-drawn diagram (figure 4.4), in which he defines *kuyō* as an act of separation born from a recognition of the interconnection of people and things in the world. He writes (my translation):

Figure 4.4. A quick diagram prepared by President Takimoto to explain his understanding of *kuyō*. Above the line, the words 感謝 (gratitude) and 願い (hope) are circled. Below the line, from left to right, are the words 過去 (past), 現在 (present), and 未来 (future).

Within the concept of *kuyō* there are the components of "gratitude" [感謝 *kansha*] and "hope" [願い *negai*]. Expressed on the axis of time, "gratitude" is looking at the past from the present, and "hope" is looking toward the future. If you can feel both "gratitude" and "hope," then thinking about humanity's long history and future, you begin to understand your place in the present. . . .

In general, *kuyō* is enacting the separation of people or things. By performing *kuyō*, a grateful heart is born, you know your own existence, and at the same time, hopes toward the future are born.

What President Takimoto's words capture is the underappreciated dimension of *kuyō* that ties it to the physical as well as spiritual labors involved in the practice of waste disposal. Although relations of exchange are often framed through acts of gifting, disposal is equally generative of sociality, and equally an act of care. In his ethnography of life at an American landfill, Joshua Reno describes the "distancing effect" of waste treatment in this manner:

To see waste as a social relationship means recognizing the subtraction of unwanted material from our lives as a form of care provided by others. They care for us by absorbing the unstable risks and benefits that mass waste proliferates. (2016, 14)

As Japanese temples receive shipments of headstones from around the country or collect old and abandoned *butsudan* from customers, they now absorb the risks of mass (sacred) waste on a scale not previously imagined.

For President Takimoto, feelings of concern generated by this waste might be somewhat alleviated by the process of incineration (焚き上げ *takiage*). At Takimoto, burnable *butsudan* components such as silk hangings, sutra books, and wooden frames are cremated each quarter at the company's headquarters in Fukui. Restrictions on open burning in urban centers, introduced under Japan's Fire Service Act (消防法 *shōbōhō*), mean that today *takiage* can only be performed on a restricted number of days per calendar year or in select rural locations. President Takimoto once described the experience of watching *takiage* as "feeling relieved, because the form [カタチ *katachi*] of the thing disappears." Transforming *butsudan* into ash, destroying its recognizable form, appears to lessen its hold over people. Katja Triplett, describing this process, argues that "the destructive force of the fire aims at those elements of the material object that need to be expelled and sent off in a process of purification. In other words, we could see it as a kind of exorcism" (2017, 150).

Incineration is a common method of disposal practiced at temples and shrines, which serve as a collection place for unwanted or expired religious goods. Accompanying the lantern burning described in chapter 3, priests at Sensōji also burned wooden prayer tablets and small amulets. During the busy New Year period, when crowds of people visit shrines to wish for good fortune in the coming year, large bins are often set up to receive these goods. Indeed, so popular is this method of disposal for religious items, temples and shrines frequently erect signs warning that they only accept goods previously purchased from their institution, in an attempt to stem the influx of random religious detritus. Rambelli describes the origins of this ritual incineration practice as an adaptation of tantric *goma* (護摩) rituals for the sacrificial burning of offerings as practiced within the Shingon school of Buddhism (2007, 254). Less commonly, such objects might be buried, floated away along a river or at sea, or even, in the case of old printed materials, dissolved into water to make new paper pulp (Rambelli 2007, 248–50). On special days like the spring and autumn equinoxes and on "*Butsudan and Butsugu* Day" (March 27), *takiage* services are held at temple grounds around the country.[5] Notably, incineration is also how Japan deals with much of its (profane) domestic waste, with "burnable" and "nonburnable" rubbish being the major categories used during sorting (Siniawer 2018).

But the alchemy of cremation does not work for all kinds of sacred waste. The human body, for one, does not appear to entirely lose its potency when transformed through fire, for ash and bone themselves become sacred objects that demand further ritual attention and performances of *kuyō*. Further, many elements of the *butsudan* assemblage persist beyond cremation. Metalwork and ceramics present a challenge to the practicality and emotional effect of *takiage* in both their distinctiveness and durability and must be dealt with through alternative methods. At Takimoto Bukkōdo, porcelain urns for human cremains and other ceramics are broken into small pieces and buried, ideally in a location like a cemetery, which people will not walk over frequently. Some elements, like brass bells that still produce a good sound, can be repaired and resold, but this is only done at a customer's explicit request for secondhand goods. Japanese scrap metal companies do accept used altar goods. However, it is difficult to ascertain from *butsudan* stores exactly how these two markets connect, given the discomfort created by inquiries into this area. And while metal *butsugu* can be melted down and remade, modern implements are often manufactured from plastic. This makes them lighter, cheaper, and easier to clean but has the negative consequence of making them harder to destroy or remake.

When *kuyō* works, it provides a means to express gratitude for, and ultimately disentangle, the bonds between people and things. But as we have seen, following the rites of disposal can incur high costs, financially but also in the form of renewed, burdensome bonds with religious authorities, or the risk of *bachi* (misfortune) in the event of improper disposal. Further, the sheer number of unwanted or excess *butsudan* and graves might overwhelm established ritual disposal practices. The result is blockages in the circulation of goods through the process of disposal, when people choose to store objects, sometimes indefinitely, rather than complete *kuyō* rites. Unwanted *butsudan* may be kept for years in an unused room or empty home, gathering dust until somebody finally decides to invest in their disposal. Occasionally, this occurs in dramatic fashion. When I was living in Kanazawa, the discovery of a *butsudan* in an old house generated days of gossip. A young family, new to the area from Tokyo, purchased a home in the countryside that had been vacant for nearly a decade. A week into their move, they discovered a false wall erected in the formal sitting room, and behind it, a boarded-up *butsudan* complete with *go-honzon*, *ihai*, and ritual implements. As it transpired, rather than properly dispose of the altar, the childless, elderly man who once lived there had decided to conceal it. The new family thus inherited both the *butsudan* and the responsibility for its disposal. The foreign-born husband wanted to keep the altar as a "cool" and "authentic" feature of the home, but his Kanazawa-born wife was substantially less enthused by the proposition. Angry calls made to the real estate agent saw them eventually take responsibility for the altar's disposal, enlisting the help of a local temple. Less dramatically, Daisuke's and Kiki's families have kept urns of ash on a "temporary" funeral altar in their living rooms for the past few years, both troubled by the prospect of securing a grave. And Buddhist priests often store abandoned ancestral tablets or Buddhist statutory in the antechamber to the main hall for many years, without finding a suitable solution to their disposal or remaking.

Of course, there is limit to the number of *butsudan*, *ihai*, urns, and especially gravestones that individuals, cemeteries, or temples can take in. Many shrines and temples now enforce strict guidelines about what kinds of sacred waste they can accept (figure 4.5). Fukuyama's grave of the graves has almost exhausted the space of its current allotment, with less organized sections beginning to spring up outside the neatly arranged rows. Storage is no final resolution to the problem of disposal, after all, but rather a kind of suspended animation that leaves the future of these sacred goods uncertain. On a recent trip to visit the grave of the graves, our party stopped off at a local stone mason, who often, albeit reluctantly, sent stones to rest there. He was reluctant because another grave refuge in the region had itself recently been abandoned, after the son of the man who established it decided to sell the business. The fate of *that* refuge is now uncertain. Is there now

Figure 4.5. Collection bays for spent or unwanted religious goods
at Atsuta Shrine, Nagoya.

need for a grave of the grave of the graves? Or is there are a way to manage
the excess of graves and *butsudan* that puts things to rest, once and for all?
Could unwanted *butsudan* find another circulation route through the material economy?

RECYCLING SACRED WASTE

Having observed the hours of hand labor that go into their crafting, it is difficult for me not to see the incineration of unwanted *butsudan* as a waste;
these objects appear to have so much life yet to live. But secondhand altars have an extremely limited circulation in contemporary Japan. Very few
listings appear on Japanese e-commerce auction sites, and I have found no
brick-and-mortar stores that display secondhand altars for purchase.[6] Exchanges of altars within families (such as the passing down of old *butsudan*
to a branch family, as with the Yamashitas in chapter 1) and between close
confidantes are not unheard of, but neither are they common. Kobayashi of
Takimoto explained to me that the existence of unwanted or excess *butsudan* can imply that the original owners' family has broken up or their business has failed, and people generally do not wish to inherit this bad fortune

with the altar. Further, as subsequent misuse or neglect could rebound to the original owner, families are unlikely to donate altars to secondhand services in the first place. For this reason, despite retail prices of tens of thousands of dollars, *butsudan* have almost no resale value. Indeed, the more elaborately decorated and expensive the *butsudan*, often the greater the cost of its disposal.

The rarity of secondhand *butsudan* can be interpreted as evidence of a broader cultural discomfort with secondhand goods in Japan (Clammer 1997, 24). In her ethnography of Japanese domestic economies, Daniels reports that most of her informants expressed "a strong dislike for things that had been used" (2010b, 174), largely because they could not discern how the object had been treated in the past. If the objects were mistreated or entangled in some kind of misfortune, this bad luck might extend to future owners. This is not to say that secondhand economies do not exist in Japan. Eiko Maruko Siniawer argues that popular rhetoric about Japanese people's distaste for secondhand goods is, in many cases, erroneous; she documents how flea markets and recycling shops have been a part of Japanese life for many decades, falling and rising in popularity in accordance with the economic outlook and frugality discourses (2018, 179–80). Religious goods like *butsudan* are perhaps just the most extreme examples of terminal commodities that cannot circulate secondhand.

There are, of course, exceptions to this rule, and discrete pathways via which *butsudan* might be reclaimed or diverted from immanent disposal and destruction. Many *butsudan* retailers have begun to collect altars that display particularly high levels of craft or exemplify a (perhaps endangered) regional style. Hasegawa Ginza hosts a corporate museum on the top floor of its showroom, where several altars are displayed as historic examples of fine craftsmanship. Their presentation in this setting involved lengthy negotiations with the former owners, as well as the performance of desacralization rites. Framed as antiques and art pieces, *butsudan* also find second homes through markets for overseas visitors. As Daniels documents, at flea markets held in temple grounds across Japan, religious goods can begin a second life "as antiques, folk crafts, or exotic Japanese souvenirs for foreign tourists" (2003, 631). Although I have yet to see an entire, decorated *butsudan* for sale, stalls selling *butsugu*, particularly golden candlesticks and incense braziers from the Ōtani school, are plentiful at Kyoto's temple markets (figure 4.6). This foreign-facing secondhand economy also extends online to e-commerce stores like eBay, via which *butsudan* and *butsugu* circulate far beyond their original contexts of production and use.

When I showed pictures of *butsugu* for sale at flea markets to my coworkers at Takimoto, they were shocked, not, as I had assumed, due to the taboos

Figure 4.6. Buddhist implements for sale at Tōji Market, Kyoto, 2017.

around resale, but because of what they perceived to be the poor quality and extravagant prices. Despite his personal discomfort with secondhand *butsugu*, Kobayashi could understand both their resale as art objects and collectibles, and the unconcern of non-Japanese people with the misfortune that could arise from mishandling such objects. He only wished that *butsudan* were represented in private collections by better-quality artifacts. Fabio Gygi similarly attests that flea-market vendors thought foreign tourists' unconcern with potential *bachi* made them the most suitable market for secondhand religious goods (2018, 16). Offloading such wares to outsiders is thus a viable prospect. A number of estate-cleaning companies I interviewed admitted to sending old *butsudan* to Southeast Asia for sale as secular furniture. That being said, the profane foreign afterlives of altars can still cause alarm. A *butsudan* craftsman and retailer in Kanazawa told me tales of foreign tourists and even visiting governmental dignitaries who wanted to purchase *butsudan* to use as wine racks, display cases for whiskey, and bookcases. He had politely refused to sell a golden *butsudan* to a Mexican official who wanted to use it as a shoe cupboard, because "it just wouldn't feel right."

Rather than enter secondhand economies as art objects or antiques, *butsudan* can find a second life through being physically recycled or remade. The innovative *butsudan* and *zushi* (reliquary) maker Alte Meister recently launched a new service in which its craftspeople disassemble elaborate, grand-scale *butsudan* into their component parts, then reconstruct them as more compact (often desktop) models better suited to their owners' situations. Any particularly distinctive or sentimental carved-wood or gold lacquer panels are preserved and incorporated into the final design, maintaining subtle resonances with the original. When I discussed the project with the company president, Hoshi-san, he was eager to stress that as yet, these remade altars are not for resale on the open market. Rather, like the smaller *butsudan* purchased by couples in chapter 2, this is a means of downsizing intended to fit altars into modern floorplans, and thus increase the chances that they will be inherited and cared for by future generations. Still, I think it not inconceivable that altar recycling practices will expand to general sales in future years.

More radically, Kumada Butsudan, based in Nagoya, has launched what it calls "a new type of *kuyō*," which involves disassembling and wood-chipping *butsudan*, then reconstituting the material into chipboard that is used to make new products. The marketing for this venture invokes themes of reincarnation and environmentalism (figure 4.7), as altars are "transformed into a new life" through death. Kumada stresses the care afforded to tendered altars throughout the whole process, including hiring a priest to perform *tamashii-nuki* (even if *kuyō* rites have already been performed) and tasking specialist *butsudan* craftspeople with the disassembly. When I visited in 2018, President Kumada Koshin was keen to distinguish his service from more general recycling companies: "Those stores are not specialist, they don't know how to treat the altar—it's quite a difficult thing to do, it takes skill. They just lump it together with other furniture." Kumada suggests that customers can receive peace of mind (安心 *anshin*) in entrusting *butsudan* to the respectful, expert care of his company. Unlike some retailers, he does

Figure 4.7. Customer-facing infographic to explain the *butsudan* recycling process at Kumada Butsudan, Nagoya.

not shy away from embracing a new future of *butsudan* retail, in which disposal forms a core part of the business: going forward, he says, "this is just as important as selling *butsudan*." His company has grown since its launch a decade or so ago from receiving ten disposal requests per month to a hundred. "Other butsudan stores see [disposal] as a burden, as a bothersome [めんどうくさい *mendōkusai*] part of the industry," he explains. "But we are happy to do this for customers." As with Fukuyama's Fudōin and its grave refuge, there is lively activity and money to be made in caring for expired graves and altars.

ABANDONING SACRED WASTE

These are not stories I should tell, and maybe questions I should not ask, according to the workers at Takimoto. It is all a "matter of Hannah's curiosity," Mitsume cautions one evening, as I join the delivery team at a local *izakaya*. We have just finished our game at the local bowling alley—my rather ill-advised proposal for a social gathering, given my general lack of hand-eye coordination. Over beers, charred edamame, and other small plates, I have the chance to ask team members about some of their most surprising or challenging cases. From delivering *butsudan* to dilapidated or hoarding houses, to stepping over a grandmother sleeping on the tatami to (silently!) install an altar, my coworkers seem to have witnessed the whole breadth of humanity and human responses to grief. There are stories, too, about the mountains of sweets and tea they are obligated to receive, and rumors about *butsudan* workers and Buddhists priests developing diabetes because they eat too many cakes at work.

The latter stories are recounted with laughter, but the atmosphere is more difficult, and people's language more circumspect, when discussing disposal. On delivery trips throughout central Japan, Takimoto workers occasionally spot *butsudan* left on the side of the road, placed out for collection by municipal councils through the "large waste" service. This is one of the more boundary-pushing means of *butsudan* disposal, in that it acknowledges the continuities between the afterlives of spent religious items and regular domestic waste or *gomi* (ゴミ). *Butsudan* workers were skeptical about the proposition. If one placed *butsudan* at community waste collection spots, they warned me, there was no guarantee municipal waste workers would be willing to collect it. Indeed, many etiquette guidebooks simply state that this practice is banned. For example, *The Housewives' Guide to Graves and Butsudan* states that "disposing of *butsudan* as general oversized waste is strictly prohibited" (Shufunotomo 2011, 179) and advises consumers to proceed through conventional channels by contacting their temple. Despite these declarations, most municipal websites do give directions for the disposal of religious waste. For example, the Osaka City website lists *butsudan* as an allowable "oversized waste" item.[7] Residents need only pay a specified fee and post the receipt of payment on the altar. The Kanazawa City waste guide lists a similar handling fee, but also states that only "post-*kuyō*" (供養済み *kuyō-zumi*) *butsudan* are accepted as waste—although how waste workers are to judge whether this metaphysical transformation has taken place is unclear.

Several popular Q & A websites and consumer advocates also provide advice on disposing of *butsudan* in this manner. One such organization, Reset Soul, stresses the finality of *kuyō*, which it states transforms the altar into "a mere container/box." Thus, one "should not worry about what the neighbors may think or about one's own psychological resistance to disposing of this object."[8] Such hesitancy and fear of censure is well founded, given the social nature of domestic waste disposal in contemporary Japan (see Siniawer 2018). In most parts of urban Japan, domestic waste must be sorted into various categories, placed into open crates or transparent plastic bags (sometimes labeled with the family name), and carried to a dedicated location on the street at specific days and times (usually between 6 a.m. and

8 a.m., on different days two to four times per month). Depending on municipal rules and community inclinations, a local resident might even be designated as responsible for supervising the disposal and sorting process at the collection spot. Domestic waste management is at times an arduous task. During fieldwork, I collected various city ward guides for rubbish, each with its own standards for how various items should be treated (from washing and flattening milk cartons to puncturing aerosol cans) and widely different numbers of categories into which waste should be sorted (as few as three, as many as forty-five).[9] The system places a high burden on individuals for the management of their waste. Making a mistake can incur neighborly censure and, in some cases, a dreaded "red flag" posted to one's garbage.[10] As with many other tasks, the responsibility for managing domestic waste and the censure caused by mistakes overwhelmingly "sticks to women" (Siniawer 2018, 297).

Friends and relatives regularly struggle within Japan's waste-disposal laws. I swap stories with friends of breaking waste items into smaller pieces to disguise their identity, wrapping them in opaque plastic, or taking rubbish to communal bins at train stations. Kiki told me a rumor about somebody driving to a different ward on the eve of collection day to deposit waste far from their own residence. But some waste cannot be disguised, and the challenge of disposal is greater for conspicuous items like *butsudan*. Wirtz describes the waste items generated by Cuban ritual as "quite mundane in their appearance, much like other garbage in a gutter" (2009, 439). Indeed, it is this covert biography of engagement in ritual practice that she says makes these objects dangerous (2009, 477). Some ephemera produced by *butsudan* ritual, like matches and flowers, can perhaps be characterized in this way and easily added to domestic waste. However, the *butsudan* frame and many decorative implements are not only durable but elaborately decorated. Deconstructing the altar frame into wood panels might make them less recognizable, but I have never seen or heard of families attempting this themselves; in any case, disassembly would likely fail to hide the lacquer and gold of *kin butsudan*. The disposal of altars in public, then, is almost always a conspicuous act.

Attempts to deidentify waste (sacred or mundane) and to obscure its ownership suggest that the disposal of sacred waste has the potential to generate significant feelings of shame, anxiety, or fear of *bachi*. Further, as we have seen, performing *kuyō* and following conventional disposal practices can incur high costs, financially and in the form of renewed, burdensome bonds with religious authorities. It is not surprising, then, to hear stories of people abandoning or "dumping" unwanted graves and altars. In late 2014, NHK reported on the illegal dumping of over fifteen hundred tons of abandoned tombstones on vacant land on Awaji Island.[11] Unceremoniously dumped on the roadside, the tombstones presented a practical and financial burden to the municipal authorities who own the land, as well as more indeterminate, spiritual risks. Even more troubling and transgressive is the abandonment of cremated remains, the human body being perhaps the most potent form of sacred waste (Paine 2014, 242). Crematoria across Japan now serve as repositories for thousands of sets of cremated remains that people either neglect or refuse to collect, a practice known as "zero interment" (ゼロ葬 *zero sō*) (Shigematsu 2016), or for which there is no identifiable next of kin. A report for Asahi Newspaper states that in Osaka City, the local government with the highest number of uncollected remains, nearly 8.3 percent of people who die — one in twelve — do so without anybody to collect their remains, a sevenfold increase since 1990 (Kotani 2019). Even cremated remains collected from the crematoria might later be abandoned. According to a 2017 article, across Japan between 2014–2016, there were at least 203 cases reported to police of human remains abandoned in public spaces like trains, a phenomenon called *ikotsu okizari* (遺骨置き去り). Little information is usually recovered about these cases, but Mainichi Shimbun (2017) notes that they frequently involve family members who feel burdened by the responsibility to properly dispose of the ash.

These, I am told, are the stories that most worry Buddhist priests and *butsudan* workers, stories that pop up in the media every few years as evidence of the monumental task of sacred waste disposal as well as the burdens and failings of the current system. Sacred waste may, as Irene Stengs argues, "always demand . . . special treatment" (2014, 235), but such demands are tough, and as such, are not always received or acted upon. Not everyone is equally motivated or equally concerned with the negative consequences of mistreating sacred waste. Further, what constitutes respectful disposal or mistreatment is open to redefinition and contestation. Like iconoclasm, I think that clandestine disposal practices and cases of dumping or abandonment tend to confirm, rather than undercut, the numinous quality of graves, altars, and ash in Japan today. But boundary-pushing forms of disposal are also revelatory of the delicate balance people strike between desiring to rid themselves of unwanted religious goods and to fulfill their obligations to objects and the dead.

DEATH IN RUINS

Somewhat paradoxically, disposal both highlights the declining fortunes of *butsudan* in contemporary Japan and affirms their continued status as sacred waste (if not always sacred goods). As Gygi notes, it is on the brink of disposal that "forgotten, 'unperformed' objects" might suddenly become "sticky" (2018, 3), in the sense that they attract moral relations. It is at the point of disposal that many people are forced to confront the cultural and spiritual significance of these objects and the future of their relations with them. For many generations, ritual disposal pathways of *kuyō* and cremation have facilitated this process, allowing the living to renegotiate their relationship to the dead and to deal with the practical remains of human and nonhuman persons.

This chapter emphasizes the importance of the dynamic of disconnection in a conceptualization of *kuyō*, by pointing out how unfinished or improper disposal can breed anxiety or discomfort. Conventional means of dealing with ritually charged waste, however, require that people reinvest in the costly, extended ritual practice of *kuyō* that produced artifacts like *butsudan* and graves in the first place. Further, systems of disposal require there to be someone in the circuit to perform the work of distancing and obscuring the afterlife of waste. In the case of *butsudan* and graves, this labor is performed by clergy and by workers at stores like Takimoto, who take on the burdens and risks of handling sacred waste. Of course, not all elements of the *butsudan* are treated with the same level of regard, nor does everybody deem these actions necessary. The burdens of conventional disposal rites can motivate consumers to put off disposal indefinitely, or to illegally dump sacred goods. New methods of recycling or remaking that promise to "do the right thing" by waste *butsudan* without significant financial and social costs are only slowly emerging to find popular appeal.

In mounds of gravestones and boarded-up *butsudan*, the collapse of a necromaterial tradition leaves remains. In this sense, we should not really think of *butsudan* as a "vanishing" tradition (see Ivy 1995) that might evaporate without a trace. The remains of graves and *butsudan* are all too visible, too weighty, too cumbersome in their state of decay. By its very nature, sacred waste cannot easily be dealt with. Somebody is always left holding the pieces. Some remains are portable and mutable; they can be remade and recirculated or stored away. Others create monumental landscapes, even if they those landscapes are hidden away on a mountainside. Perhaps the Japanese public is not ready to confront the material consequences of tens of thousands of abandoned graves and altars, and all they represent, about the ancestors, the household, the nation. Walking through the grave of the graves, it is tempting to despair, to ponder how new life may emerge from the ruins. But given the growing rubble, perhaps the more pressing question is where "new deaths" will emerge, that is, new processes of death and disposal. In the next chapter, I tackle this question by examining how new necromaterial designs emerge within the industry and travel outward.

CHAPTER 5

Remaking

"Demonstration corpse" is not a role I expected to occupy when I began my research. But it's where I find myself during the 2018 Life Ending Industry Expo (エンディング産業展 *Endingu Sangyōten*), or ENDEX, in Tokyo, as I am whisked through the packed convention center to a stage occupied by one of Japan's mortuary schools, Okuribito Academy, to undergo a demonstration encoffining ritual (納棺 *nōkan*). A throng of expo visitors congregate around the tatami mat in anticipation. A woman in a three-piece suit helps me shed my outer layers and wraps me in a cotton robe. I lay down on the futon, close my eyes, and endeavor to "act dead" for the next ten or so minutes as two encoffiners poke, prod, roll, and dress me. It is, I must admit, a task I fail at almost immediately, being overcome by ingrained habit to return the encoffiner's bow. I am promptly reminded that corpses do not bow and resolve to remain motionless.

Encoffining is one part of a larger rite involving washing and dressing the body, blocking the bodily orifices, and making up the face. It is usually performed before the viewing and funeral. During the ENDEX demonstration, a silk kimono is draped over me, an apron is covertly tied around my waist, and the cotton robe is then whisked out from underneath (the move reminds me of a tablecloth being pulled from underneath a dinner service). The kimono is tied and straightened, and the dresser lightly massages my hands into a prayer position (I suspect more force is required for corpses affected by rigor mortis) and shapes them around prayer beads. Still trying to fake death, I am dimly aware of the quiet, dignified struggle to fit silk coverings over my large feet. The skill of the *nōkanshi* (納棺師 "encoffiner") is to completely change the dress of the deceased with a visible performance of respect, which means preventing any bare flesh from showing to the mourners seated before the body during the ritual. In Western, industrial deathcare systems, preparing the body through washing or embalming is typically a "backstage" process. But in Japanese encoffining, the skill of concealment has become a ritualized art, with only a thin piece of silk to act as border

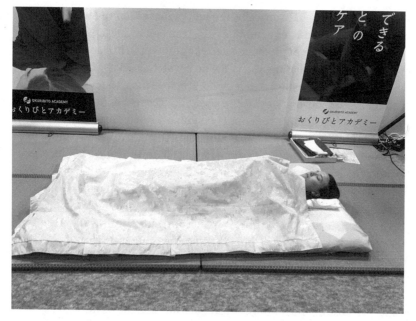

Figure 5.1. My first performance as a "demonstration corpse" for an encoffining ceremony. Tokyo, 2018.

between living and dead. From my perspective, the overall process feels like a rough massage, with hands jostling and fabric stuffed beneath my body. It strikes me that the *nōkanshi* never has to worry about what the process actually *feels like*.

Inspirational cello music streams through loudspeakers during the demonstration. It is the soundtrack to the 2008 Oscar-winning film *Departures* (おくりびと *Okuribito*), which made this mortuary ritual internationally famous and is responsible for its contemporary resurgence. *Okuribito* tells the story of a classical musician who moves to the countryside with his wife after the orchestra he performs in disbands. Responding to a newspaper advertisement for work in "departures services," which he assumes refers to a travel agency, he is unexpectedly hired as an encoffiner. The film probes questions of family, obligation, and the pollution of death, as characters struggle to accept, and ultimately learn to respect, his new profession. If the classic film *The Funeral* (1984) takes a critical, albeit comedic, look at the rigid structure of traditional Japanese funeral rites, then *Departures* (2008) completes a redemption arc, celebrating the intricacies of the encoffining rite as representative of a refined, compassionate approach to mortality.

The tradition *Departures* celebrates is far more modern and "invented" than it might appear. Historically, the full, public *nōkan* rite was only ever practiced in a few rural communities in Japan, and was usually undertaken by family members, not professionals (Okuyama 2013). It is only in the wake of the film's success that the son of the man who trained its actors, Kimura-san, opened the Okuribito Academy to promote the rite across the mainstream funeral industry.[1] Today, the academy accepts hundreds of trainees each year, and customers seek out encoffining service even from overseas. Ruth Toulson (2022), for example, describes how *Departures* inspired one Singaporean funeral home to begin offering "Showers of Love," in which families wash and dress the body and address the dead with words of affirmation and love. At ENDEX, Okuribito is a distinguished company and success story that injects vitality into a sector often concerned with decline.

This chapter considers the remaking of death rites through the design and launch of new necromaterial products and services. Beginning at the ENDEX convention, I follow two strands of experimental design ("at hand" goods and automatic conveyance columbaria) out into the world, tracking where they have found purchase or failed, and considering their potential to transform relations between the living and the dead.

Anthropologists have not typically paid much attention to spaces like industry conventions when studying the creation of ritual. Perhaps we are disinclined to see the rituals we perform and the objects we buy for the dead as subject to market research, global trends, or advertising campaigns. I wonder if it is because the discipline still finds distasteful the combination of grief and finance, commerce and care that pervades these spaces, or if we remain wedded to an imaginary of ritual preceding capital. As I have described, religious third actors are key to the transmission of necromaterial traditions, putting substantial efforts into imagining, designing, prototyping, and advertising new necromaterials and rituals. Industry events like ENDEX draw together established commercial players, religious institutions, start-ups, independent designers, media, and sometimes even members of the public. They are where new product lines are launched, gossip is shared, and the social networks necessary to conduct business in Japan are formed. Writing about funeral industry expos in the USA, UK, and Australia, the DeathTech Research Team describes these events as where "anxieties about the current industry are rehearsed and different imagined futures converge" (van Ryn et al. 2019, 37). In this chapter, I spend some time on the convention-center floor, attempting to capture this atmosphere at ENDEX, in an ethnographic pastiche of my attendance (interrupted by COVID) between 2017 and 2022. What causes anxiety for the sector, and what generates hope? How do these impulses translate into new necromaterials?

After attending ENDEX for many years, one thing becomes clear:

remaking death ritual is a difficult task. Émile Durkheim's axiom that "society never stops creating new sacred things" (1912, 215) may be true post facto, but it does skip over the substantial labor, as well as luck, involved in such creation. On more than one occasion, I attended the enthusiastic launch at ENDEX of a new product or service, only to watch it disappear without a trace by the next convention. Few of these propositions to reinvigorate or remake (Buddhist) death ritual, which John Nelson (2013) aptly characterizes as "experiments," make a successful transition to market, and even fewer achieve widespread uptake. The number of failed necrotechnologies continues to rise (Gould et al. 2019). Launching new products requires substantial capital and social resources, and very few ventures have Oscar-winning films to bolster them.

In Japan, as elsewhere, it is tempting to read emerging death phenomena, from fungi burial suits and human composting to jewelry made from ash and memorials in virtual reality, as representative of radical shifts in culture or, indeed, a "new death" (Dawdy and Kneese 2022, 5). Examples of innovative, "sometimes radical" *butsudan* have indeed been described as representing "a paradigm shift in how families and individuals should interact with ancestral spirits" (Nelson 2008, 305). I am generally wary of such pronouncements and of the allure of the seemingly new or outlandish. New products do not necessarily represent new modes of death, particularly when those products fail to capture mainstream attention. The two innovations I consider in this chapter, however, have, I think, received sufficient uptake to warrant interpretation as markers of the future direction of Japanese necromateriality. While their permanence has yet to be determined, their development has something interesting to teach about the work of reimagining and remaking death ritual. What is perceived as malleable about Japanese death, and what is perceived as immutable? What is remade in new necromaterials? How do new designs, intentionally or unintentionally, transform the sensory relationship between the living and the dead? What do people do to make new necromaterials meaningful, ritually efficacious, or popular?

SOCIALITY AND SPECTACLE

Arriving bright and early on the first day of ENDEX, I make my way to the middle of the convention center to survey the room. Middle-aged men in three-piece suits and priests in summer robes circulate between stalls, picking up flyers and performing the occasional ritualized exchange of business cards. I pick up a promotional black coffee from a nearby stand, where beans are being ground using a millstone recycled from an abandoned tombstone. As with every ENDEX, the first task is to peruse the map and schedule.

Alongside the permanent exhibition hall is a program of live demonstrations, seminars, and professional development workshops. ENDEX runs for three days in mid-August, after the busy O-bon period. It is always scheduled to fall across one day classified as *tomobiki* (友引) on the Japanese auspiciousness calendar. This is viewed as a good day for business and lawsuits but an unfortunate day for funerals, as it homophonically implies that "a friend will be drawn (toward the grave)." As very few ceremonies take place on such days, industry members are free to attend.

Each year, up to fifteen thousand attendees visit approximately 150 exhibits, arranged throughout the Tokyo Big Sight Convention Centre by theme, from "ceremony hall facilities and services" and "pet funerals" to "bereavement services" and "religious organizations." A whole section displaying the boxed snacks commonly distributed to funeral guests is located next to an area specializing in avant-garde urn designs, including soccer balls and diamanté-encrusted Hello Kitty statues. A particularly fragrant quadrant is occupied by incense companies, whose presence has increased in recent years, as the practice of sending boxed incense sticks to the bereaved (for offering at the *saidan*) found renewed popularity amid COVID-19 restrictions on house visits. ENDEX is regularly cohosted by the Memorial Stone Show (メモリアルストンショー), which builds massive displays of abandoned graves surrounded by overgrown, fake grass. But the most visually striking area is undoubtedly that of the florists. Elaborate flower altars are very popular at upscale funerals and funerals for celebrities, signifying the social status of the deceased (Yamada 2007, 295–306). For reasons that never become clear to me, in 2018 one company created a colossal floral T-Rex, with signage evoking the Jurassic Park film franchise, complete with red glowing eyes and smoke (figure 5.2); in 2022, a display was based on Hayao Miyazaki's animated film *My Neighbor Totoro*.

The space occupied by incense vendors and priests speaks to the ongoing power of religious institutions in Japanese deathcare. Pure Land Buddhist schools in particular have a large showing at ENDEX, regularly occupying a whole corner of the convention center and running a slate of seminars. In comparison, when the Church of England exhibited at a recent UK funerary convention, attempting to reassert a clerical stake in a rapidly secularizing marketplace, its participation "caused a stir" (Arnold et al. 2018, 107). Not all religious organizations or services are equally embraced on the convention-center floor.[2] The bold launch of the "rent-a-priest" service (お坊さん便 *O-bōsan bin*) at ENDEX 2017 attracted enthusiastic foreign media coverage and some internal disquiet. Hosted on Amazon Japan, the service enabled people to circumvent temples and funeral homes to hire individual priests for rites for a transparent, low cost, starting at 35,000 yen for a basic

Figure 5.2. T-Rex flower arrangement by For Seasons Flowers, ENDEX. Tokyo, 2018.

package. The group behind it, Yorisō, has promoted similar "direct to consumer religion" trends, including AI home speakers that connect users to a priest for live counseling. Such innovations have slowly faded into the background at ENDEX, however, as the shock value of experimental combinations of religion and technology has declined.

To the outside observer, the evolving convention is perhaps notable for some of its absences. For one, ENDEX is dominated by men, as is middle and senior management at funeral and *butsugu* companies. Men also make up the majority of ordained priests. That said, the perceived desires of female consumers generate considerable discussion. Women, particularly single women and those without descendants, have historically encountered difficulties in establishing their own graves in Japan, and contemporary configurations of bilateral belonging and acts of refusal challenge the patrilineal basis of this system. According to one long-running study of Japanese family dynamics, in 1988, 64.6 percent of women surveyed thought it best to enter their husband's family grave, while in 2018, that percentage had fallen to 42.0 percent (Ceremonial Occasions Research Institute 2021, 132). There has also been (somewhat sensational) media coverage of "posthumous divorce" (死後離婚 *shigo rikon*), whereby women decide not to enter the patrilineal grave of their husband or refuse the obligation to care for his ancestors, sometimes only after his death (Kikkawa et al. 2017). Some women choose instead to enter their natal household grave or to pursue alternative routes to secure their posthumous care, such as communal graves. Over the years, several ENDEX seminars have been dedicated to this "women problem," bringing activists into conversation with mainstream figures. However, the overall presence of women remains marginal.

Environmental offerings also occupy relatively marginal real estate, confined usually to solutions for industry (better light bulbs or reusable caskets), rather than consumer-facing offerings that promise a "green ending." In general, an accounting of environmental impact plays a minor role in the mainstream Japanese deathcare market, certainly when compared to the UK or Australia, which have seen significant social movements to embrace "natural" or "woodland" burial (see Davies and Rumble 2012). Of course, almost all Japanese are cremated (several ENDEX attendees expressed shock to me that Australians "still put people in the ground"), and innovations to crematorium technology tend to concern limiting the local impact of emissions. Even so, products and services evoking "a return to nature" as a metaphor for death are represented, with both "ocean scattering" (Kawano 2014) and "tree burial," whereby cremated remains are interred in proximity to a mature tree or other planting (Boret 2014; Miyazawa forthcoming), becoming more popular in recent years.

Laughter is heard across the hall as a group of colleagues slap each other on the back and reminisce outside a stall promoting drone technology for shooting video of cemeteries. Picking up another "gravestone-ground" coffee, I head to a meeting with anthropologist Anne Allison and Daisuke Uriu, a scholar of human-computer interaction at Tokyo University and designer of high-tech *kuyō* goods. Anne and I often find ourselves at similar field sites as we investigate, respectively, the social (Allison 2023) and material dimensions of transformations in Japan's death rites. Uriu, together with his wife Amico (herself a designer and funeral celebrant), has long been my guide at industry events, helping me decode the social hierarchies and rivalries that shape the success or failure of particular innovations, as well as sharing industry rumors. I take in his advice on the seminar program, which includes explorations of emerging social justice issues, such as "Memorial services after 3/11" and "Meeting the needs of LGBT+ customers"; insider analysis of industry trends, such as "Death in an age of no successors"; and technical presentations on business management, such as "Maximizing your online retail strategy." Although individual sessions vary, the overall themes have remained largely unchanged across the years. The seminars are usually presented by prominent industry leaders and attended by colleagues, members of nonprofit organizations, and, very occasionally, inquisitive researchers.

The atmosphere is collegial, with business cards collected before each seminar, so that presenters can check up on their audience afterward. I have rarely attended a session with a disinterested crowd, and it is commonplace for presenters to call out by name somebody in the audience with greater expertise or social standing. Often, the seminars become a movable feast, transitioning seamlessly into business lunches or evening drinking sessions, which appear, at least for some, to be the real attraction of attending each year.

Through its annual repetition as a social ritual, ENDEX works to reinforce industry norms and social hierarchies, as much as it might disrupt them. As he cycles through familiar greetings to colleagues and friends on the convention floor, Uriu (not for the first time) expresses some hesitancy about the role of ENDEX in fostering innovation. A few years ago, he posted this assessment on social media:

> When you attend the same conference year upon year, you inevitably meet the following people:
> 1) people you make courtesy calls on, saying "long time no see!"
> 2) people whose idea/product clearly has no future, but who are still trying to gain new clients/networks
> 3) Competitors to the people you work for, who you should avoid
> 4) People doing new things who are fascinating
> 5) People who are doing commonplace things at the moment (including me) but if they got together with somebody, could do awesome things immediately.
>
> But you only talk to 1) and 2), and during that time it all ends.

Exhibitors come and exhibitors go, but by and large, the same main players remain. I have occasionally met new external exhibitors with little previous experience or few contacts in the industry.[3] Armed with a piece of technology—a hologram projector, a drone, an AI speaker—and a dream, they spend the convention searching for partners to help adapt their technology for the death space. Very rarely, in my experience, do such ventures bear fruit. Foreign companies exhibiting at ENDEX appear to face similar challenges—not just the language gap but an absence of established networks in the Japanese sector. Uriu's comments suggest a more pointed critique: the extent to which ENDEX functions as an echo chamber for industry insiders. The public, for example, are largely absent, however much their changing desires and mercurial nature are the constant topic of conversation. But perhaps expansion and disruption are not the main draws, when catching up with colleagues and drinking are equally available.

Music, lights, and good-looking priests burst onto the stage to interrupt the regular business on the convention floor. In 2017 (and several years subsequently) ENDEX hosted competitions for best funerary floral display, best encoffining performance, "hottest priest" (イケメンお坊さん *ikemen obōsan*), and "Miss Kuyō" (for funeral attendants). These competitions, sponsored by the Okuribito Academy, draw a large crowd. Although the judging criteria remain somewhat opaque to me, the hottest priest and Miss Kuyō contests show striking analogies to a beauty pageant. Contestants parade down a runway in formal robes or suits, answer questions about the meaning of life and death, and put on displays of correct bowing technique. While a bow angling the back to thirty degrees might be appropriate for greetings, at least forty-five degrees is judged necessary for bereavement, and a full ninety degrees is reserved for making apologies. But not everything is so easy to quantify. Before announcing the results, the judges describe one key characteristic of the winners from these two categories: the *kokoro* (心) they display in their work. *Kokoro* is a ubiquitous but ambiguous concept within Japanese religion and spirituality. The term has several glosses, including "heart" and "heart-mind," but Helen Hardacre favors the translation "self," which combines faculties of mind, will, and emotion and "includes the soul (*tamashii*) but is not identical to it" (1988, 19). Timothy O. Benedict's recent study of hospice workers in Japan shows how *kokoro* has become a key focus of end-of-life care for an aging, secular population. "*Kokoro* care," Benedict notes, has significant affective dimensions aimed at helping patients *feel* valued, worthy, or themselves, as much as it is about resolving existential questions (2022, 29–30). It is this same quality that is also invoked in the assessment of new products launched at ENDEX and cultivated by *butsudan* workers in customer service (see chapter 2).

For the encoffiners, a rigorous display of technique across two rounds is required, with a full, sequential performance of dressing a body, first in a suit and then a kimono, followed by an interview. The encoffining contest is emceed by the Okuribito president, who explains the history and contemporary appeal of *nōkan*. This event, he notes, is an opportunity to demonstrate professionalism and expertise to fellow industry members, who may rarely themselves witness the practice. All of the entrants are women in their twenties; the announcer jokes that they will have to wait until next year for an *ikemen nōkanshi* (handsome guy encoffiner). All the while, the *Departures* soundtrack plays in the background. As the music swells, the seven encoffiners performing in the final raise their arms inside of the silk kimono, stretching the fabric out to the sky like a flag. Audience members snap photos, and there is murmured approval for one young encoffiner who appears to be outperforming the rest in the grace of her draping technique. Coming to the interview portion, entrants speak of their experiences of death work. A desire to send the dead off with respect and a "kind heart" (優しい心 ya-sashii kokoro) is a common motif. Talking to some contestants afterward, I learn that many are also (or primarily) motivated by the desire to find stable employment in a precarious economy; Japan's aging society appears to make the deathcare sector a relatively safe career choice. At the end of the competitions, the winners are paraded on stage to copious applause.

Although these competitions have not been held post-COVID, almost all editions of ENDEX feature some measure of pageantry. Some years are livelier than others, but usually one event or stall manages to capture the attention of the conventiongoers. Most such appeals are aimed at the business-to-business (B-to-B) market. At the encoffining competition, for example, the first two rows of the audience were occupied by funeral company delegates flown in from Taiwan and Hong Kong. Occasionally, however, industry spectacles rise up to capture public attention. On the opening morning of one ENDEX convention, I found myself in the middle of an international media scrum focused on Softbank's Pepper, one of Japan's more advanced semihumanoid robots, who was being exhibited in a new role as a Buddhist priest. Dressed in formal monastic silk robes with a mallet strapped to one arm, Pepper chanted excerpts of the Heart Sutra (般若心経 hannya shingyō) in a strange, digitized voice as it struck a large wooden glockenspiel and brass bell in time to the phrases. Next to Pepper, a (human) priest surveyed the performance; he was there, he later told reporters, to see if Pepper could "impart the 'heart' aspect . . . because I believe that the 'heart' is the foundation of religion" (quoted in Gibbs 2017). A new service being advertised by Nissei Eco promised to deliver Pepper to homes across the country to perform memorial services or funerals. The robot's performance, repeated several times a day, drew large crowds of convention delegates as well as external media. But to this day, the use of humanoid robots within the Japanese funeral sector is extremely rare. Pepper in particular appears an impractical offering—expensive, cumbersome, and reliant on accompanying programmers to function (see Gould et al. 2021). Then again, the practicalities of the Pepper priest service are perhaps less important than the charged atmosphere that even its brief appearance at ENDEX created. Yuji Sone's work on Japanese robotics describes industry conventions as "spectacularised robot events," in which robotic devices emerge as "emblems of futurity" presented to an awaiting audience (2017, 22). In this light, Pepper's presentation as a priest served to symbolically project the traditional craft object of bu-tsudan into a bright future of technological innovation. As a publicity stunt, the launch of Pepper allowed Nissei Eco to gently entice people to view their other, more practical, offerings, including a live-streaming funeral platform and an e-commerce portal for funeral homes.

Every year I return to ENDEX to witness this atmosphere of deep anxiety over the future of the sector and "business as usual" social networking and drinking, interspersed with the occasional, spectacular performance of futurity. While the collective efforts of the sector generate great desires and energies to innovate, they are also significantly limited by the pull of convention and the brutal realities of monumental demographic change in Japan. As noted, the road from the convention center to people's hearts and homes is slow and uncertain, and littered with failed prototypes. In the next section, I explore two categories of necromaterials which have, over many decades of remaking and revision, rather successfully made this jump: at-hand *kuyō* goods (手元供養品 *temoto kuyōhin*) and automatic conveyance columbaria (自動搬送納骨堂 *jidō hansō nōkotsudō*). In different ways, these products are designed to remake, reject, or replace the graves and altars introduced in chapter 1. Collectively, they represent an emerging trend in Japanese necromaterials toward the amalgamation of the multiple locations (graves and *butsudan*) for the enshrinement of the dead in multiple objects (ashes and ancestral tablets) into a single site. In redesigning the necromaterial form, they can also limit or creatively extend the sensory experience of *kuyō*.

AT-HAND *KUYŌ* GOODS

My husband Daisuke's family were shocked to discover that they are part of a new trend in Japanese death rites. "Oh, I thought we were just lazy," Daisuke jokes when I tell him over Zoom. Its 2022 and I am in Hiroshima visiting his family and find out that some five years after his grandfather died, the cremated remains of his grandparents remain, "temporarily stored," in the second bedroom of the family home. The cardboard funeral *saidan*, at least, has been replaced by a *karaki butsudan* that was eventually transported from his paternal grandparents' house. The *butsudan* enshrines the two ancestral tablets, and the urns of cremains, wrapped in silk brocade, are placed to the side on the tatami mat floor.

This practice of keeping cremains in the home as a focus of ritual activity, called *temoto kuyō* (手元供養; literally "at-hand *kuyō*"), is becoming more and more common in Japan. Sometimes, *temoto kuyō* is centered around not ash but another sentimental item, like a wristwatch or wedding ring. Naitō dates this trend to around 2005, when the practice became a serious talking point in mass media (2013, 203–5). During house visits, my colleagues at *butsudan* stores are no longer surprised to find a silk-wrapped urn stowed in the *tokonoma* (display corner) or to extract small containers of ash from *butsudan* drawers. Still, workers occasionally field objections from clergy or customers that this practice contravenes national legal frameworks for the disposal of human remains.[4] (Current consensus is that it falls within a gray area.) The domestic storage of cremains occurs for number of different reasons and in different styles. For some families (like Daisuke's), the financial and social obligations associated with erecting a new grave, along with concerns about the line of succession, may move people to delay interment.

Ash scattering appears another alternative, but it is heavily restricted across Japan and is currently possible only at sea.[5] In the past, organizations and individuals promoting ash scattering faced accusations of selfishness, lack of filial piety, and Westernization (Kawano 2014, 85–86), although these critiques were tempered as the practice grew more popular. *Temoto kuyō* may occur alongside scattering or interment in a grave, as sometimes only a small amount of remains are retained in the home.

Cremains might also be retained for sentimental reasons, as was the case with Kiki, who wanted to keep her mother close by for several years. The expression used by Kiki is *yorisō* (寄り添う), meaning "to get close to," "nestle close to," or even "cuddle." It is the same phrase she used when she described wearing her mother's retro jacket around town. It is also the expression Takimoto and Hasegawa used when describing the affective skills fostered by the work of *butsudan* stores. But for many working in and writing about the sector, feeling *yorisō* in relation to cremated remains is a surprising sentiment. It appears contrary to deep-rooted ideas about the pollution (汚れ *kegare*) generated by death, and in particular, contact with the corpse, that give rise to taboos and purification rites before and after funerals (Suzuki 2000, 27–29; Shintani 1992; Yamada 2007). More and more, the dead and the living are coming together in unexpected ways within the space of the home.

In response, Japan's deathcare sector has designed and produced a huge array of objects for the storage and display of cremains (or sentimental items) in the home, known broadly as *temoto kuyōhin* (手元供養品). Walk up and down the aisles at ENDEX, or enter any funeral home or *butsudan* store, and the volume and diversity of *temoto kuyōhin* on display points to the great creative energies devoted to remaking necromaterials today. Some products cleave to the structure (if not the aesthetics) of *butsudan*. For example, the *Musubi Butsudan* (結び仏壇), developed by the floristry company Tenmac, incorporates a brilliant display of vacuum-sealed flowers above a single drawer with space for the storage of at least two full sets of cremains. It is particularly marketed to women without siblings who find

Figure 5.3. The "Potterin" *temoto kuyō* product. Image courtesy of Seo Inc., 2022.

themselves responsible for the care of their parent's remains. The design is overtly feminine; the compact, desktop altar is available in sky blue, pink, and red vinyl, and decorated with crystalline offering dishes.

Most *temoto kuyōhin* do away with the "box" structure of *butsudan*, moving the memorial instruments into the space of the home. Most also are designed to preserve only a few grams of ash. This includes a vast range of miniature urns and containers, crafted in delicate porcelain or pottery and often decorated in pastel colors. Many are sold as decorative sets of objects, which may echo the ritual instruments found at *butsudan*, remade in miniature size and minimalist aesthetics. For example, the "Potterin" set, made by Seo Ltd. for its brand Sotto (figure 5.3), first appears to be a flower vase crafted from white unglazed porcelain and brass. But it can be disassembled to reveal a set of three ritual instruments: an incense stick holder, a candle, and a brass bell with mallet. Seo is a Takaoka-based maker of brass bells and altar fittings, founded in 1935. As with the traditional artisans discussed in chapter 1, Seo has had to transform its product line; the "*kuyō* tools" (供養の道具 *kuyō no dōgu*) it now produces highlight traditional artisanal skills while attending to modern domestic space constraints and aesthetics. Placed before a personal photograph or combined with one of the company's delicately crafted urns, Potterin is easy to incorporate into the home and, indeed, might be mistaken for just a floral display.

There are also jewelry options for *temoto kuyōhin*, including pendant necklaces with tiny receptacles to hold a few grams of ash. A Japanese company offers to compress human ash into a sapphire. Algordanza, a Swiss-based company, offers to compress ash into a single diamond. The latter process requires approximately 300 grams of ash to produce a one-carat diamond over the course of six months, and costs up to 2.7 million yen. Yet another company, operating out of Aichi Prefecture, Inori Shinju, promises to transform human cremains into pearls. Approximately 15 grams of human ash is finely ground and formed into balls, which are dried, cured, and inserted into oysters. The company raises the oysters at its farm over the course of a year, finally inviting the bereaved family to be part of the process of harvesting the pearl and making fine jewelry.

The aesthetic presentation of these objects reigns supreme at ENDEX and on online retail sites, where the companies' sales are concentrated. In these arenas, Naitō notes that *temoto kuyōhin* are marketed equally as objets d'art and funerary goods, and often incorporate an element of interactivity or DIY (2013, 203). In lush marketing campaigns, porcelain *temoto kuyōhin* are displayed next to vases of flowers in a brightly lit living room, while jewelry is matched to fashionable outfits and sunny backdrops. On Seo's Sotto online store, the *kuyōhin* are integrated into the home and into everyday activities (figure 5.4): they are photographed on a kitchen bench while somebody cooks, or beside a bed where somebody sits listening to music, or on a coffee table while somebody reads a book.

Figure 5.4. A promotional image for *temoto kuyō* goods in the Sotto range.
Image courtesy of Seo Inc., 2022.

This is very much how I have encountered *temoto kuyōhin* in people's spaces. In someone's workspace at a university, I saw a beautiful photograph-centric display for a beloved grandfather built into a bookshelf. A friend once took me to their parent's home in Kobe, where a small display of a wedding ring, flowers, and a bell was placed on a ledge between the kitchen sink and the pantry. One rainy day in early 2019, sixty-year-old Tanaka-san, a friend of old high-school exchange partners living in Kobe, led me upstairs to see the *kuyōhin* for her mother arranged atop the family piano. The careful display centers on a beautiful portrait of Tanaka's mother and a spherical porcelain urn (no larger than a golf ball), which I was told contains a small amount of ash. The majority of Tanaka's mother's cremains remain with her father and extended family, but plans to establish a grave are unclear, given Tanaka's status as only child and daughter. Immediately before the urn is a small dish, which on my visit contained a single yellow bloom, floating in water, as well as an incense burner. But Tanaka also likes to burn incense to "refresh the atmosphere" and "relax after a long day," so she sometimes moves the burner to the dining table, where the scent can better dissipate. The floral display is similarly mobile, with vases swapped in and out depending on the blooms that are in season.

Absent from the usual retinue of ritual goods is a bell or candle. There is no particular reason for this, Tanaka says; they are just not so important to her. When I ask what *is* important, she recalls the altar from her maternal grandmother's house: "I remember my grandmother sitting there each morning, with this curling pillar of smoke rising to the ceiling. So that's the thing that should be there, for me." In abundance at this display are photographs, which extend the assemblage to the edges of the piano. They feature the family at different times and places; some focus on her mother, but others are group shots, showing the children at New Year's or a trip to Universal Studios Japan. I spy at least one Snoopy figurine nestled among the photos, a onetime contribution, I suspect, from Tanaka's (now adult) children. There are strong resonances between this space and the one maintained by Kiki (chapter 3). Both have evolved over time, updated with life events and family travel, and both blur the line between altar and the broader space of the home. This display is perhaps less regularly attended to; there are no daily offerings of food or Buddhist sutras. On birthdays, anniversaries, and Mother's Day, Tanaka says she makes a point of offering flowers and lighting incense, but the evolution of this assemblage is also driven by profane patterns of life in the home. From the outside, one might find barely any visual traces of "Buddhist materiality" at all.

Not everyone likes the idea of keeping cremains in the home, even if it is sometimes necessary to do so. The sustainability of this practice also comes into question. When I talked to Tanaka, I did not think to ask what might happen to her mother's ashes in the future, how that might be contingent even on her own mortality. Will the ashes find their way into a grave, or might they be scattered? The future of necromaterials stored outside the bounds of the household grave system appears uncertain. With *temoto kuyōhin* there is no promise of resolution, of securing future *kuyō* or cleanly dispensing with one's obligations to the dead (as is promised by other services that I explore in the next section). This ambiguous ending to the life-course of cremains can be troubling. Indeed, at least one nonprofit organization, the Japanese Sonkotsushi Association (日本尊骨士協会 *nihon sonkotsushi kyōkai*), led by Kawamoto Yasuo, has been set up to retrieve and dispose of cremains found in the homes of the recently deceased.

There are also practical challenges posed by the creation of *temoto kuyōhin*, particularly the division of cremains into portions that are then incorporated into new designs. Crematoria in Japan return to families a mixture of bones (遺骨 *ikotsu*) and ash (遺灰 *ihai*). But what is needed for many *temoto kuyōhin* (or indeed, for ash scattering) is powdered ash. Other products, like the *Musubi Butsudan* and new forms of columbaria or collective grave (discussed below) have the capacity to store more, but only if the cremains are pulverized and compressed. While crematorium workers in the US, UK, and Australia almost always grind cremains into a fine ash via the use of a cremulator machine (Davies 2005, 152; Prothero 2001, 149–50), in Japan this process is neither conventional nor institutionally supported: whole bone fragments are preserved and returned to the family (Namihara 2013). Indeed, bone fragments play a crucial role in the "bone picking ceremony" (骨上げ *kotsuage*) at the crematorium, in which bereaved family members transfer bones into an urn using long chopsticks.[6]

How, then, are people to make ash? Some early advocates of ash scattering recommended DIY bone crushing. Satsuki Kawano (2014, 118–19) reports that members of the nonprofit Grave Free Promotion Society were advised to place the cremains in a cloth bag and pulverize them by hand using a personal article of the deceased (such as a paperweight or golf club). Suffice it to say, the suggestion provoked mixed reactions among the membership, and professional services for bone milling (粉骨 *funkotsu*) and bone cleaning (洗骨 *senkotsu*) have multiplied in recent years.[7] Norizuki-san, the manager of Norizuki Butsudan in Shizuoka expanded his company's services into this area at the direct request of his customers. Norizuki crafts a huge range of traditional and modern *butsudan* but has recently expanded into manufacturing more and more *temoto kuyōhin*, particularly beautiful wooden boxes decorated with photographs and engravings of Buddhist posthumous names, in the style of ancestral tablets. The company also produces thin wooden "books" for cremains that can easily fit into the drawers beneath a traditional *butsudan*. But Norizuki-san came to "feel troubled," he says, about selling these products to families who were struggling with how to handle the cremains in their possession. And so, he entered the bone-crushing business: purchasing new equipment, erecting a ventilated building at the back of the factory, and upskilling his workforce. Today, the company offers both machine and "by-hand" bone milling, from which families receive back small packages of compressed ash for further storage or scattering. While a new range of products and services promises to make *kuyō* more meaningful and less burdensome, then, the process of holding the dead "close by" can still require significant investment and professional assistance. And further, it leaves the question of the future of these necromaterials unresolved.

AUTOMATIC CONVEYANCE COLUMBARIA

"No, really, thank god for that," Hiyama intoned. "The ashes were becoming quite a *nayami*," that is, a trouble, bother, or burden. Hiyama, a literature teacher in his mid-forties, unbuttons his suit jacket and relaxes at the Starbucks in Shinanomachi train station, five minutes from Ingyōin, a Buddhist temple in Tokyo. After several years' absence from Japan due to COVID-19, I have returned to continue my fieldwork, and to visit with Hiyama the columbarium where he recently chose to inter his father's and grandmother's remains. Evidently, he is happy to have this part of his life and obligations squared away. Some years previously, when I met Hiyama at a local *izakaya*, he was struggling with the seemingly inevitable prospect of commissioning a new family grave. In 2010, the average cost to establish a gravesite in central Tokyo was 10 million yen (in Boret 2014, 90), a figure that already well exceeded Japan's average annual household income. And even then, gravesites within commutable distance of urban centers were in short supply. As the descendant of a second son, Hiyama's family had not established a grave before his father died. Further, although the original stem family (*honke*) owned a grave, it was some distance away. With social mobility and postwar urbanization, the social condition of *hakabanare* (墓離れ), or living away from one's grave, is a growing concern for temples and the deathcare sector. In recent years it has prompted large numbers of people to "close" (墓じまい *hakajimai*) or "move" (墓引っ越し *hakahikkoshi*) their ancestral graves, while others hesitate over whether and where to establish one in the first place. According to one report, in the past fifteen years, some eighty thousand graves in Japan have been moved or closed (NHK 2018). Apart from the distance, Hiyama confided, it would be awkward to ask his older brother to accommodate several more sets of remains in the ancestral gravesite.

And so one of my very first conversations with Hiyama revolved around alternatives to the ancestral grave system. In particular, he was interested in columbaria (納骨堂 nōkotsudō), which allow for the storage of many hundreds, or even thousands, of sets of cremated remains within a relatively small space. The rise of new forms of interment have dramatically transformed Japan's grave system over the past decade. In 2011, conventional graves (一般墓 ippanhaka) still represented 91.0 percent of all new grave purchases, but by 2019, only 27.4 percent of new purchases were of conventional graves, while 24.9 percent were of columbarium niches and 41.5 percent were of tree burial sites (Ceremonial Occasions Research Institute 2021, 134).

Despite recently rising in popularity, columbaria are not a new phenomenon. The headquarters of the Nishi (West) Pure Land school in Kyoto has maintained a multistory necropolis since the 1950s, and in regions such as Hokkaido (where cold weather can make outdoor grave visitation a challenge), they are fairly common. Most columbaria in Japan are the "locker-type," where families purchase a small steel or aluminum locker set into a wall. At some locations, these walls are mobile, operating on a sliding-track system similar to library stacks. At many temples, like the Nishi-Hongan-ji, there is a communal butsudan built into each row, providing visitors a space to make offerings, adjacent (or at least proximate) to their dead.

Hiyama was aware of this type of columbarium before we started talking, but the prospect of purchasing a locker raised several concerns. First, many of the columbaria near his home were sold out, and some planned facilities had long waiting lists even before their construction. Where there were vacancies, the available lockers were located in the very bottom row, closest to the ground. For Hiyama, being stored so close to the ground and the feet of passersby seemed "somehow disrespectful," and the prospect of having to bend over or kneel to pay respects was laughable. As one funeral hall owner told me, the major problem with locker-style columbaria is the spatial hierarchy. While lockers in the middle rows sell quickly and attract a premium, those in the bottom two rows, which are located near the feet, and lockers located in awkwardly high rows, must be heavily discounted. Further, as with high school hallways in the minutes between classes, busy periods of ritual activity in Japan can flood locker columbaria with streams of families clambering over one another to access their dead.

But now, several years after introducing this facility to Hiyama, I found myself back at Ingyōin, Tokyo.[8] Here, the Hasegawa company has purpose built an alternative system for the perpetual storage of remains, known as

Figure 5.5. The viewing booths at *Ichigyōin* automated columbarium, Tokyo.
Image courtesy of Hasegawa Co. Ltd., 2022.

an "automatic conveyance columbarium" (henceforth, ACC; 自動搬送式納
骨堂 *jidō hansōshiki nōkotsudō*). ACC emerged in the 1990s as an alternative
to the traditional grave system in densely populated urban areas, particularly
Osaka and Tokyo-Yokohama. Ingyōin is a small urban temple in Shinanomachi, sandwiched between a train station and Meiji Jingu Gaien Gardens. Its
new set of minimalist buildings peek out from beneath the concrete onramp
for an intercity freeway. The natural wood walls and sweeping tiled roof
were designed by renowned architect Kengo Kuma, famous for his design of
the 2020 Olympic Stadium. Warm lights and deep bows greet us as we enter
the building. The design of the lobby hovers somewhere between temple,
wellness center, and luxury hotel. The main hall of the temple with its large
golden Buddha is off to the right, but Hiyama heads instead for an open com-
puter terminal and taps a neat black ID card to the reader. In response, the
machine displays details of his family account, and large video screens on
the wall direct us to a viewing booth downstairs. Urns held at Ingyōin have
no fixed location for visitation; rather they can be conveyed to any of eight
viewing booths. This eliminates the spatial hierarchy of locker columbaria,
although some issues persist: peak visitation periods like O-bon and New
Year's can limit availability. According to Ueno-san, the facility manager,
some customers prefer to use the same booth for every visit. But Hiyama
lets the system allocate whichever is free, and we proceed to the elevators.

What happens during that elevator ride is what makes ACC extraordinary.

Activated by the ID card, the system locates, within a multistory storage rack that runs through the center of the building, the corresponding metal vault containing the family urns. ACC like Ingyōin can store many thousands of sets of cremains, contained within metal vaults called *zushi* (厨子), approximately 30 centimeters wide and 60 centimeters deep. A series of mechanical claws and belts, similar to systems used in large distribution warehouses, the deliver the vault to the designated viewing booth.

Of course, none of these moving parts are visible to us as we descend. Alighting on the second basement floor, we walk to the viewing booth, where the selected vault has been slotted into place in the center of a gravestone. Only the front of the vault is visible, decorated with a stone plaque engraved with the Hiyama name (other families may choose an aphorism like "thank you" or "memories"). In fact, the elevator ride is exactly timed such that families reach the relevant floor only when the moving parts have stopped and the vault is in place. Even as a researcher, it took several visits and a series of increasingly high-profile introductions to be allowed to see "behind the curtain" and watch as the vaults travel on conveyor belts between storage and viewing booth.

The viewing booth is centered on a black marble gravestone, recessed into the wall behind metal doors (already open when we arrive). On either side of the stone are small vases of flowers. In front sits a vessel containing fine woodchips of incense and an electronic brazier; open flames for incense or candles are against fire regulations for buildings in Tokyo. There is no central Buddhist image or statue; instead, a digital monitor set off to one side cycles through images of a seated Buddha, a stylized ancestral tablet, and photographs of the deceased. We are greeted at Hiyama's booth with the warm smiling face of his father, first in the style of a formal funeral portrait (遺影 *iei*) and then in family photos—meals under the *kotatsu* at home, his wedding, a very old trip to Disneyland. Hiyama approaches the grave and gingerly pinches some incense chips, holding them momentarily to his forehead before sprinkling them atop the brazier where they heat, but do not smoke. He gently strikes a brass bell, and we join our hands together in prayer for a moment or two.

"Well, that's about it," Hiyama laughs. In truth, there's not much to be done during a visit to an ACC grave. A large part of visiting and caring for traditional outdoor graves is the cleaning: pouring buckets of water over the stones, removing any leaves or debris, and replacing the flowers. Even if there's no visible dirt, water might renew and purify the grave and slake the continual thirst of the dead. Here, of course, there's nothing to wash. Indeed, because this "time-share grave" is occupied by multiple families in turn, many customary practices of grave visitation are limited. Visitors to Ingyōin are discouraged from bringing personalized offerings to the dead, like their favorite sweets, alcohol, or tobacco. But visitors (perhaps unaware of these rules) do keep bringing flowers, so the temple has had to erect an offering site outside in the garden, before a statue of *Jizo Bosatsu* (a beloved Buddhist figure in Japan, the guardian of children and travelers).

Visiting an ACC is a sensory experience distinct from visiting a traditional grave. The building is heated in winter, air-conditioned in summer, sheltered from the rain year-round. There are toilet facilities, convenient parking, and rooms for shared meals. Each booth at Ingyōin has a bench that can be pulled in front of the grave to support those with limited mobility or for longer visits. It's a far cry from some ancestral gravesites, located in the middle of a rice paddy or on the side of a mountain. The facilities are clean, neat, and contained.

The use of electric incense and candles is emblematic of this redesigned material interface between the living and the dead. These devices have also become popular for household *butsudan*. At Buddhist goods retailers, electric candles range from two-foot monuments to tiny ornaments for Tokyo-style altars, all powered by lithium batteries that illuminate yellow-tinted LEDs. The key selling point is fire safety. Many elderly Japanese live alone in wooden houses, and the fear of fire lingers in intergenerational memory of bombings and earthquakes. Electric devices afford peace of mind (安心 *anshin*) for adult children living apart from their elderly parents, minimizing the risk that caring for the dead will lead to their own untimely departure. But electric devices offer entirely different engagements than do wick, wax, fragrance, and flame. Sometimes the wiring buzzes slightly, but they do not burn or smoke. And they flicker, not randomly or in response to movement, signaling the presence of another, but in a preprogrammed algorithmic pattern.

Hiyama and I stay in the booth for no more than ten minutes before pressing a button to close the metal doors and making our way back to the elevator. It feels like a short visit but turns out to be fairly typical. Since the ACC's grand opening in 2016, the facility manager has tracked the frequency and length of visits using anonymized data collected each time an ID card is used. At Ingyōin, remains are called up to viewing booths, on average, six times per year; visits to traditional outdoor graves occur, he notes, far less frequently. This is perhaps unsurprising: Ingyōin is located along Hiyama's regular train commute, halfway home, not multiple train connections and five-plus hours away in the countryside. Because the ACC is so conveniently located, Hiyama has not yet felt the need to purchase a *butsudan* for his home. Most ACC are strategically constructed near public transport—several advertise how many minutes or even steps they are from the station exit. But the statistic that surprised me more than the frequency of visits was their average *length*: just five minutes from the time the ID card activates the system to the moment the booth doors close, including time spent in the elevator.

My colleague Daisuke Uriu and I had an opportunity to discuss these early statistics with clergy overseeing various ACC facilities in Tokyo (see Uriu et al. 2018). Most priests did not seem to consider short visits unusual or concerning. Indeed, overly long or frequent visitation appeared a greater locus of concern. One priest working at a long-established ACC reported that some visitors, especially elderly, widowed men, stayed for hours in the booth, looking through the photographic display and lingering in the presence of the deceased. Of course, similarly extended vigils before a *butsudan* in the home or at a remote gravesite might go unnoticed, but in the semiprivate, time-stamped, climate-controlled space of the columbarium, it raised concern. The priest worried that such extended visits could foster unhelpful kinds of attachment between the living and deceased. Buddhist commemorative rites, he explained, occur at successively larger intervals: seven days, fourteen days, thirty-three days, forty-nine days, one year, and so on. Might the relationship between the living and dead at ACC become too permanent?

Of course, permanence, or at least perpetual care for the dead, is a key selling point of many new cemetery facilities and *kuyō* services, including ACC. For Hiyama, one great attraction of Ingyōin was the option to ensure ongoing care for his relatives, even after he himself is gone. At Ingyōin, customers pay an initial fee of 900,000 yen for each vault and an annual fee of 18,000 yen for facilities services and management. Leases on vaults usually last thirty-three years and can be purchased in advance. After this period, if there is no objection from the current custodian (if one exists), the remains are transferred to a communal grave at the facility, where they continue to receive daily offerings and prayers from clergy. In this respect, ACC are one form of *eitai kuyōbo* (永代供養墓), or "graves with 'permanent' ritual care" (Kawano 2014, 421), that have emerged in Japan in recent decades. These facilities, offering perpetual *kuyō* for the dead either as individuals or in a collective grave (共同墓 *kyōdō haka* or 集合墓 *shūgō haka*), take many forms, from tree burials (樹木葬 *jumokusō*) to monumental statues of the Buddha composed of ash (骨仏 *kotsubotoke*). If we are to read *kuyō* as a practice of both care and separation, then, as Satsuki Kawano (2014) indicates, this combination of perpetuity and *kuyō* appears contradictory. The dead, meant to move toward ancestorhood through successive generations of ritual activity, are instead held in place by their ongoing relation to the living. For Hiyama, who is currently unmarried and childless, the future-proofing that this service offers is appealing:

> At least this way, somebody will look after my dad and grandmother, even after I am gone. I don't really care about it for me, but I think maybe they would be sad to have nobody around to look after the grave. And it's not like they got to see me get married or have kids or something.

ACC thus deliver the present and future of *kuyō* for their consumers by containing cremated remains and the ritual activity that surrounds them in a clean, accessible facility. An ongoing resting place for the dead is secured, while responsibility for their care is supported by, and eventually outsourced to, ritual professionals outside the family line.

Some of the designs for new necromaterials that I describe in this chapter no doubt appear radical departures from the tradition and form of *butsudan*. ENDEX certainly makes room for the fantastical: floral dinosaurs, robot priests, and hologram projectors, outlandish designs presented to a crowd of industry insiders in the hope of garnering enough financial resources to make them viable. But viability is not necessarily the point. The public spectacle and spirit of renewal created by such experiments might be just as important for an industry experiencing financial and existential unease.

There are, however, developments in Japanese necromateriality that have, in recent years, moved beyond spectacle and become the technologies and practices through which people meet their dead. While the variety of new products is immense, taken together, they speak to notable shifts in death culture. These include a trend toward combining the grave and the altar into a single site, whether within the home (as with *temoto kuyōhin*) or at a convenient outside location (as with the ACC). Both moves are, I think, consistent with a desire to "keep the dead close." This should counter any assumption that the rejection of traditional graves and *butsudan* means Japanese people no longer care, or care less, about the dead. Indeed, *temoto kuyōhin* signal a trend toward incorporating cremains into domestic space, implying a reassessment of assumed taboos around the pollution of the dead body.

Constructing and caring for multiple, grand necromaterials (graves and *butsudan*) is simply no longer possible or desirable for many. In contrast, *temoto kuyōhin* are relatively private, open to improvisation, and readily available for retail purchase. Online access, in particular, allows people to sidestep many of the professional religious services or relations involved in purchasing graves and altars (although some *temoto kuyōhin* require bone milling). In accepting people of all or no Buddhist faith, and requiring no affiliation with temples, ACC (and tree burial facilities) similarly offer customers a transactional relationship and sense of finality, with the additional benefit of eternal veneration.

The remaking of Japanese necromateriality is ongoing, not just in the sense that new products and services are continually between designed, made, and marketed, but in the sense that the practice and experience of mediating the dead via new necromaterials is still being worked out. Although I emphasized the role of design and designers in the first part of this chapter, the intentions behind the (re)making, as we have seen throughout this book, are only one part of what necromaterials are or could be. New necromaterials transform social and sensory exchanges between the living and the dead in ways that I suspect were not predicted by their designers. At ACC, there are sensory modalities in which the dead can no longer appear, and acts of service the living can no longer perform. But the presence of the dead might also be more frequent (if brief), and subject more to work commutes and train timetables than annual seasonal holidays. Similarly, in *temoto kuyōhin*, the presence of the dead is crafted through personal memories or ideas about what offerings or acts are important. The dead are integrated into the everyday life of the living but take up less visually demarcated space in the domestic sphere.

New necromaterials may keep the dead close, but they offer no easy solutions to the ongoing life of death stuff beyond the limits of human mortality. In the remaking of necromaterials, we see an emerging reliance on horizontal communal or commercial ties, in place of vertical patrilineal ties, for securing the future welfare of both the dead and death stuff. Several new forms of ACC and grave do this by promising to provide perpetual *kuyō* for the deceased. But time and again as we have seen, even the most stable of arrangements for the perpetual care of the dead (like the household) can collapse. And even institutions made to gather the remains of this collapse, like the grave of the graves, can decay. People find new ways to come together and care for the dead, but the limits to the futures of care that the living can offer the dead are becoming clearer.

When Death Falls Apart

The death of a way of dying, or of living with the dead, can be painful. Piers Vitebsky's twin ethnographies of death rites among the Sora people of southern Odisha, set over twenty years apart, *Dialogues with the Dead* (1993) and *Living without the Dead* (2017), speak to how dramatic transformation of death ritual can reshape people's cultural identities, linguistic repertoires, and daily routines. In Vitebsky's initial fieldwork, he encountered a community invested in elaborate daily acts of conversation, argument, and reminiscence with the dead, often conducted via a shaman mediator. However, after widespread conversion to Baptist Christianity and Hinduism, the Sora people's animist cosmology and ways of relating to the dead have all but been abandoned, a change that to Vitebsky "feels like a great loss" and leads him to ask, "How can people abandon the beliefs that constituted their identity and seemed to match their innermost feelings?" (2017, 2). His later book thus unfolds as equal parts thick description, salvage ethnography, and act of personal mourning. There is a palpable sense of anguish in the final pages, as Vitebsky questions his right to speak for the (now silent) ancestors and contemplates the loss of the world his earlier informants shared with him: "People like Ononti will never exist again. However, such people did exist, and they were my friends" (2017, 323).

As I noted in the introduction, my work is not intended as a eulogy for *butsudan*, nor for the artisan tradition of crafting golden altars and carving Buddha statues, nor for the ritual tradition of multigenerational ancestor veneration. It is—I hope—less tinged with sadness than Vitebsky's later work. For one thing, I cannot declare *butsudan* "dead." Across Japan, sales of new altars remain on an upward (albeit plateauing) trajectory. When a family member dies, most people still turn to Buddhist temples, retailers, or funeral homes, and invest in the services of priests, ancestral tablets, altars, and graves. There is still so much life lived at the altar.

But *butsudan* no longer move through the world as they did in the past. There are changes in how people engage *butsudan* in ritual, changes to their material form, changes to religious economies, and most notably, changes to the trajectory of the *butsudan* lifecourse. This book thus articulates a period of extended and intense uncertainty for the *butsudan* tradition and industry. I say "extended" because transformations to the lifecourse of necromaterials, absent any major natural disaster or revolution, usually unfold in the relations between generations. *Butsudan* are time machines; people make or purchase altars in the present to project a past life into the future. In that sense, the kind of "death" *butsudan* face, if any, is paradigmatic of *rōsui* (老衰), or a "gradual decline," rather than *pokkuri* (ぽっくり), a "sudden death" (Long 2004).

The uncertainty is also "intense" because change to necromaterial traditions is so often encountered as a loss, no more so than for those invested (emotionally, economically, professionally) in its continuity. There are many who mourn keenly what they encounter as the death of *butsudan*. This view is perhaps most intensely expressed by artisans, for whom retail trends can mean a loss of livelihood and an end to business dynasties. One might also mourn the loss of *techne*, a skill and way of making transmitted through an intimate relationship between bodies and *butsudan*. At various points in their history, *butsudan* and ancestor veneration have been deployed by the state to block foreign religious incursion, to encourage loyalty to the emperor, and to construct a unified ethnic identity. It is no surprise, then, that discussions about the precarious present often extend to the changing composition of the Japanese nation-state, the country's defeat in World War II, and the impact of changing gender roles. At this grander scale, the collapse of a system of ancestral graves and *butsudan* speaks to the demographic failure of twenty-first-century Japan to reproduce the nation and the socioreligious structure of the household that long organized people's lives and afterlives.

But how people react to changes affecting the stuff of death is far from simple. Vitebsky appears to struggle with the gap between his sorrow at the loss of an animist cosmology and his informants' acceptance of new ways of being and dying. Throughout this journey, I have encountered many who express conflicted feelings about the decline of *butsudan* and related ritual practice. Like the elderly Sora people who Vitebsky reports fear that their children "will no longer converse with them beyond the Christian grave or the Hindu pyre" (2017, 1), many elderly Japanese can no longer depend on their descendants, if any exist, to care for *butsudan* and perform *kuyō*. At the same time, some elderly Japanese couples are concerned about burdening younger generations with the financial and social costs of these rites. Avoiding becoming either *muen* (bondless) or *mendō* (burdensome) appears a difficult balancing act, one that has driven attempts to make *butsudan* and *kuyō* more convenient, fashionable, economical, and inclusive of modern family structures.

There are equally those who are entirely happy to see Japan's necromaterial traditions changed, if not entirely revolutionized. There is significant popular distrust of the contemporary deathcare industry. For those conventionally excluded from or disadvantaged by the patrilineal household system, the current pace of change might indeed appear inadequate. Put simply, the emotional response to the uncertain fate of *butsudan* is heterogeneous. I regularly encounter both those who praise *butsudan* as "the spiritual foothold" (拠り所 *yoridokoro*) of the Japanese people and those who argue (sometimes simultaneously) that altars are archaic and onerous, and that the temples and industry connected to them are extortive.

Why should people's reaction to change in Japanese death rites skew so bleak? There are significant considerations of economic livelihood and cultural heritage. In the case of the Sora, Vitebsky further argues that conversion to world religions represents a loss of theo-diversity (2017, 332). But Vitebsky's grief, and that of my informants, feels like a particular kind of anguish, generated by confronting the mortality of death stuff. I am not immune here. In the introduction, I asked, "how could something once so fundamental to how the living relate to the dead, die?" At the end of this work, perhaps the question I should ask is "why should necromaterials, of all things, be presumed to persist?" Permanence appears strangely wound around death. Zygmunt Bauman suggests that permanence is the ultimate product of human confrontation with mortality:

> Culture is precisely about transcendence, about going beyond what is given and found before the creative imagination of culture sets to work; culture is after the permanence and durability which life, by itself, so sorely misses. Whereas death (more exactly, awareness of mortality) is the ultimate condition of cultural creativity. It makes permanence into a task, into an urgent task, into a paramount task—a fount and a measure of all tasks—and so it makes culture, that huge and never stopping factory of permanence. (1992a, 4)

The particular form of permanence produced by Japanese ancestral deathways is one in which the social structure of the household endures, despite the birth and death of individual (non)human persons therein. At least, it is this model that lingers as part of the normative vision of a good death. Ultimately, Bauman suggests, culture's quest for permanence never succeeds. The "ultimate failure of rationality" is our inability to reconcile the "transcending power of time-binding mind" with its "time-bound fleshy casing"

(1992b, 1). *Butsudan* are less fleshy casing than works of wood and gold, but like bodies they are subject to time and move through a lifecourse that contradicts the transcendence of any spiritual forces they are said to enshrine. Greater attention to the material conditions and contradictions of the stuff of death makes the ultimate impermanence of death ritual plain.

To view the lifecourse of *butsudan* from this zoomed-out perspective is not to erase the anguish caused by the death of death things. This book owes its title to Buddhist teacher Pema Chödrön, whose famed work *When Things Fall Apart* was something I picked up after my father died. In one particularly striking paragraph, Chödrön asks people to make room for the reality of death and change, rather than trying to fix things in place:

> Things falling apart is a kind of testing and also a kind of healing. We think that the point is to pass the test or to overcome the problem, but the truth is that things don't really get solved. They come together and they fall apart again. It's just like that. The healing comes from letting there be room for all of this to happen: room for grief, for relief, for misery, for joy. (1996, 9)

Framing the lifecourse of necromaterials in this manner, as a "falling apart and coming together" rather than an end, is a move that creates space for a more empathetic account of the constellation of emotions that transformation brings forth. *Butsudan* come together and they fall apart, and there is grief, relief, misery, and joy.

No matter how people emotionally respond to the current trajectory of *butsudan*, there is growing popular awareness of their mortality. This pathos for the passing of things (*mono no aware*) motivates acts of professional and personal mourning. It is also a powerful force shaping contemporary death practice. The collapse of *butsudan* tradition and the remains this generates are now significant factors in how people navigate relations with the (human) dead in Japan. Facilities like automatic conveyance columbaria (chapter 5) or mass ossuaries are premised on an understanding that the patrilineal household line will end and that both mourners and their memorial goods will die. Put simply, awareness of the mortality of necromaterial traditions has become a feature of how people in Japan negotiate death today.

Uncertainty surrounding the ultimate fate of *butsudan* does not preclude creativity and experimentation. New *butsudan* designs and funeral services are launched with great fervor, and aging individuals might be actively engaged in planning their own posthumous care. Theorists of modernity working in the lineage of Anthony Giddens (1991) typically position death customs outside the realm of creative endeavors, even upon the collapse of structures of meaning provided by institutional religion, because of their abject qualities. My experiences in Japan suggest a need to rethink this sequestration. At least for some, death ritual has become a site of creative remaking, although these experiments do not all point in the same direction. While monumental golden *butsudan* like President Yamashita's altar (chapter 1) are still being commissioned, altars designed by furniture makers capture record sales across the country (chapter 2) and people forgo *butsudan* to have their loved ones made into fashionable jewelry (chapter 5). Even the ritual disposal of abandoned graves and *butsudan* (chapter 4) has become a source of new ventures and profits for certain organizations. There is life to be found in the "death" of *butsudan*.

Where is this all heading? Robert J. Smith, at the close of his magnum opus on the Japanese ancestors, walks bravely, eyes open, into the task of future predictions.[1] With different visions of the future jostling for industry and popular attention, I am more reticent to do so. Rather than charting a new course for Japanese death rites, I want instead to suggest two matters that should direct future study: the stuff and the workers.

NECROSOCIALITY FROM THE ALTAR

The task of examining contemporary Japanese necrosociality "from the altar" requires taking seriously the messy, sensory, improvised activities that take place there. Entrenched biases in the study of religion mean that, historically, this kind of work has been relatively uncommon. Further, when transformations to *butsudan* have been studied, they tend to be interpreted primarily as reflections of bigger changes to Japanese economy, religion, and society. If I were to examine *butsudan* in this manner, as symbols of a precarious age, I am not entirely sure what conclusions could be drawn, except in the very broadest strokes. The problem is not just that *butsudan* are polysemous or that most people volunteered little that is conclusive about their meaning or use (although these are significant methodological hurdles). Rather, it is that my attempts to map patterns of necrosociality onto changes in materiality were nearly always confounded by how these objects are engaged in practice.

On one level, this research supports other scholars' arguments that *butsudan* practice has become more secular, focused on the nuclear family and bilateral relations, inexpensive, and personalized. However, I have also described a grandiose *butsudan* stored for years behind a motorcycle in an artisan's garage (chapter 1) and a tiny box *butsudan* that is lavished with daily readings of Buddhist sutras and offerings of incense (chapter 3). I have described how ashes are handed over to temples, in lieu of descendants, for *eitai* (perpetual) *kuyō*; how personal photographs are removed from the altar to avoid angering visiting priests (chapter 3); and how altars might become difficult-to-dispose-of burdens (chapter 4). What these encounters teach is that abstracting necromaterials from their contexts of use flattens the complexity that characterizes how people navigate Buddhist traditions of death in Japan today. It also flattens out the richness ethnography can add to the study of religion and of death. Attempts to read artifacts in a semiotic manner miss something fundamental about *butsudan* that scholars of material religion are primed to acknowledge: they are not signs but stuff (Daniels 2010a, 19–20; Toulson and Newby 2019, 11). *Butsudan* are touched, sensed, used, neglected, broken, discarded, rejected, and reinvented. They are also expensive, musty, and haunting. As Raquel Romberg (2018, 156) argues, altars live and work, and *do* something. Or, I would add, fail to do something. Altars can surprise and confuse, prompt people to redecorate their homes, reminisce about the past, or feel intense discomfort. Beginning at the altar means building an understanding of death culture from this intimate engagement between people and things.

My experiences at the altar inform my understanding of the practice of *kuyō* as an affective response to death that operates on the bonds between the living and the dead. In making the dead present, *butsudan* become a site for engaging with their absence, enabling people both to nurture the dead and to negotiate their gradual disentanglement from the world of the living. This is not a strict translation of *kuyō* from Buddhist teachings but one that resonates with more expansive readings of popular religious practice and laypeople's orientation toward the dead. It is also distinct from memorialization. *Kuyō* is a different mode of necrosociality that positions the living and the dead within interdependent relations of exchange. Of course, memorialization is an equally multifaceted (and overlapping) mode of being with the dead. By highlighting the particularities and limitations of memorialization, my goal has been not to reject this productive concept but to provoke deeper reflection on how often it is unconsciously applied in English-language scholarship, particularly in the still Eurocentric field of death studies. By particularizing *kuyō* and memorialization, we create space to describe many more modes of relation for thinking about death and material culture.

It has been tempting to describe *kuyō* teleologically, as aimed at the ontological metamorphosis of the dead. The interdependent relationship between the living and the dead, in which the former shepherds the latter through a series of stages that transform them from spirits to *hotoke*, and then to ancestors or gods, is a foundational narrative in studies of Japanese death rites. Correspondingly, the mental transformation of the living from an immediate state of shock or grief to a restored homeostasis has been suggested in the psychological literature. However, just as semiotic readings of *butsudan* reduce these artifacts to signs, overly functionalist readings of material culture risk reducing altars to tools. This too easily slips into what Jeremy Stolow calls the "instrumentalist model" (2012, 8), which begins with religious goals, then judges how technology might meet or fail to meet them.

One interesting corollary of an instrumental framing is that *kuyō* so often appears to fail. No matter how many times an icon is cleansed by *butsudan* workers, it does not return to being "just a thing" (chapter 4). The human dead appear to require even more performances of *kuyō*, spread across years and generations. Some deaths demand more attention than others; human cremains generate a timeline of obligation that waste *butsudan* do not, and certain people's deaths, or the unfortunate circumstances of their passing, weigh more heavily. However, the realization that attempts to "slake the thirst" of the dead, as Mark Rowe (2011) would have it, never seem to work, always came as a surprise. Not only does *kuyō* fail to dispense with one's duties to the dead, it can also generate new bonds. Caring for the dead in this manner requires people's investment in new relationships with religious specialists or retailers and, often, the purchase of more stuff. Just like *butsudan* or *temoto kuyōhin*, which were created to ritualize the death of another and themselves one day will die and be ritualized, this cycle appears to have no end. Such sticky sociality is not always welcome. Indeed, rather than a condition of social disconnection and bondlessness (*muen*), I have often encountered people deeply troubled by social adhesion and the moral weight of bonds. The workings of *kuyō* in this regard can be described as contingent. *Kuyō* is a process of settling one's obligations, born from the strength of one's interconnections. A more cynical reading might point to the sustained financial opportunity that such apparent failure creates for *kuyō* providers. By selling graves, *butsudan*, and ritual performances, religious professionals market a treatment, but not a cure, to the affective pull of the dead. It is a treatment course that some people now choose to reject. Some innovators and outliers seek out less taxing means of settling their obligations to the dead, such as dumping altars and graves on the side of the road (chapter 4), or never purchasing a grave and scattering ashes at sea (chapter 5). These actions suggest a considerably more finite resolution to *en*.

Rather than frame *kuyō* as a ritual designed to fail, however, I wonder if the instrumental framing might be set aside to give closer attention to the emotional, experiential dimension of *kuyō*. During fieldwork, as I reached again and again to define *kuyō*, people continually told me how to perform *kuyō* and what it *feels like*. Often, their description began and ended with miming hands folded in prayer. The phrase *te o awaseru* (手を合わせる)

quickly became code for an appropriate response to the dead. Intergenerational memories of multisensory experiences at the altar, of one's grandmother offering incense or striking a bell, provided additional language for people to talk about *kuyō*. Such explanations were sometimes presented apologetically, by industry outsiders or young people who lacked confidence or expertise regarding altars. But I see no reason why such encounters should be valued less as explanations of contemporary necrosociality than diagrams charting the progression of the dead toward ancestorhood. So much of what I discovered about *butsudan* practice was described to me as "matters of feeling/sensation" (気持ちの問題 *kimochi no mondai*). These feelings help explain why the purchase of altars and performance of certain rites produces a sense of relief (chapter 2) and why unwanted altars and graves—or even spent matches—cannot simply be disposed of as regular waste (chapter 4). They help explain why the specter of the abandoned dead (*muenbotoke*) and ritual goods provoke visceral discomfort. Framing *butsudan* simply as incarnations of evolving kinship structures or tools to bring about the ontological transformation of the dead misses out on these crucial matters of context and feeling. Let us start, then, at the altar, with the lifecourse of this object that animates the dead.

RELIGIOUS THIRD ACTORS

The people who work in the space between temples and families in contemporary Japan have become my friends, and they remain my teachers (plate 8). I have grown to appreciate the crucial role they play in holding together religious life and in the practice of caring for the dead. These workers increasingly have the ability, if not always the authority, to define what *butsudan* are and how they should be used. They respond to evolving consumer demands when crafting this vision, just as members of the public adapt and personalize altar practice in conversation with family members and religious institutions. The making of *butsudan* has thus shifted from artisan-crafted, inherited forms to aesthetically driven "designs" as retail companies draw on market research and cosmopolitan aesthetics to develop products, and as they make selective decisions about what to preserve and what to elide from new *kuyō* goods. Whether or not these new designs are worthy heirs to artisan tradition is a matter of some debate, with criteria extending beyond Buddhist symbols or aesthetic features to the capacity of modern *butsudan* to inspire *kuyō*, to get people to "fold one's hands in prayer." Indeed, the capacity of contemporary altars to reproduce this sensational relation between *butsudan* and body is an important arbiter of their value. Of course, retailers also praise modern *butsudan* for supporting their bottom line and praise traditional altars for preserving artisan traditions. Time and again, dueling values of commerce and care are interwoven in *butsudan* retail.

Butsudan retail shows *kuyō* to be a collective effort. Workers help to bridge the gap in ritual expertise, confidence, and social distance between laypeople and clergy. They translate expectations around payment, field customer inquiries about ritual etiquette, and do the behind-the-stage work of disposing of waste and preparing offerings. In contemporary Japan, Buddhist goods companies are not secondary actors relative to temples; rather, they are perhaps the most publicly accessible source of ritual advice for laypeople (alongside online sources). Given the substantial work they perform, the labors and experiences of these actors are severely understudied. Any analysis of Buddhism's economic dimensions will be impoverished if it continues to focus only on temples and neglects retail and service industries and, beyond them, broader networks of primary suppliers and waste workers extending around the world.

One emerging form of labor performed by *butsudan* retailers is as ritual proxies, who execute the work of caring for the dead (both human and nonhuman) alongside or instead of customers. This is a potentially lucrative space for *butsudan* companies but one that can be taxing on workers. Not all ritual proxies are equal, and companies must work hard to establish their legitimacy. Workers are regularly forced to defer to both customers and clergy, even in areas where they have superior expertise. *Butsudan* workers appear acutely aware of the tensions within which their industry operates, and the industry has thus developed strong narratives about the virtues of investing in *kuyō* in order to combat accusations of self-interest. In particular, the consumption of altars and graves is framed as benefiting the dead as much as the bereaved. Cultivating ongoing relations with customers is vital to attracting new sales and encouraging repeat purchases, but this desire can come into conflict with that of the customers, who may wish to maintain the transactional nature of commercial relationships. The work of ritual proxy thus demands a careful approach.

Sometimes, these proxies are not formal or acknowledged. While most of my time in the field was spent with male *butsudan* retail staff, women emerge as some of the most powerful actors driving change in Buddhist death ritual. Care for the ancestors, *butsudan*, and grave are nominally inherited through the paternal line, but women take on significant labors in care for the (non)human dead. From communal graves and *kuyō* for single women to the push to legalize ash scattering or altars that enshrine bilateral sets of relations, female consumers' desires now set much of the agenda within the industry, even if women do not occupy its power structures. The role of these rebel women in transforming death rites, and the challenges they face, is a theme deserving of deeper theoretical engagement and field-work in the future.

A work structured around the lifecycle of an object, no less a Buddhist object, might be expected to come full circle. I began this work with the story of my first interment ceremony, working with Enomoto at a cemetery on the outskirts of Osaka, surrounded by gravestones, altars, and ash. In thinking about necromaterials in Japan and engaging with scholarship on memorial goods, gravestones first appeared to me to be the natural archetype for theorizing the stuff of death. The monumentality of gravestones demarcates a place for the dead in the landscape. Their durability preserves a trace of the dead through time, transcending the limits of human memory and mortality. But then gravestones, like memories, erode. The permanence they offer might exceed an individual human lifespan, but these artifacts are subject to a lifecourse of their own.

Upon reflection, I now find ash to be the better metaphor. Ash is both hard to wholly preserve and hard to wholly dispense with. Something always escapes our grasp and lingers on. In this book, I have reached toward understanding the stuff that is suspended between the living and the dead. Inevitably, some of that stuff will have slipped through my fingers. *Butsudan* are made, sold, used, destroyed, and remade. They come together and they fall apart. And at the altar, in the smoke of incense and the strike of a bell, the dead and the living meet, if only for this moment.

Acknowledgments

Ethnographic research is a practice of making connections and accruing debts. I am sure I will never repay the kindness that has been shown to me over the past seven years of research. I can only hope that this book is received as an offering of thanks.

This work would not have been possible without the support of the Japanese religious goods industry. My initial success in fieldwork was entirely dependent on President Takimoto Yoshiyuki of Takimoto Bukkōdō, who extended his trust to an unknown researcher and welcomed me into the industry. The delivery team at Takimoto—Kobayashi, Tan, Enomoto, and Mitsume—trained me and supported me throughout the project. Ōgoshi Norio of Ōgoshi Butsudan expanded my understanding of the care and craft required to make altars. I am indebted to Hasegawa Fusao of Hasegawa Co. Ltd., who models excellence in the industry, and to Shimoyamada Akinari and the whole team at Hasegawa Ginza, as well as Ueno Masahiro of Ingyōin, who have taught me what it means to serve both customers and the dead. My ongoing engagement with the field, both before and throughout the COVID-19 pandemic, has been facilitated by Sumida Kotato of Shūkyō Kōgeisha, who I cannot thank enough for championing my work. To Kawamoto Yasuo, Hoshi Yasunori, Kimura Kōki, and the countless other artisans, retailers, priests, encoffiners, funeral assistants, and funeral directors who gave their time to this project: thank you.

The intellectual contributions in this book are born of fruitful conversations throughout my career and at various locations with colleagues, mentors, and friends. I want to particularly acknowledge Anne Allison, Laura Clark, Inge Daniels, Kate Falconer, Gwyn McClelland, Paulina Kolata, Melyn McKay, Aki Miyazawa, John Nelson, Sally Raudon, Saki Tanada, and Ruth Toulson for their mixture of blistering intellect and compassion. I further received support from the scholastic communities of Kanazawa, Toyo, Nanzan, and Tokyo Universities. Daisuke Uriu deserves special thanks for his support and insight.

During my time at the University of Melbourne, I have had the great privilege of working with mentors who have both encouraged and challenged me. Even more surprisingly, Tamara Kohn and Richard Chenhall appeared willing to learn infinitesimal details of *butsudan* construction. For this, I can only express my apologies and endless gratitude. Tammy: thank you for being not only a brilliant ethnographer and teacher but a tireless mentor and friend. This text has been vastly improved as the result of comments from early readers, my editorial team at the University of Chicago Press, and the anonymous reviewers of this manuscript. I am further indebted to the wider Melbourne academic community and the DeathTech Research Team. My thanks to Alexandra Anastatsov, Fraser Allison, Michael Arnold, Martin Gibbs, Elizabeth Hallam, Samuel Holleran, Bjørn Nansen, Jun Ōhashi, and Carolyn Stevens.

This research was supported by funding from the Australian Government Research Training Program (RTP) Scholarship, the Japan Foundation Fellowship, and the Melbourne University Fieldwork Grant. Portions of this work have previously appeared in the *Enshrining the Sacred: Microarchitecture in Ritual Spaces*, edited by Ilia M. Rodov (Peter Lang Verlag, 2022), and in the journal *Japanese Religions* (2019).

On a personal note, this book would not exist without the support of Honor Coleman, Sarah Gosper, Bryonny Goodwin-Hawkins, Sami Jayd, Cynthia Sear, Devony Schmidt, Christine Thompson, Su Ying Xie, and many, many more.

My love (to the end of all the numbers) to my mum, who raised me to seek first to understand and then to be understood, and to my big brother, for teaching me the importance of small places and big issues. To Daisuke and Mochi: thank you for being my home. Finally, I deeply wish that my Dad was alive to see this book published. He would have been so proud.

Notes

INTRODUCTION

1. In 2017 the Japanese Coast Guard reported the arrival of ninety-five boats carrying at least twenty-seven corpses (Watson 2017).

2. Japanese custom for the treatment of cremains (bones and ash) shows distinct regional variation. For example, in Kansai (including Osaka), cremains might be directly interred in the ground or transferred from a ceramic urn into a cloth bag, whereas in Kanto (including Tokyo) the urn itself is usually placed in the grave.

3. The vast majority of contemporary Japanese funerals are conducted in the Buddhist idiom, with at least some involvement of a Buddhist priest.

4. *Butsudan* assemblages vary widely between Buddhist schools, regions, and households. The most significant exception to the general description given here is altars for Jōdo Shinshū (浄土真宗), or True Pure Land Buddhism, which do not, by official accounts, enshrine ancestral tablets. As I describe, however, such official accounts are frequently disproven by practice.

5. For accessible accounts of these histories of invention, see Bernstein (2006) on cremation and Mori (1993) on funerals and graves.

6. Although the 1948 Burial and Tombs Law allows for burial, almost all people in Japan today are cremated. Municipal regulations make burial, if desired, inaccessible to most outside of select burial grounds (e.g., MGIJ Muslim Graveyard Ibaraki). Burials also occurred after the March 2011 earthquake, tsunami, and nuclear disaster in Japan, when local crematoria ran over capacity (Suzuki 2011). Outside of intense crises, demand at some central metropolitan crematoria (like facilities in Tokyo-Yokohama) has pushed waiting times for cremation out to a week or more after death.

7. This multiplicity is even clearer in selected regions of Japan that have historically practiced the "double grave system" (両墓制 *rōbosei*), of constructing two distinct graves, a "burial grave" (where remains are interred—usually buried) and a "ceremonial grave" (where offerings are made), often in a more convenient location for visitors.

8. Dore (1958, 306–16) estimated that *butsudan* were present in 80 percent of Tokyo homes. According to 2019 data from the Ministry of Economy, Trade and Industry "Census of Industry," the value of religious equipment manufacturing and shipping in Japan (for offices with four or more employees) is 30.9 billion yen. According the latest (2016) METI commercial statistics for the retail industry, nationwide sales of religious items account for approximately 154.6 billion yen. Shūkyō Kōgeisha (the Religious Craft Association) estimates that approximately half this figure can be attributed to *butsudan*

sales, with approximately 270,000–280,000 *butsudan* sold each year (Sumida Kotato, personal communication, October 2022).

9. A more substantive history of this turn would recognize the significant and sustained contributions of archaeologists in particular in the study of grave goods.

10. I have encountered a small number of *butsudan* located in community centers or nursing homes, where they serve different kinds of social "households."

11. Survey of 1,955 male and female chief mourners aged forty or older from across Japan who conducted funerals between March 2020 and March 2022.

CHAPTER 1

1. Although *butsudan* are not usually sold or transferred (see chapter 4), excess *butsudan* are sometimes passed down from the head family to a branch family. The branch family (分家 *bunke*) separates from the main family (本家 *honke*) via male descendants born after the first son. Secondhand *butsudan* are more common in some overseas communities (Gould 2019; Wilson 2022).

2. The *Nigabyakudō*, a common decorative motif in Jōdo Shinshū temples, refers to a seventh-century Chinese parable about a traveler whose faith is tested as he attempts to cross a white road to paradise located between two rivers, one of water (wrath) and one of fire (greed) (Graham 2007, 64).

3. The first character of *karaki*, also read as *tang*, is an archaic word for China. Exotic wood is typically imported from Southeast Asia through China, apart from Yakushima cedar, which is a protected Japanese natural resource.

4. In the teachings of Jōdo Shinshū, people are said to travel to the Pure Land (浄土 *jōdo*) upon death and thus do not require ongoing care. *Butsudan* should be reserved "for the living" and especially self-improvement through veneration of Amida (Taniguchi 2013, 3–15). However, I have found that among lay practitioners, regional and family custom often trump doctrinal distinctions. Not only do *ihai* sometimes appear in Jōdo Shinshū *butsudan*, but care for the recent dead and ancestors can be a significant part of followers' daily practice.

5. In Mahayana Buddhism, Bodhisattvas (Jp. 菩薩 *bosatsu*) are compassionate being who have committed themselves to the enlightenment of all sentient beings, often at the sacrifice of their own enlightenment.

6. Most people purchase *go-honzon* from *butsudan* stores, though some schools of Buddhism sell these items through their head temple and some even encourage followers to go on pilgrimage to receive them.

7. Ooms (1967) and Kretschmer (2000a) provide excellent summaries of work on ancestor veneration from Japanese folklore studies for English readers.

8. *Japan Historical Text Initiative*, University of California Berkeley, chap. 29, p. 181, https://jhti.berkeley.edu (accessed June 2021).

9. The word Kobori uses is *mushūkyō* (無宗教), which denotes a lack of a formal religious affiliation but should be distinguished from atheism. The term "religion" (宗教 *shūkyō*) has a contested history in Japan, with scholars arguing it emerged in the Meiji period with reference to Christianity and thus does not describe (preexisting) folk religious practice (see Krämer 2013; Josephson 2012). More broadly, scholars have stressed the importance, when discussing Japan, of expanding the definition of religion beyond belief or doctrine to include affiliation and practice, which are not necessarily congruent (Reader and Tanabe 1998).

10. The term *sōshiki bukkyō* was popularized in a 1963 publication by Tamamuro Taijō, who used it condemn contemporary Buddhism as one-dimensional and archaic, divorced from everyday life and focused almost exclusively on death. Largely shedding the critical tone of this work, funeral rites remain a key site of inquiry for scholars of Japanese Buddhism.

11. For the year 2019, approximately 236,000 of the total altars sold (approximately 268,000) were imported, based on estimates supplied by Shūkyō Kōgeisha (the Religious Craft Association) (Sumida Kotato, personal communication October 2022). This number is affected by global events, including the 2011 tsunami, which destroyed many altars, leading to an influx of imports to replace them, and COVID-19, which significantly stunted imports from China.

12. Yamada Shōji (2002) makes a further distinction between *kata* as the pattern itself and *katachi* (形) as the mastery of that pattern.

13. Notably, Shinto domestic shrines, or *kamidana*, are regularly sold at garden centers and home-goods stores across Japan, although the central talismans must be purchased through Shines.

14. The intended meaning of this product name is unclear to me. It is an example of 和製英語 (*wasei eigo*), or pseudo-English phrases coined in Japanese.

15. The Japanese Religious Goods Association (全日本宗教用具協同組合 *zen nihon shūkyō yōgu kyōdō kumiai*) is a national corporate cooperative approved by METI under the Small Business Cooperative Law.

CHAPTER 2

1. Mark Rowe calls scholarly statements about people's ignorance of their family's Buddhist affiliation "almost a cliché" (2011, 4).

2. As of October 2022. Information on Hasegawa, a publicly traded company, is available via its investor relations website (https://corp.hasegawa.jp/ir/), as well as the published corporate history (Hasegawa Co. Ltd. 2013).

3. See Suzuki (2000, 85) for a table expressing the appropriate amount of money to spend according to one's age and relationship to the deceased. At the time of her ethnography, this ranged from ¥3,000 (a business colleague in one's twenties) to ¥59,600 (a brother or sister in one's fifties).

4. Surveys were conducted annually before the impact of COVID-19. The latest survey, published in May 2019, contains responses from 433 people who downloaded a coupon to apply toward the purchase of a new *butsudan*. See https://www.e-butsudan.com/questionnaire/18.html.

5. The rate of *butsudan* replacement for *honke* families can rise steeply after certain natural disasters, including the 2011 earthquake, tsunami, and nuclear disaster.

6. A second "religion boom" in the 1980s similarly saw a rise in what have been called "new new religions" (新新宗教 *shin shin shūkyō*).

7. The international spread of Sōka Gakkai has also been one of the routes via which *butsudan* have traveled overseas (Gould 2019), alongside Zen Buddhism (Rocha 2010).

8. Morioka Kiyomi (1984) introduces class into the discussions of ancestor veneration. Morioka argues that lower-class families who are less likely to benefit from an intergenerational transfer of wealth are accordingly less likely to practice reciprocity toward the ancestors. Wealth may determine whether or not the ancestors are thanked and "prayed to" or are seen as pitiful, as "prayed for" (after Smith 1974). However, im-

proper or insufficient ancestral veneration can also be interpreted as a cause of house-hold decline. Therefore, Morioka suggests, the "central function of ancestor worship for lower class people was to relieve themselves of tension concerning their present plight as well as possible further disaster and misfortune" (1984, 203). While my research collected insufficient data on class, it is a dimension that should be pursued further, given growing generational inequalities in Japan and elsewhere.

9. If the altar is too small, it might not be able to accommodate the *ihai* and *butsugu*. Although many schools of Japanese Buddhism teach that the ancestors lose their personal identity after thirty-three or one hundred years, at which time tablets may be (carefully) disposed of, older *ihai* are often retained in the back of altars. For families with long lineages and crowded *butsudan*, a consolidated ancestral tablet, known as *kuridashi ihai* (繰り出し位牌) is one solution.

10. *Manzai* (漫才) is a traditional style of stand-up comedy in Japan performed by two-person teams: a "straight man" and a "funny man." Kobayashi was the latter.

11. The *rokuyō* (六曜) calendar, originating in the Kamakura period (1185–1333), is based on a six-day cycle. *Taian* is the most auspicious day in the cycle, and thus often chosen for marriages and other momentous events, including installing a new *butsudan* (see Hayashi 1996).

CHAPTER 3

1. In Hamabata's ethnography of a Japanese business dynasty, family achievements are reported to the ancestors by placing report cards, salary envelopes, and diplomas in the drawer beneath the butsudan. Mischievous children are dragged before the altar and asked, "Do you think you can give any excuse to the ancestors for doing that?" (1990, 79–80).

2. The dance of access and ethics in the study of *butsudan* in Japan is highlighted by ongoing discussions of Robert J. Smith's fieldwork. For his landmark study *Ancestor Worship in Contemporary Japan* (1974), Smith went door-to-door in a Tokyo neighborhood, asking residents to show him their *butsudan* and take out the *ihai* for closer inspection, a method that resulted in a rich data set that shocked even some of his informants. On more than one occasion, Japanese colleagues referred to Smith's work as "something only a foreigner could do." I gained the distinct impression that they were both shocked and envious of the direct approach. Ultimately, I felt uncomfortable breaking this social taboo and reproducing Smith's approach, given the bonds I maintained to both *butsudan* companies and my in-laws in Japan.

3. The first characters of these two words are the same. The second character of *kuyō* means "foster" or "bring up"; the second character of *kugi* means "sacrifice" or "give up."

4. Although this term is written in katakana script, which typically indicates a loan word into Japanese, it is derived from the Japanese funerary industry.

5. See Venbrux 2007, discussing on Hertz, death, and materiality in Melanesia in introducing a special issue of *Journal de la Société des Océanistes*.

6. On special occasions, *o-zen* (御膳), a tray laden with rice, miso soup, a braised dish, pickles, and a vegetable side dish, is offered at the altar.

7. The *kaimyō* for Daisuke's grandmother was revealed at the dining room table the night before. With nine characters, two of which are shared with her husband's name, it was judged suitable for someone with close ties to temple life. It was also, the family noted, a hefty expense.

8. My statement is primarily based on observations in Tokyo, Hiroshima, Kanazawa, and Osaka. Smith's 1974 work was in Kansai; he later reported (1983, 36) that he was made aware of significant regional variation, such as a preference in the Tōhoku region that the head of the household tend to the altar and a prohibition on women doing so. Whether this remains the case some thirty years later is unclear; more extensive study of women and domestic religion in Japan is much needed.

CHAPTER 4

1. The proliferation of "conduct literature" in Japan makes it a powerful normative force in regulating etiquette, especially for its target audience of women (Bardsley and Miller 2011, 15–16), who bear the prime burden of managing domestic waste.

2. Buddha nature is a teaching common to Mahayana Buddhism and particularly important to Jōdo Shinshū. Put simply, it states that all beings have within them an enlightened Buddha, or state of awakening filled with compassion and wisdom.

3. The classification of Shintoism as animist, or indeed a cohesive religion, is controversial, even more so when it is deployed as a blanket explanation of popular phenomena in Japan and overseas. A recent flashpoint through which to examine these debates is public commentary on the spiritual dimensions of organizational guru Marie Kondō's Netflix series (Thomas 2019; Gould 2022). A recent collection, *Spirits and Animism in Contemporary Japan* (Rambelli 2019), explores the uses and abuses of the animism concept.

4. A notable exception to this process is *go-honzon* belonging to Sōka Gakkai, a popular new religious movement derived from Nichiren Buddhism. In the teachings of Sōka Gakkai, the *go-honzon* is the literal manifestation of the teachings of the Buddha, such that its mistreatment or destruction is a grave offense (Wallinder-Pierini 2018). When approached with a Sōka Gakkai *butsudan* for disposal, many of the stores will direct customers to the organization directly to arrange collection.

5. This event, organized by the Japanese Religious Goods Association, commemorates the day in 685 when Emperor Tenmu is said to have ordered a Buddhist image be enshrined in every home.

6. Within Japan, Sōka Gakkai is a notable exception to this rule. Not only do altars crafted in this recognizable style (with an extra set of doors around the icon) regularly appear on secondhand auction websites, but a number of stores associated with the group purchase old *butsudan* for resale to members. Overseas, Jeff Wilson (2022) describes the established economy of secondhand altars in North American Buddhist communities.

7. See http://www.city.osaka.lg.jp/kankyo/page/0000384507.html.

8. See http://reset-soul.com/useful/butudan-gomi.

9. The town with forty-five categories was Kamikatsu, Shikoku, which in recent years has gained worldwide fame as the "zero waste town."

10. The politics of domestic waste management in Japan are demonstrated by the recent fate of Airbnb, which was forced to close nearly 80 percent of its listings in Japan in the first half of 2018; one of the major reasons local residents cited for opposing rentals was incorrect disposal of domestic waste (Takada 2017). As Douglas (1966) reminds us, dirt as "matter out of place"—literally sorted into the wrong categories in this case—has long been used as a boundary-drawing device within and between communities.

11. A small island in the Seto Inland Sea between Honshu and Shikoku.

CHAPTER 5

1. Other rituals, like bathing the dead body, have been similarly (re)invented. There are histories of ritual bathing of the sick and dying at Buddhist temples dating back to the Heian period, but the rite largely disappeared after World War II. Hikaru Suzuki (2000, 179–202) describes the efforts of one funeral home to reinvent and market this rite, in the process changing its form (from submersion to washing) and meaning (from sanitation to purification).

2. Perhaps the clearest example is the participation of the controversial right-wing new religious movement Happy Science (幸福の科学 *kōfuku no kagaku*), which presented a demonstration funeral service at the 2017 ENDEX satellite event in Osaka. The group's booth and enthusiastic promoters seemed to be treated with a mixture of fascination and suspicion by other participants, who studiously avoided approaching the booth for networking but showed interest in viewing the demonstration funeral rite.

3. Booths at ENDEX are not cheap, costing close to 360,000 yen for a small space of eight square meters (see http://ifcx.jp/exhibitor/plan.php).

4. Article 190 of the penal code (Destruction of Corpses) states, "A person who damages, abandons or unlawfully possesses a corpse, the ashes or hair of a dead person, or an object placed in a coffin is punished by imprisonment for not more than 3 years" (Ministry of Justice 1962). (See https://www.japaneselawtranslation.go.jp/en.)

5. The Ministry of Justice has ruled that scattering does not violate article 190, "since the aim of the law is to protect the religious feelings of the people" (Suzuki 1998, 186). Nonetheless, the practice remains tightly regulated.

6. How much of the cremains make it into the urn depends on regional custom. In Kansai, families may receive only a small portion taken from the feet, knees, hips, sternum, and hyoid (the Buddha bone). In Kanto, all of the bone and ash produced in cremation is retained, while some communities retain only the hyoid bone (Kawano 2014, 118–20). As a result, the standard sizes of urns vary significantly across Japan. Remnant ash may be collected into the urn or, in many locations, left at the crematorium and deposited in a communal grave (集合墓 *shūgo haka*).

7. Cleaning is generally recommended for ashes that were interred directly in the ground rather than contained in an urn, a common practice in some parts of Japan, including Kansai. In some cases, customers send Norizuki Butsudan material indistinguishable from soil, which they carefully wash and sieve to separate out small ash and bone fragments.

8. The temple belongs to the Jōdoshū, or Pure Land, school, but the columbarium accepts remains from people of all Buddhist schools or other religions, as well as people of no faith.

CONCLUSION

1. "Those who have predicted the future course of events in Japan over the past century have generally been wrong. However, they are not an unworthy group, and I have little hesitation in joining such good company" (Smith 1974, 225).

Works Cited

Ahern, Emily M. 1973. *The cult of the dead in a Chinese village.* Stanford, CA: Stanford University Press.

Allison, Anne. 2006. *Millennial monsters: Japanese toys and the global imagination.* Berkeley: University of California Press.

———. 2013. *Precarious Japan.* Durham, NC: Duke University Press.

———. 2018. "Not-waiting to die badly: Facing the precarity of lonely death in Japan." In *Ethnographies of waiting: Doubt, hope and uncertainty,* edited by Manpreet K. Janeja and Andreas Bandak, 164–81. London: Bloomsbury.

———. 2023. *Being dead otherwise.* Durham, NC: Duke University Press.

Ambros, Barbara. 2012. *Bones of contention: Animals and religion in contemporary Japan.* Honolulu: University of Hawai'i Press.

Anderson, Richard, and Elaine Martin. 1997. "Rethinking the practice of *mizuko kuyō* in contemporary Japan: Interviews with practitioners at a Buddhist temple in Tokyo." *Journal of Japanese Religious Studies* 24, nos. 1/2: 121–43.

Appadurai, Arjun, ed. 1986. *The social life of things: Commodities in cultural perspective.* Cambridge: Cambridge University Press.

Araki, Kuniomi [荒木國臣]. 2005. 日本仏壇工芸産業の研究 [*Nihon butsudan kōgei-sangyō no kenkyū*]. Tokyo: Akaiwa Publishing.

Ariès, Philippe. 1974. *Western attitudes toward death in the Middle Ages to the present.* Baltimore: John Hopkins University Press.

Arnold, Michael, Martin Gibbs, Tamara Kohn, James Meese, and Bjørn Nansen. 2018. *Death and digital media.* London: Routledge.

Asquith, Pamela J. 1986. "The monkey memorial service of Japanese primatologists." In *Japanese culture and behaviour: Selected readings,* edited by Takie Sugiyama Lebra and William P. Lebra, 29–32. Honolulu: University of Hawai'i Press.

Bailey, Tara. 2010. "When commerce meets care: Emotion management in UK funeral directing." *Mortality* 15, no. 3: 205–22.

Bardsley, Jan, and Laura Miller. 2011. "Manners and mischief: Introduction." In *Manners and mischief: Gender, power, and etiquette in Japan,* edited by Jan Bardsley and Laura Miller, 1–28. Berkeley: University of California Press.

Barraud, Cecile, Daniel de Coppet, Andre Iteanu, and Raymond Jamous. 1994. *Of relations and the dead: Four societies viewed from the angle of their exchanges.* Translated by Stephen J. Suffern. Oxford: Berg.

Bauman, Zygmunt. 1992a. *Mortality, immortality and other life strategies.* Stanford, CA: Stanford University Press.

———. 1992b. "Survival as a social construct." *Theory, Culture & Society* 9, no. 1: 1–36.

Benedict, Timothy O. 2022. *Spiritual ends: Religion and the heart of dying in Japan.* Oakland: University of California Press.

Benjamin, Walter. 1936 [2008]. *The Work of Art in the Age of Mechanical Reproduction.* Translated by J. A. Underwood. London: Penguin.

Bernstein, Andrew. 2006. *Modern passings: Death rites, politics, and social change in imperial Japan.* Honolulu: University of Hawai'i Press.

BKSSK [Butsuji kōdinētā shikaku shinsa kyōkai; 仏事コーディネーター資格審査協会], ed. 2015. 仏壇仏具ガイダンス：よりよい仏壇店を目指して [*Butsudan butsugu gaidansu: Yori yoi butsudanten o mezashite*], 4th edition. Tokyo: National Japanese Religious Goods Association.

Bokhoven, Jeroen [ボクホベンヨルン]. 2005. 葬儀と仏壇：先祖祭祀の民俗学的研究 [*Sōgi to butsudan: Senzo saishi no minzokugakuteki kenkyū*]. Tokyo: Itō Shoin.

Boret, Sébastien Penmellen. 2014. *Japanese tree burial: Ecology, kinship and the culture of death.* London: Routledge.

Broom, Alex. 2012. "Gender and end-of-life care." In *The Palgrave handbook of gender and healthcare*, edited by Ellen Kuhlmann and Ellen Annandale, 224–38. London: Palgrave Macmillan.

Brox, Trine, and Elizabeth Williams-Oerberg, eds. 2022. *Buddhism and waste: The excess, discard, and afterlife of Buddhist consumption.* London: Bloomsbury.

Caillois, Roger. 1939 [2001]. *Man and the sacred.* Translated by Meyer Barash. Urbana: University of Illinois Press.

Ceremonial Occasions Research Institute [冠婚葬祭文化振興財団]. 2021. データから知る冠婚葬祭をとりまく環境変化：データブック2021年版 [*Dēta kara shiru kankonsōsai o torimaku kankyō henka: dētabukku 2021 nenhan*]. Tokyo: Ceremonial Occasions Research Institute.

Chidester, David. 2014. "The accidental, ambivalent, and useless sacred." *Journal of Material Religion* 10, no. 2: 239–40.

Chödrön, Pema. 1996 [2016]. *When things fall apart: Heart advice for difficult times.* Boulder: Shambala.

Clammer, John. 1997. *Contemporary urban Japan: A sociology of consumption.* London: Wiley & Sons.

Cobbi, Jane. 1995. "Sonaemono: Ritual gifts to the deities." In *Ceremony and ritual in Japan: Religious practices in an industrialized society*, edited by Jan van Bremen and Dolores P. Martinez, 201–9. Oxford: Routledge.

Connerton, Paul. 1989. *How societies remember.* Cambridge: Cambridge University Press.

Covell, Stephen G. 2009. "The price of naming the dead: Posthumous precept names and critiques of contemporary Japanese Buddhism." In *Death and the afterlife in Japanese Buddhism*, edited by Jacqueline I. Stone and Mariko Namba Walter, 293–324. Honolulu: University of Hawai'i Press.

Cox, Rupert. 2007. "Introduction." In *The culture of copying in Japan: Critical and historical perspectives*, edited by Rupert Cox, 1–18. London: Routledge.

Cox, Rupert, and Christoph Brumann. 2010. "Introduction." In *Making Japanese heritage*, edited by Christoph Brumann and Rupert Cox, 1–18. Abingdon: Routledge.

Dahl, Shayne A. P. 2017. "Summits where souls gather: Mountain pilgrimage in post-disaster Japan." *Journal of Religion in Japan* 6:27–53.

Danely, Jason. 2008. "Departure and return: Abandonment, memorial and aging in Japan." PhD diss., University of California.

———. 2014. *Aging and loss: Mourning and maturity in contemporary Japan.* New Brunswick, NJ: Rutgers University Press.

Daniels, Inge. 2003. "Scooping, raking, beckoning luck: Luck, agency and the interdependence of people and things in Japan." *Journal of the Royal Anthropological Institute* 9, no. 4: 619–38.

———. 2009. "The 'social death' of unused gifts: Surplus and value in contemporary Japan." *Journal of Material Culture* 14, no. 3: 385–408.

———. 2010a. "'Dolls are scary': The locus of the spiritual in contemporary Japanese homes." In *Religion and Material Culture*, edited by David Morgan, 153–70. London: Routledge.

———. 2010b. *The Japanese house: Material culture in the modern home.* Oxford: Berg.

Davies, Douglas J. 2005. "Cremulation." In *Encyclopedia of cremation*, edited by Lewis H. Mates and Douglas J. Davies, 152–53. Aldershot: Ashgate.

Davies, Douglas, and Hannah Rumble. 2012. *Natural burial: Traditional-secular spiritualities and funeral innovation.* London: Bloomsbury.

Dawdy, Shannon Lee, and Tamara Kneese, eds. 2022. *The new death: Mortality and death care in the twenty-first century.* Santa Fe: School of Advanced Research Press.

Deal, William E., and Brian Ruppert. 2015. *A cultural history of Japanese Buddhism.* Chichester: Wiley Blackwell.

DeNicola, Alicia Ory, and Clare M. Wilkinson-Weber. 2016. "Introduction: Taking stock of craft in anthropology." In *Critical craft: Technology, globalization, and capitalism*, edited by Clare M. Wilkinson-Weber and Alician Ory DeNicola, 1–16. London: Bloomsbury.

Desjarlais, Robert. 2016. *Subject to death: Life and loss in a Buddhist world.* Chicago: University of Chicago Press.

Doi, Takeo. 1973. *The anatomy of dependence.* Translated by John Bester. Tokyo: Kodansha International.

Dore, Ronald Phillip. 1958 [1998]. *City life in Japan: A study of Tokyo ward*, volume 2. London: Routledge.

Dorman, Benjamin. 2007. "Representing ancestor worship as 'non-religious': Hosoki Kazuko's divination in the post-Aum era." *Nova Religio: Journal of Alternative and Emergent Religions* 10, no. 3: 32–53.

Doughty, Caitlin. 2015. *Smoke gets in your eyes: And other lessons from the crematorium.* New York: W. W. Norton.

Douglas, Mary. 1966. *Purity and danger: An analysis of concepts of pollution and taboo.* London: Routledge.

Durkheim, Émile. 1912 [1995]. *The Elementary Forms of Religious Life.* Translated by Karen E. Fields. New York: Free Press.

Duteil-Ogata, Fabienne. 2015. "New technologies and new funeral practices in contemporary Japan." In *Asian religions, technology and science*, edited by István Keul, 227–44. London: Routledge.

Eades, Jeremy Seymour, Carla Eades, Yuriko Nishiyama, and Hiroko Yanase. 2000. "Houses of everlasting bliss: Globalization and the production of Buddhist altars in Hikone." In *Globalization and social change in contemporary Japan*, edited by Jeremy Seymour Eades, Tom Gill, and Harumi Befu, 159–79. Melbourne. Trans Pacific Press.

Field, Nigel P. 2006. "Unresolved grief and continuing bonds: An attachment perspective." *Death Studies* 30, no. 8: 739–56.

Fortes, Meyer. 1976. "An introductory commentary." In *Ancestors*, edited by William H. Newell, 1–16. The Hague: Mouton.

Foulk, T. Griffith. 2008. "Ritual in Japanese Zen Buddhism." In *Zen ritual: Studies of Zen Buddhist theory in practice*, edited by Steven Heine and Dale S. Wright, 21–82. Oxford: Oxford University Press.

Fukuhara Dōji [福原 堂礎]. 1997. 真宗門徒の墓づくり [*Shinshū monto no hakadzukuri*]. Tokyo: Tokishobo.

Garvey, Pauline. 2017. *Unpacking IKEA: Swedish design for the purchasing masses.* London: Routledge.

Gerhart, Karen M. 2009. *The material culture of death in medieval Japan.* Honolulu: University of Hawaii Press.

Gibbs, Samuel. 2017. "The future of funerals? Robot priest launched to undercut human-led rites." *Guardian*, August 24, 2017. https://www.theguardian.com /technology/2017/aug/23/robot-funerals-priest-launched-softbank-humanoid -robot-pepper-live-streaming

Giddens, Anthony. 1991. *Modernity and self-identity: Self and society in the late modern age.* Stanford, CA: Stanford University Press.

Goody, Jack. 1962. *Death, property and the ancestors: A study of the mortuary customs of the Lodagaa of West Africa.* London: Routledge.

Gorai, Shigeru [五来重]. 1994. 日本人の死生観 [*Nihonjin no shiseikan*]. Tokyo: Kadokawa shoten.

Gould, Hannah. 2019. "Domesticating Buddha: Making a place for Japanese Buddhist altars (butsudan) in Western homes." *Journal of Material Religion* 15, no. 4: 488–510.

———. 2022. "Modern minimalism and the magical Buddhist art of disposal." In *Buddhism and waste: The excess, discard, and afterlife of Buddhist consumption*, edited by Trine Brox and Elizabeth Williams-Oerberg, 53–74. London: Bloomsbury.

Gould, Hannah, and Melyn McKay. 2020. "An introduction to bad Buddhism." *Journal of Global Buddhism* 21;141–51.

Gould, Hannah, Martin Gibbs, Bjørn Nansen, Tamara Kohn, and Michael Arnold. 2021. "Robot death care: A study of funerary practice." *International Journal of Cultural Studies* 24, no. 4: 603–21.

Gould, Hannah, Tamara Kohn, and Martin Gibbs. 2019. "Uploading the ancestors: Experiments with digital Buddhist altars in contemporary Japan." *Death Studies* 43, no. 7: 456–65.

Graham, Barbara. 2016. *Death, materiality and mediation: An ethnography of remembrance in Ireland.* New York: Berghahn Books.

Graham, Patricia J. 2007. *Faith and power in Japanese Buddhist art, 1600–2005.* Honolulu: University of Hawai'i Press.

Grasseni, Cristina. 2007. "Introduction." In *Skilled visions: Between apprenticeship and standards*, edited by Cristina Grasseni, 1–22. New York: Berghahn Books.

Guth, Christine M. E. 2014. "Theorizing the Hari *Kuyō*: The ritual disposal of needles in early modern Japan." *Design and Culture* 6, no. 2: 169–86.

Gygi, Fabio. 2018. "The metamorphosis of excess: 'Rubbish houses' and the imagined trajectory of things in post-bubble Japan." In *Consuming life in post-bubble Japan: A transdisciplinary perspective*, edited by Katarzyna J Cwiertka and Ewa Machotka, 129–51. Amsterdam: Amsterdam University Press.

————. 2019. "Things that believe and how to get rid of them: Towards a material ecology of the numinous in Japan." *Japanese Journal of Religious Studies* 45, no. 2: 1–26.

————. 2022. "The great Heisei doll massacre: Disposal and the production of ignorance in contemporary Japan." In *Buddhism and waste: The excess, discard, and afterlife of Buddhist consumption*, edited by Trine Brox and Elizabeth Williams-Oerberg, 103–24. London: Bloomsbury.

Hallam, Elizabeth, and Jenny Hockey. 2001. *Death, memory and material culture*. Oxford: Berg.

Hamabata, Matthews Masayuki. 1990. *Crested kimono: Power and love in the Japanese business family*. Ithaca, NY: Cornell University Press.

Hardacre, Helen. 1988. *Kurozumikyo and the new religions of Japan*. Princeton, NJ: Princeton University Press.

————. 1999. *Marketing the menacing fetus in Japan*. Berkeley: University of California Press.

Hasegawa Butsudan. 2005. *Annual report 2001*. Tokyo: Hasegawa Investor Relations Department.

Hasegawa Co. Ltd. 2013. *Uketsugu kokoro to inochi ashita e* [受け継ぐ心といのち 明日へ]: 1929–2013. Tokyo: Bunkasha Publishing Company.

Hayashi, Makoto [林淳].1996. "暦の変遷と六曜 [*Koyomi no hensen to rokuyō*]." In 消費される「宗教」 [*Shōhi sareru shūkyō*], edited by Shimazono Susumu [島薗 進] and Ishii Kenji [石井 研士], 1–6. Tokyo: Shunjusha.

Heine, Steven. 2012. *Sacred high city, sacred low city: A tale of religious sites in two Tokyo neighborhoods*. Oxford: Oxford University Press.

Hendry, Joy. 2000. *The Orient strikes back: A global view of cultural display*. Oxford: Berg.

Hertz, Robert. 1907 [1960]. *Death and the right hand*. Translated by R. Needham and C. Needham. Glencoe: Free Press.

Hetherington, Kevin. 2004. "Secondhandedness: Consumption, disposal, and absent presence." *Environment and Planning D: Society and Space* 22, no. 1: 157–73.

Himonya, Hajime [碑文谷創]. 1994. 「お葬式」の学び方 [*O-sōshiki manabikata*]. Tokyo: Kodansha.

Hirayama, Toshijirō [平山敏治郎]. 1949. 神棚と仏壇 [*Kamidana to butsudan*]. *Shirin* [史林] 32, no. 2: 42–70.

————. 1959. "家の神と村の神 [*Ie no kami to mura no kami*]." In 日本民俗学大系 [*Nihon minzokugaku taikei*], volume 8. Tokyo: Heibonsha.

Hobsbawm, Eric, and Terence Ranger. 1992. *The invention of tradition*. Cambridge: Cambridge University Press.

Hochschild, Arlie Russell. 1979 [1983]. *The managed heart: Commercialization of human feeling*. Berkeley: University of California Press.

Howarth, Glennys. 1996. *Last rites: The work of the modern funeral director*. Amityville: Baywood.

Hur, Nam-Lin. 2007. *Death and social order in Tokugawa Japan: Buddhism, anti-Christianity and the Danka system*. Cambridge: Harvard University Asia Centre.

Hyland, Liam, and Janice M. Morse. 1995. "Orchestrating comfort: The role of funeral directors." *Death Studies* 19, no. 5: 453–74.

Ikegami, Yoshimasa [池上良正]. 2014. "Shūkyōgaku no kenkyū kadai toshite no 'segaki' [宗教学の研究課題としての「施餓鬼」]." *Komazawa daigaku bunka* [駒沢大学文化] 32:69–94.

Irizarry, Joshua A. 2014. "Signs of life: Grounding the transcendent in Japanese memorial objects." *Signs and Society* 2, no. 1: S160–S187.

———. 2022. *Sōjiji: Discipline, compassion, and enlightenment at a Japanese Zen temple.* Ann Arbor: University of Michigan Press.

Ishii, Kenji [石井研士]. 2007. データブック現代日本人の宗教 [*Dētabukku gendai nihonjin no shūkyō*]. Tokyo: Shinyō-sha.

Itami, Juzu, dir. 1984. お葬式 [*O-sōshiki*]. Motion Picture.

Itoh, Mayumi. 2018. *The Japanese culture of mourning whales: Whale graves and memorial monuments in Japan.* Princeton, NJ: Palgrave MacMillan.

Ivy, Marilyn. 1995. *Discourses of the vanishing: Modernity, phantasm, Japan.* Chicago: University of Chicago Press.

Jensen, Casper Bruun, and Anders Blok. 2013. "Techno-animism in Japan: Shinto cosmograms, actor network theory, and the enabling powers of non-human agencies." *Theory, Culture & Society* 30, no. 2: 84–115.

Jeremy, Michael, and Michael Ernest Robinson. 1989. *Ceremony and symbolism in the Japanese home.* Honolulu: University of Hawaii Press.

Jindra, Michael, and Joël Noret, eds. 2011. *Funerals in Africa: Explorations of a social phenomenon.* New York: Berghahn Books.

Josephson, Jason Ānanda. 2012. *The invention of religion in Japan.* Chicago: University of Chicago Press.

Kamakura Shinsho [鎌倉新書]. 2018. エンディング産業展 [*Endingu Sangyōten*]. Tokyo: Kamakura Shinsho.

———. 2022. お葬式に関する全国調査第 5 回 [*O-sōgi ni kansuru zenkoku chōsa daigokai*]. *E-Sogi*, May 30, 2022. https://www.e-sogi.com/guide/46028/

Kamata Tōji [鎌田東二], ed. 2009. モノ学の冒険 [*Monogaku no bōken*]. Tokyo: Sogensha.

Kawano, Satsuki. 2010. *Nature's embrace: Japan's aging urbanites and new death rites.* Honolulu: University of Hawai'i Press.

———. 2014. "'Who will care for me when I am dead?' Ancestors, homeless spirits, and new afterlives in low-fertility Japan." *Journal of the German Institute for Japanese Studies Tokyo* 26, no. 1: 49–69.

Kendall, Laurel. 2017. "Things fall apart: Material religion and the problem of decay." *Journal of Asian Studies* 76, no. 4: 861–86.

Kerner, Karen. 1976. "The malevolent ancestor: Ancestral influence in a Japanese religious sect." In *Ancestors*, edited by W. H. Newell, 205–17. The Hague: Mouton.

Kidron, Carol A. 2009. "Toward an ethnography of silence: The lived presence of the past in the everyday life of Holocaust trauma survivors and their descendants in Israel." *Current Anthropology* 50, no. 1: 5–27.

Kieschnick, John. 2003. *The impact of Buddhism on Chinese material culture.* Princeton, NJ: Princeton University Press.

Kikkawa, Mitsuko [吉川美津子], Serizawa Kensuke [芹沢健介], and Nakamura Asami [中村麻美]. 2017. 死後離婚 [*Shigo rikon*]. Tokyo: Yosensha.

Kim, Jieun. 2016. "Necrosociality: Isolated death and unclaimed cremains in Japan." *Journal of the Royal Anthropological Institute* 22, no. 4: 843–63.

Kirby, R. J. 1910. "Ancestral worship in Japan." *Transactions of the Asiatic Society of Japan* 38 (1910–22): 233–58.

Klass, Dennis. 1996. "Ancestor worship in Japan: Dependence and the resolution of grief." *OMEGA: Journal of Death and Dying* 33, no. 4: 279–302.

———. 2001. "Continuing bonds in the resolution of grief in Japan and North America." *American Behavioral Scientist* 44, no. 5: 742–63.

Klass, Dennis, Phyllis R. Silverman, and Steven L. Nickman, eds. 1996. *Continuing bonds: New understandings of grief.* Philadelphia: Taylor & Francis.

Kobori, Kenichi. [小堀賢一]. 2017. 日本人が誇る無宗教 [Nihonjin ga hokoru mushū-kyō]. Tokyo: Shūkyō Kōgeisha.

Kohn, Tamara. 2021. "Decay, rot, mold and resistance in the US prison system." In *Decay*, edited by Ghassan Hage, 140–52. Durham, NC: Duke University Press.

Kopytoff, Igor. 1986. "The cultural biography of things: Commoditization as process." In *The social life of things: Commodities in cultural perspective*, edited by Arjun Appadurai, 64–91. Cambridge: Cambridge University Press.

Kolata, Paulina. 2022. "Heritage out of control: Buddhist material excess in depopulating Japan." *Allegra Lab*, February 2022. https://allegralaboratory.net/heritage-out-of-control-buddhist-material-excess-in-depopulating-japan/

Kolata, Paulina, and Gwendolyn Gilson. 2021. "Feasting with Buddhist women: Food literacy in religious belonging." *Numen* 68, nos. 5–6: 567–92.

Kotani, Midori [小谷みどり]. 2014. 墓が捨てられる～無縁化の先に何が～ [*Haka ga suterareru~muenka no saki ni naniga~*]. *NHK Modern Close Ups*, October 8, 2014. http://www.nhk.or.jp/gendai/articles/3562/1.html

———. 2018. "誰が死者を弔い、墓を守るのか [*Dare ga shisha o tomurai, haka o mamoru no ka*]." In 現代日本の葬送と墓制：イエ亡き時代の死者のゆくえ [*Gendai nihon no sōsō to bosie: Ie naki jidai no shisha no yukue*], edited by Iwayumi Suzuki [鈴木岩弓] and Kenji Mori [森謙二], 115–30. Tokyo: Yoshikawa Publishing.

———. 2019. 家族がいても引き取り手のない「無縁遺骨」が増える事情 [*Kazoku ga itemo hikitorite no nai muenihai ga fueru jijō*]. Asahi News. June 11, 2019. https://www.asahi.com/relife/article/12431896

Krämer, Hand Marin. 2013. "How 'religion' came to be translated as shukyo: Shimaji Mokurai and the appropriation of religion in early Meiji Japan." *Japan Review: Journal of the International Research Centre for Japanese Studies* 25:89–111.

Kretschmer, Angelika. 2000a. *Kuyô in contemporary Japan: Religious rites in the lives of laypeople.* Göttiingen: Civillier Verlag.

———. 2000b. "Mortuary rites for inanimate objects: The case of Hari *Kuyō*." *Japanese Journal of Religious Studies* 27, nos. 3/4: 379–404.

Kuwayama, Takami. 2004. *Native anthropology: The Japanese challenge to Western academic hegemony.* Melbourne: Trans Pacific Press.

LaFleur, William R. 1992. *Liquid life: Abortion and Buddhism in Japan.* Princeton, NJ: Princeton University Press.

Latour, Bruno. 1991 [2000]. "The Berlin Key or how to do words with things." In *Matter, Materiality and Modern Culture*, edited by P. M. Graves-Brown, 10–21. London: Routledge.

———. 1993. *We have never been modern.* Translated by Catherine Porter. Cambridge, MA: Harvard University Press.

Lebra, Takie Sugiyama. 1976. "Ancestral influence on the suffering of descendants in a Japanese cult." In *Ancestors*, edited by W. H. Newell, 219–30. The Hague: Mouton.

Lee, Harper. 1960 [1989]. *To kill a mockingbird.* London: Mandarin Paperbacks.

LIMO. 2019. "お仏壇で知られる、はせがわの給料はどのくらいか [*O-butsudan de shirareru, Hasegawa no kyūryō wa donokurai ka*]." *LIMO Life & Money*, May 4, 2019. https://limo.media/articles/-/10432

Long, Susan Orpett. 2004. "Cultural scripts for a good death in Japan and the United States: Similarities and differences." *Social Science & Medicine* 58, no. 5: 913–28.

———. 2005. *Final days: Japanese culture and choice at the end of life.* Honolulu: University of Hawaii Press.

———. 2008. "Someone's old, something's new, someone's borrowed, someone's blue: Tales of elder care at the turn of the 21st century." In *Imagined families, lived families: Culture and kinship in contemporary Japan,* edited by Akiko Hashimoto and John Traphagan, 137–58. Albany: SUNY Press.

Luckman, Susan, and Nicola Thomas. 2018. "Crafting economies: Contemporary cultural economies of the handmade." In *Craft economies,* edited by Susan Luckman and Nicola Thomas, 1–14. London: Bloomsbury.

Maeda, Takashi. 1976. "Ancestor worship in Japan: Facts and history." In *Ancestors,* edited by W. H. Newell, 139–61. The Hague: Mouton.

Mainichi Shimbun. 2017. "人の遺骨 置き去りか 8 割以上 「落とし主」 が見つからず [*Hito no ikotsu okisari ka hachiwari ijō 'otoshinushi' ga mitsukarazu*]." *Mainichi Shimbun,* September 9, 2017. https://mainichi.jp/articles/20170909/k00/00m/040 /201000c

Maldonado-Estrada, Alyssa. 2020. *Lifeblood of the parish: Men and Catholic devotion in Williamsburg, Brooklyn.* New York: New York University Press.

Mansfield, Becky. 2003 "'Imitation crab' and the material culture of commodity production." *Cultural Geographies,* no. 10, 176–95.

Marcus, George. E., and Erkan Saka. 2016. "Assemblage." *Theory, Culture & Society* 23, no. 2–3: 101–6.

Matsuzaki Kenzō [松崎憲三]. 1996. "動植物の供養覚書: 供養碑建立習俗をめぐって [*Dōshokubutsu no kuyō oboegaki: Kuyōhi konryū shūzoku o megutte*]." In民俗的世界 の探求 [*Minzokuteki sekai no tankyū*], edited by Kamata Hisako [鎌田久子], 162–85. Tokyo: Keiyūsha.

Mauss, Marcel. 1925 [2002]. *The gift: The form and reason for exchange in archaic societies.* Translated by W. D. Halls. London: Routledge.

Mayer, Paul, Hagin, and Yasuyo Ishiwara. 1970. "Introduction." In *About our ancestors: The Japanese family system.* Tokyo: Japan Society for the Promotion of Science.

McDannell, Colleen. 1995. *Material Christianity: Religion and popular culture in America.* New Haven, CT: Yale University Press.

Metcalf, Peter, and Richard Huntington. 1991. *Celebrations of death: The anthropology of mortuary ritual,* 2nd edition. Cambridge: Cambridge University Press.

Meyer, Brigit. 2006. "Religious sensations: Why media, aesthetics, and power matter in the study of contemporary religion." Inaugural lecture, Vrije Universiteit Amsterdam. http://www.fsw.vu.nl/nl/Images/Oratietekst%20Birgit%20Meyer_tcm30 -36764.pdf

———. 2012. "Mediation and the genesis of presence: Towards a material approach to religion" [speech]. Utrecht: University of Utrecht.

Meyer, Brigit, David Morgan, Crispin Paine, and S. Brent Plate. 2011. "The origin and mission of material religion." *Religion* 40, no. 3: 207–11.

Miller, Daniel, and Fiona Parrott. 2009. "Loss and material culture in South London." *Journal of the Royal Anthropological Institute* 15, no. 3: 502–19.

Ministry of Economy, Trade and Industry [METI, 経済産業省]. 2016. 商業統計 [*Shōgyō tōkei*]. Last modified July 4, 2018. https://www.meti.go.jp/statistics/tyo/syougyo /result-2.html

Ministry of Justice. 1962. *The Civil Code of Japan*. Tokyo: Ministry of Justice.

Mitford, Jessica. 1963. *The American way of death*. New York: Simon & Schuster.

Miyazawa, Aki. Forthcoming (2024). *Natural burial in the UK and Japan: A comparative study of postmodern funerals*. Sapporo: Hokkaido University Press.

Moeran, Brian. 1997. *Folk art potters of Japan: Beyond an anthropology of aesthetics*. Abingdon: Routledge.

Morgan, David. 2016. "Materializing the study of religion." *Religion* 46, no. 4: 640–43.

Mori, Kenji [森謙二]. 1993. 墓と葬送の社会史 [*Haka to sōsō no shakaishi*]. Tokyo: Kōdansha.

Morioka, Kiyomi. 1984. "Ancestor worship in contemporary Japan: Continuity and change." *Senri Ethnological Studies* 11:201–13.

Morita, Natsumi. 2011. "Kimochi: Capturing elderly Japanese dialysis patients' experiences." In *Faces of aging: The lived experiences of the elderly in Japan*, edited by Yoshiko Matsumoto, 170–93. Stanford, CA: Stanford University Press.

Murata, Daisuke. 2015. "The Kogei tragedy." *Journal of Modern Craft* 8, no. 1: 9–28.

Nagano, Hironori [長野浩典]. 2015. 生類供養と日本人 [*Shōrui kuyō to Nihonjin*]. Fukuoka: Genshobo.

Naitō, Rieko [内藤理恵子]. 2013. 現代日本の葬送文化 [*Gendai Nihon no Sōsō Bunka*]. Tokyo: Itō Shōin.

Nakamaki, Hirochika. 1983. "The 'separate' coexistence of Kami and Hotoke: A look at Yorishiro." *Japanese Journal of Religious Studies* 10, no. 1: 65–86.

———. 2003. *Japanese religions at home and abroad: Anthropological perspectives*. London: Routledge.

Nakamura, Ikuo [中村生雄]. 2010. 日本人の宗教と動物観：殺生と肉食 [*Nihonjin no shūkyō dōbutsukan: Sesshō to nikushoku*]. Tokyo: Yoshikawa Publishers.

Namihara, Emiko. 2013. "The characteristics of Japanese concepts and attitudes with regard to human remains." In *Japanese and Western bioethics: Studies in moral diversity*, edited by Kazumasa Hoshino, 61–72. New York: Springer.

Nelson, John. K. 2008. "Household altars in contemporary Japan: Rectifying Buddhist "ancestor worship" with home décor and consumer choice." *Japanese Journal of Religious Studies* 35, no. 2: 305–30.

———. 2013. *Experimental Buddhism: Innovation and activism in contemporary Japan*. Honolulu: University of Hawaii Press.

Nelson, Robert S., and Margaret Olin, eds. 2003. *Monuments and memory, made and unmade*. Chicago: University of Chicago Press.

NHK. 2018. 急増する "墓じまい" 新たな弔いの形とは [*Kyūzōsuru hakajima aratana momurai no katachi to wa*]. NHK News, April 8, 2018. https://www.nhk.or.jp/gendai/articles/4112/index.html

Nobushige, Hozumi. 1901. *Ancestor worship and Japanese law*. Tokyo: Maruzen.

Obinata, Sumire. 1990. "Women's role in ancestor worship in contemporary Japanese families." Masters diss., Indiana University.

Okuyama, Yoshiko. 2013. "Shinto and Buddhist metaphors in *Departures*." *Journal of Religion & Film* 17, no. 1: 39.

Ooms, Herman. 1967. "The religion of the household: A case study of ancestor worship in Japan." *Contemporary Religions in Japan* 8, nos. 3/4: 201–333.

———. 1976. "A structural analysis of Japanese ancestral rites and beliefs." In *Ancestors*, edited by William H. Newell, 61–90. The Hague: Mouton.

Orsi, Robert A. 2013. *Between heaven and earth: The religious worlds people make and the scholars who study them.* Princeton, NJ: Princeton University Press.

Ōsaki, Tomoko [大崎智子]. 1997. "ハサミ供養をめぐって―東京都港区芝増上寺 [*Hasami kuyō o megutte: Tōkyōto Minato-ku Shibazōjō-ji*]." *Mingui Matsuri* 30, no. 1: 14–24.

Osterfeld Li, Michelle. 2012. "Human of the heart: Pitiful *Oni* in medieval Japan." In *The Ashgate research companion to monsters and the monstrous,* edited by Asa Simon Mittman and Peter J Dendle, 173–98. Surrey: Ashgate.

Paine, Crispin. 2014. "Sacred waste." *Material Religion* 10, no. 2: 241–42.

Parsons, Brian. 2003. "Conflict in the context of care: An examination of role conflict between the bereaved and the funeral director in the UK." *Mortality* 8, no. 1: 67–87.

Plath, David. W. 1964. "Where the family of god is the family: The role of the dead in Japanese households." *American Anthropologist* 66, no. 2: 300–317.

Prothero, Stephen. 2001. *Purified by fire: A history of cremation in America.* Berkeley: University of California Press.

Rambelli, Fabio. 2007. *Buddhist materiality: A cultural history of objects in Japanese Buddhism.* Stanford, CA: Stanford University Press.

———. 2010. "Home Buddhas: Historical processes and modes of representation of the sacred in the Japanese Buddhist family altar (butsudan)." *Japanese Religions* 35, nos. 1–2: 63–86.

———. 2017. "Materiality, labor, and signification of sacred objects in Japanese Buddhism." *Journal of Religion in Japan* 6, no. 1: 1–26.

———, ed. 2019. *Spirits and animism in contemporary Japan: The invisible empire.* London: Bloomsbury.

Reader, Ian. 1991. *Religion in contemporary Japan.* Honolulu: University of Hawai'i Press.

———. 2011. "Buddhism in crisis? Institutional decline in modern Japan." *Buddhist Studies Review* 28, no. 2: 233–63.

———. 2012. "Secularisation, R.I.P.? Nonsense! The 'rush hour away from the gods' and the decline of religion in contemporary Japan." *Journal of Religion in Japan* 1, no. 1: 7–36.

Reader, Ian, and George Tanabe Jr. 1998. *Practically religious: Worldly benefits and the common religion in Japan.* Honolulu: University of Hawai'i Press.

Reider, Noriko T. 2009. "Animating objects: *Tsukumogami ki* and the medieval illustration of Shingon truth." *Japanese Journal of Religious Studies* 36, no. 2: 231–57.

Reno, Joshua O. 2016. *Waste away: Working and living with a North American landfill.* Berkeley: University of California Press.

Repp, Martin. 2010. "Socio-economic impacts of Hōnen's Pure Land doctrines: An inquiry into the interplay between Buddhist teachings and institutions." In *The social dimensions of Shin Buddhism,* edited by Ugo Dessi, 11–58. Leiden: Brill.

Robertson, Jennifer. 2018. "Robot reincarnation: Rubbish, artefacts, and mortuary rituals." In *Consuming life in post-bubble Japan: A transdisciplinary perspective,* edited by Katarzyna J. Cwiertka and Ewa Machotka, 153–73. Amsterdam: Amsterdam University Press.

Rocha, Cristina. 2010. "Can I put this Jizo together with the Virgin Mary in the altar? Creolizing Zen Buddhism in Brazil." In *Issei Buddhism in the Americas,* edited by Duncan Ryūken Williams and Tomoe Moriya Williams, 5–26. Urbana: University of Illinois Press.

Roemer, Michael 2009. "Religious affiliation in contemporary Japan: Untangling the enigma." *Review of Religious Research* 50, no. 3: 298–320.

Romberg, Raquel. 2018. "Introduction: Shrines and altars that happen, do, and cease." *Magic, Ritual, and Witchcraft* (Summer): 1–10.

Ronald, Richard, and Allison Alexy. 2017. "Continuity and change in Japanese homes and families." In *Home and family in Japan: Continuity and transformation,* edited by Richard Ronald and Allison Alexy, 1–24. London: Routledge.

Rosaldo, Michelle Zimbalist. 1974. "Women, culture, and society: A theoretical overview." In *Women, culture, and society,* edited by Michelle Zimbalist Rosaldo and Louise Lamphere, 17–47. Stanford, CA: Stanford University Press.

Rowe, Mark. 2011. *Bonds of the dead: Temples, burial, and the transformation of contemporary Japanese Buddhism.* Chicago: University of Chicago Press.

Sanders, George. 2012. "Branding in the American funeral industry." *Journal of Consumer Culture* 12, no. 3: 263–82.

Sasaki, Kōkan [佐々木宏幹]. 1993. 仏と霊の人類学：仏教文化の深層構造 [*Hotoke to tama no jinruigaku: Bukkyō bunka no shinsō kōzō*]. Tokyo: Shunjūsha.

———. 1996. 神と仏と日本人：宗教人類学の構想 [*Kami to hotoke to nihonjin: Shūkyō jinruigaku no kōsō*]. Tokyo: Yoshikawa Kōbunkan.

Satō, Dōshin. 2011. *Modern Japanese art and the Meiji state: The politics of beauty.* Translated by Hiroshi Nara. Los Angeles: Getty Research Institute.

Sennett, Richard. 2008. *The craftsman.* New Haven, CT: Yale University Press.

Shigematsu, Kiyoshi [重松清]. 2016. "あなたの遺骨はどこへ～広がる"ゼロ葬"の衝撃～ [*Anata no ikotsu wa doko e ~hirogaru "zerosō" no shōgeki*]." NHK, September 21, 2016. https://www.nhk.or.jp/gendai/articles/3865/1.html

Shimazono, Susumu [島薗進]. 2009. "生きているモノの宗教学―アニミズムを開く愛・愛を身体化するモノ [*Ikiteirumono no shūkyōgaku: animizumu o hiraku ai, ai o shintaika suru mono*]." In モノ学の冒険 [*Monogaku no bōken*], edited by Katama Tōji [鎌田東二編], 121–35. Sogensha: Tokyo.

Shintani, Takanori [新谷尚紀]. 1992. 日本人と葬儀 [*Nihonjin to sōgi*]. Tokyo: Kinokuniya.

———. 2007. "民俗学からみる慰霊と追悼 [*Minzokugaku kara miru irei to tsuitō*]." 明治聖徳記念学会紀要 [*Meiji seitoku kinen gakkai kiyō*] 44:171–80.

Shufunotomo [主婦の友]. 2011. お墓と仏壇選び方・建て方・祀り方 [*O-haka to butsudan erabikata, tatekata, matsurikata*]. Tokyo: Shufunotomo-sha.

Shūkyō Kōgeisha [宗教工芸社]. 2019. "第２９回業界動向調査～時代に対応する仏壇店 [*Dai 29 kai gyōkai dōkō chōsa~ jidai ni taiōsuru butsudanten*]." 宗教工芸新聞 [*Shukyō Kōgei Shimbun*], January 15, 2019.

Simpson, Bob. "Death." In *The Cambridge encyclopedia of anthropology.* 23 July, 2018. http://doi.org/10.29164/18death

Siniawer, Eiko Maruko. 2018. *Waste: Consuming postwar Japan.* Ithaca, NY: Cornell University Press.

Slater, David H. 2020. "Vulnerable populations under COVID-19 in Japan: A lull in the storm?" *Asia-Pacific Journal* 18, no. 2: 1–15.

Smith, Robert John. 1974. *Ancestor worship in contemporary Japan.* Stanford, CA: Stanford University Press.

———. 1983. "Ancestor worship in contemporary Japan." *Nanzan Bulletin* 7:30–40.

Solnit, Rebecca. 2006. *A field guide to getting lost.* Penguin.

Sone, Yuji. 2017. *Japanese robot culture: Performance, imagination, and modernity.* New York: Palgrave Macmillan.

Starling, Jessica. 2019. *Guardians of the Buddha's home: Domestic religion in contemporary Jōdo Shinshū.* Honolulu: University of Hawai'i Press.

Stengs, Irene. 2014. "Sacred waste." *Material Religion* 10, no. 2: 235–38.

Stevens, Carolyn. 2011. "Touch: Encounters with Japanese popular culture." *Japanese Studies* 3, no. 1: 1–10.

Stolow, Jeremy. 2012. "Introduction: Religion, technology and the things in between." In *Deus in machina: Religion, technology and the things in between,* edited by Jeremy Stolow, 1–24. New York: Fordham University Press.

Suzuki, Hikaru. 1998. "Japanese death rituals in transit: From household ancestors to beloved antecedents." *Journal of Contemporary Religion* 13, no. 2: 171–88.

———. 2000. *The price of death: The funeral industry in contemporary Japan.* Stanford, CA: Stanford University Press.

———. 2013a. "Introduction: Making one's death, dying and disposal in contemporary Japan." In *Death and dying in contemporary Japan,* edited by Hikaru Suzuki, 1–30. London: Routledge.

———. 2013b. "Epilogue: Price of mortality—reinvention of Japanese death rituals." In *Death and dying in contemporary Japan,* edited by Hikaru Suzuki, 226–29. London: Routledge.

Suzuki, Iwayumi. 2011. "Dealing with the dead: The reemergence of earth burials after the Great East Japan Earthquake." In *Commemorating the Dead in a Time of Global Crisis,* edited by Testuya Ohtoshi and Susumu Shimazono. Tokyo: University of Tokyo Press.

———. 2013. "Beyond ancestor worship: Continued relationship with significant others." In *Death and dying in contemporary Japan,* edited by Hikaru Suzuki, 141–56. London: Routledge.

Suzuki, Iwayumi [鈴木岩弓], and Kenji Mori [森謙二], eds. 2018. 現代日本の葬送と墓制： イエ亡き時代の死者のゆくえ [*Gendai nihon no sōsō to hakasei: ienaki jidai no shishū no yukue*]. Tokyo: Yoshikawa Publishers

Takada, Hidetoshi. 2017. "Tokyo condos shut doors on Airbnb and other vacation rental businesses." *Japan Times,* December 1, 2017. https://www.japantimes.co.jp/news/2017/12/01/business/tokyo-condos-shut-doors-airbnb-vacation-rental-businesses/

Takeda, Chōshu [竹田聴洲]. 1953. "仏壇を成立する民俗学的論理 [*Butsudan o seiritsu-suru minzokugaku-teki ronri*]." 禪學研究 [*Zengaku Kenkyu*] 40:7–30.

———. 1976. "Recent trends in studies of ancestor worship in Japan." In *Ancestors,* edited by W. H. Newell, 129–238. The Hague: Mouton.

Tamamuro, Taijō [圭室諦成]. 1963. 葬式仏教 [*Sōshiki Bukkyō*]. Tokyo: Daihorin Kaku.

Tanabe, George J. 2012. "Voices for the dead: Priestly incantations and grave discussions." In *Handbook of Japanese religions,* edited by Inken Prohl and John K. Nelson, 177–96. Leiden: Brill.

Taniguchi Kōji [谷口幸璽]. 2013. 仏壇の話 [*Butsudan no hanashi*]. 4th edition. Kyoto: Hōzōkan.

Tei, Munetetsu [丁宗鐵]. 2009. 正座と日本人 [*Seiza to Nihonjin*]. Tokyo: Kodansha

Thomas, Jolyon Baraka. 2015. "The Buddhist virtues of raging lust and crass materialism in contemporary Japan." *Material Religion* 11, no. 4: 485–506.

———. 2019. "Domesticity & spirituality: Kondo is not an animist." Marginalia: *Los Angeles Review of Books*, February 8, 2019. https://marginalia.lareviewofbooks.org/domesticity-spirituality-kondo-not-animist/

Tobin, Beth Fowkes, and Maureen Daly Goggin. 2013. "Connecting women and death: An introduction." In *Women and the material culture of death*, edited by Beth Fowkes Tobin and Maureen Daly Goggin, 1–12. Ashgate: Oxford.

Toulson, Ruth. E. 2022. "Grief transformed: New rituals in a Singaporean Chinese funeral parlour." In *The new death: Mortality and death care in the twenty-first century*, edited by Shannon Lee Dawdy and Tamara Kneese, 259–78. Santa Fe: School of Advanced Research Press.

Toulson, Ruth E., and Zahra Newby. 2019. "Introduction: Emotions and materiality in theory and method." In *The materiality of mourning: Cross-disciplinary perspectives*, edited by Zahra Newby and Ruth E. Toulson, 1–20. London: Routledge.

Traphagan, John W. 2004. *The practice of concern: Ritual, well-being and aging in rural Japan*. Durham, NC: Carolina Academic Press.

Triplett, Katja. 2017. "The making and unmaking of religious objects: Sacred waste management in comparative perspective." In *Materiality in religion and culture*, edited by Saburo Shawn Morishita, 143–54. Zurich: LIT Verlag.

Turner, Kay. 1999. *Beautiful necessity: The art and meaning of women's altars*. New York: Thames & Hudson.

Ukai, Hidenori [鵜飼秀徳]. 2016. 無葬社会 [*Musōshakai*]. Tokyo: Nikkei Business Publications.

Umesao Tadao [梅棹忠夫]. 1973 [1991]. "人の心と物の世界 [*Hito no kokoro to mono no sekai*]." In 梅棹忠夫著作集 [*Umesao Tadao Chosakushū*], volume 13, 139–58. Tokyo: Chūō Kōronsha.

Uriu, Daisuke, Ju-Chun Ko, Bing-Yu Chen, Atsushi Hiyama, and Masahiko Inami. 2019. "Digital memorialization in death-ridden societies: How HCI could contribute to death rituals in Taiwan and Japan." In *Human aspects of IT for the aged population: Design for the elderly and technology acceptance*, edited by Jia Zhou and Gavriel Salvendy, 532–50. Orlando: Springer, Cham.

Uriu, Daisuke, William Odom, and Hannah Gould. 2018. "Understanding automatic conveyor-belt columbaria: Emerging sites of interactive memorialization in Japan." In *Proceedings of the 2018 Designing Interactive Systems conference (DIS '18)*, 747–52. New York: ACM Press.

van Ryn, Luke, Bjørn Nansen, and Martin Gibbs. 2019. "'Adapt or die': The funeral trade show as a site of institutional anxiety." In *Residues of death: Disposal refigured*, edited by Tamara Kohn, Martin Gibbs, Bjørn Nansen, and Luke van Ryn, 37–51. London: Routledge.

Venbrux, Eric. 2007. "Robert Hertz's seminal essay and mortuary rites in the Pacific region." *Journal de la Société des Océanistes* 124:5–10.

Verdery, Katherine. 1999. *The political lives of dead bodies: Reburial and postsocialist change*. New York: Columbia University Press.

Vitebsky, Piers. 1993. *Dialogues with the dead: The discussion of mortality among the Sora of eastern India*. Cambridge: Cambridge University Press.

———. 2017. *Living without the dead: Loss and redemption in a jungle cosmos*. Chicago: University of Chicago Press.

Vlastos, Stephen. 1998. "Tradition: Past/present culture and modern Japanese history."

In *Mirror of modernity: Invented traditions of modern Japan*, edited by Stephen Vlastos, 1–18. Berkeley: University of California Press.

Wallinder-Pierini, Linda. 2018. "The Buddhist dharma for sale: Who owns the past? The internet and objects of worship." *Journal of Global Buddhism* 19:95–111.

Walter, Tony. 2016. "The dead who become angels: Bereavement and vernacular religion." *OMEGA–Journal of Death and Dying* 73, no. 1: 3–28.

Watson, Ivan. "Ghost ships: Bodies and boats unsettle Japanese communities." *CNN World*, December 23, 2017. https://edition.cnn.com/2017/12/22/asia/japan-north-korea-ghost-ships-intl/index.html

Weiner, Annette B. 1992. *Inalienable possessions: The paradox of keeping-while-giving.* Berkeley: University of California Press.

Weiss, Brad. 1997. "Forgetting your dead: Alienable and inalienable objects in northwest Tanzania." *Anthropological Quarterly* 70, no. 4: 164–72.

Williams, Paul, and Patrice Ladwig, eds. 2012. *Buddhist funeral cultures of Southeast Asia and China.* Cambridge: Cambridge University Press.

Wilson, Jeff. 2009. *Mourning the unborn dead: A Buddhist ritual comes to America.* Oxford: Oxford University Press.

———. 2022. "The afterlives of butsudan: Ambivalence and the disposal of home altars in the United States and Canada." In *Buddhism and waste: The excess, discard, and afterlife of Buddhist consumption*, edited by Trine Brox and Elizabeth Williams-Oerberg, 75–102. London: Bloomsbury.

Winfield, Pamela D., and Steven Heine, eds. 2018. *Zen and material culture.* Oxford: Oxford University Press.

Wirtz, Kristina. 2009. "Hazardous waste: The semiotics of ritual hygiene in Cuban popular religion." *Journal of the Royal Anthropological Institute* 15, no. 3: 476–501.

Wise, J. Macgregor. 2011. "Assemblage." In *Gilles Deleuze: Key concepts*, edited by C. J. Stivale, 91–102. Durham, NC: Acumen.

Wu, Emily S. 2018. "Chinese ancestral worship: Food to sustain, transform, and heal the dead and the living." In *Dying to eat: Cross-cultural perspectives on food, death, and the afterlife*, edited by Candi K. Cann, 17–36. Lexington: University Press of Kentucky.

Yagi, Takaharu [矢木隆晴]. 2019. "墓石びっしり「お墓のお墓」上等兵から犬まで数万基 [*Hakaishi bisshiri "o-haka no o-haka" jōtōhei kara inu made sūbanki*]." *Asahi Shimbun*, January 20, 2019. https://www.asahi.com/articles/ASLDG6HC9LDGPQIP01R.html

Yamada, Shinya [山田慎也]. 2002. "亡き人を想う—遺影の誕生 [*Nakihito o omou: Iei no tanjō*]." In 異界談義 [*Ikai Dangi*], edited by Ikegami Yoshimasa, 33–47. Tokyo: Uokawa Shoten.

———. 2007. 現代日本の死と葬儀 [*Gendai nihon no shi to sōgi*]. Tokyo: Tokyo University Press.

———. 2018. "納骨堂の成立とその集合的性格 [*Nōkotsudō no seiritsu to sono shūgōteki seikaku*]." In 現代日本の葬送と墓制: イエなき時代の使者の行方 [*Gendai nihon no sōsō to hakasei: ie-naki jidai no shisha no yukue*], edited by Iwayumi Suzuki [鈴木岩弓] and Kenji Mori [森謙二], 63–86. Tokyo: Yoshikawa Publishers.

Yamada, Shinya [山田慎也], and Hiroshi Doi [土居浩], eds. 2022. 無縁社会の葬儀と墓: 死者との過去・現在・未来 [*Muenshakai no sōgi to haka: Shisha tono kakō, gendai, mirai*]. Tokyo: Yoshikawa Publishers.

Yamada, Shōji [山田奨治]. 2002. 日本文化の模倣と創造: オリジナリティとは何
か? [*Nihon bunka no mohō to sōzō: Orijinaritei towa nani ka?*]. Tokyo: Kodokawa
Shoten.

Yamamoto, Joe, Keigo Okonogi, Testuya Iwasaki, and Saburo Yoshimura. 1969.
"Mournings in Japan." *American Journal of Psychiatry* 125, no. 12: 1660–65.

Yanagita, Kunio [柳田国男]. 1946. 先祖の話 [*Senzo no hanashi*]. Tokyo: Chikumashobo.

Yokoyama, Erica. 2022. "Long burdened by costly funerals, Japan embraces simple
goodbyes." *Japan Times*, September 26, 2022. https://www.japantimes.co.jp/news
/2022/09/26/national/social-issues/funeral-costs/

Index

191